Much Ado About Nothing

ARDEN EARLY MODERN DRAMA GUIDES

Series Editors:
Andrew Hiscock, University of Wales, Bangor, UK and
Lisa Hopkins, Sheffield Hallam University, UK

Arden Early Modern Drama Guides offer practical and accessible introductions to the critical and performative contexts of key Elizabethan and Jacobean plays. Each guide introduces the text's critical and performance history, but also provides students with an invaluable insight into the landscape of current scholarly research, through a keynote essay on the state of the art and newly commissioned essays of fresh research from different critical perspectives.

Further titles are in preparation

Much Ado About Nothing

A Critical Reader

Edited by
Deborah Cartmell and
Peter J. Smith

THE ARDEN SHAKESPEARE
LONDON • NEW YORK • OXFORD • NEW DELHI • SYDNEY

THE ARDEN SHAKESPEARE
Bloomsbury Publishing Plc
50 Bedford Square, London, WC1B 3DP, UK

BLOOMSBURY, THE ARDEN SHAKESPEARE and the Arden Shakespeare
logo are trademarks of Bloomsbury Publishing Plc

First published in Great Britain 2018
Reprinted 2018

ISBN: HB: 978-1-474-28437-0
ePDF: 978-1-474-28438-7
eBook: 978-1-474-28439-4

Library of Congress Cataloging-in-Publication Data
Names: Cartmell, Deborah, editor. | Smith, Peter J., 1964– editor.
Title: Much ado about nothing : a critical reader / edited by Deborah Cartmell and
Peter J. Smith.
Description: First edition. | London; New York : Bloomsbury Arden Shakespeare,
an imprint of Bloomsbury Publishing Plc, 2018. | Includes bibliographical
references and index.
Identifiers: LCCN 2017027591 | ISBN 9781474284370 (hardback) |
ISBN 9781474284394 (e-Book) | ISBN 9781474284387 (epdf)
Subjects: LCSH: Shakespeare, William, 1564–1616. Much ado about nothing. |
Shakespeare, William, 1564–1616—Stage history. | Shakespeare, William,
1564–1616—Criticism and interpretation.
Classification: LCC PR2828 .M825 2018 | DDC 822.3/3–dc23 LC record
available at https://lccn.loc.gov/2017027591

Series: Arden Early Modern Drama Guides

Typeset by RefineCatch Limited, Bungay, Suffolk
Printed and bound in Great Britain

To find out more about our authors and books visit
www.bloomsbury.com and sign up for our newsletters.

CONTENTS

SERIES
INTRODUCTION

The drama of Shakespeare and his contemporaries has remained at the very heart of English curricula internationally and the pedagogic needs surrounding this body of literature have grown increasingly complex as more sophisticated resources become available to scholars, tutors and students. This series aims to offer a clear picture of the critical and performative contexts of a range of chosen texts. In addition, each volume furnishes readers with invaluable insights into the landscape of current scholarly research as well as including new pieces of research by leading critics.

This series is designed to respond to the clearly identified needs of scholars, tutors and students for volumes which will bridge the gap between accounts of previous critical developments and performance history and an acquaintance with new research initiatives related to the chosen plays. Thus, our ambition is to offer innovative and challenging guides that will provide practical, accessible and thought-provoking analyses of early modern drama. Each volume is organized according to a progressive reading strategy involving introductory discussion, critical review and cutting-edge scholarly debate. It has been an enormous pleasure to work with so many dedicated scholars of early modern drama and we are sure that this series will encourage you to read 400-year-old play texts with fresh eyes.

Andrew Hiscock and Lisa Hopkins

ACKNOWLEDGEMENTS

The editors of this volume are sincerely grateful to the series editors, Professors Andrew Hiscock and Lisa Hopkins, for their initial commission, their incisive suggestions on earlier drafts and their cheerful efficiency, throughout. We would also like to thank each of our enthusiastic authors for their thoughtful and thorough contributions.

Margaret Bartley and Susan Furber of Bloomsbury Arden Shakespeare have eased the whole process from start to finish and we are grateful for their attentiveness.

NOTES ON CONTRIBUTORS

Deborah Cartmell is Professor of English, De Montfort University. Her recent publications include *Adaptations in the Sound Era: 1927–37* (Bloomsbury, 2015), *Teaching Adaptations*, ed. (Palgrave, 2014) and *A Companion to Literature, Film and Adaptation* (Blackwell, 2012). She is co-editor and founder of the international journals *Adaptation* and *Shakespeare* and series editor of the Bloomsbury Adaptation Histories.

Christy Desmet is Professor of English at the University of Georgia. She is co-editor of *Borrowers and Lenders: The Journal of Shakespeare and Appropriation* and she is the author of numerous books and articles, including *Shakespearean Gothic* (University of Wales Press, 2009).

Alison Findlay is Professor of English at Lancaster University. Among her recent publications are *Cambridge World Shakespeare Encyclopedia* (2014), *Twelfth Night: A Critical Reader* (Bloomsbury, 2013) and *Much Ado About Nothing: A Guide to the Text and Play in Performance* (Palgrave, 2011).

Brett Greatley-Hirsch is University Academic Fellow in Textual Studies and Digital Editing at the University of Leeds. He is coordinating editor of *Digital Renaissance Editions* and a co-editor of *Shakespeare*, and (with Hugh Craig) is the author of *Style, Computers, and Early Modern Drama* (Cambridge University Press, 2017).

Sarah Neville is an assistant professor of English at the Ohio State University with a courtesy appointment in Theatre. She is an assistant editor of the *New Oxford Shakespeare* (2016), for which she edited five plays, and a general textual editor of

Digital Renaissance Editions. In 2014, she founded Lord Denney's Players, an academic theatre company exploring intersections of texts, criticism and performance.

Elinor Parsons is a Lecturer in Drama at De Montfort University and has published in the field of Renaissance drama and Shakespeare adaptations. She has recently co-edited a special issue of *Adaptation*: 'From Theatre to Film and Back Again!'

Lois Potter is Ned B. Allen Professor Emerita of the University of Delaware. Her publications include the Arden edition of *The Two Noble Kinsmen*, *Shakespeare in Performance: Othello* (Manchester University Press) and *The Life of William Shakespeare* (Wiley-Blackwell). She is also a frequent reviewer of theatre productions.

Kathryn Prince is Associate Professor and Director of Undergraduate Studies in the Department of Theatre at the University of Ottawa, where she is also the Director of the Medieval and Renaissance Studies programme. She has published widely on Shakespeare performance history and reception, including a biography of Dame Judi Dench in the Great Shakespearean Series and chapters in *Shakespeare in the Eighteenth Century*, *Shakespeare in the Nineteenth Century* and elsewhere. She is the author of *Shakespeare in the Victorian Periodicals* and the co-editor of *Performing Early Modern Drama Today* and *History, Memory, Performance*.

Sara Reimers gained her PhD in Shakespeare, gender and casting from the Drama Department at Royal Holloway, University of London, where she is now a Senior Teaching Fellow. She is also a director and dramaturg working on the London fringe and regularly collaborates with Lazarus Theatre Company.

Duncan Salkeld is Professor of Shakespeare and Renaissance Literature, University of Chichester. Among his publications are *Shakespeare Among the Courtesans: Prostitution,*

Literature and Drama 1500–1650 (Ashgate, 2012) and *Madness and Drama in the Age of Shakespeare* (Manchester University Press, 1993).

Elizabeth Schafer is Professor of Drama and Theatre Studies at Royal Holloway, University of London. She has published performance histories of *The Taming of the Shrew* and *Twelfth Night* in the Cambridge Shakespeare in Production series and is currently writing a performance history of *Merry Wives* for Manchester University Press. She edited *The City Wit* for Richard Brome Online and is general editor of the online journal *Australian Studies*. She has also written a biography of Lilian Baylis and a polemic history of women directors' work, *Ms-Directing Shakespeare*.

Peter J. Smith is reader in Renaissance literature, Nottingham Trent University. He is the author of *Social Shakespeare* (Macmillan, 1995), *Between Two Stools* (Manchester University Press, 2012) and co-editor of *Hamlet: Theory and Practice* (Open University Press, 1996). He is a former trustee of the British Shakespeare Association. His essays and reviews have appeared in *Cahiers Élisabéthains*, *Critical Quarterly*, *Shakespeare*, *Shakespeare Bulletin*, *Shakespeare Survey* and *Times Higher Education*.

TIMELINE

1561   Thomas Hoby's translation of Baldassare Castiglione, *The Courtier* (published 1528), a possible source for the Beatrice and Benedick relationship in the verbal sparring between Castiglione's Gaspare Pallavicino and Emilia Pia.

1564   Birth of William Shakespeare in Stratford-upon-Avon.

1569   Matteo Bandello's *La Prima Parte de la Novelle* (1554), translated into French by François de Belleforest, contains a possible source for the Hero plot. Set in Messina, it features Sir Timbreo and his beloved Fenicia Lionata and follows from King Piero's (Peter III of Aragon) defeat of Charles of Anjou (1282).

1590   First three books of Edmund Spenser's *Faerie Queene* are published. II.iv contains a possible source for the Claudio/Hero plot, regarding Claribell, who is killed by her intemperate lover, who has been tricked into thinking her handmaiden, whom his best friend seduces, is his fiancée.

1591   John Harington's translation of Ariosto's *Orlando Furioso* (1532) is published (with a possible source for the Hero and Claudio plot in the story of Ariodante and Genevra in Book V).

1598   Francis Meres, *Palladis Tamia: Wit's Treasury* mentions *Love's Labour's Won* as a play by Shakespeare, thought by some to be *Much Ado About Nothing*. Meres does not mention *Much Ado About Nothing*.

1598	Christopher Marlowe's *Hero and Leander* entered in The Stationers' Register. Shakespeare may have borrowed the name 'Hero' from this poem.
1598–1599	Probable composition of *Much Ado About Nothing*.
1600	*Much Ado About Nothing* appears in the Quarto edition. Some of the speech headings name the comic actor, Will Kemp, in speeches intended for Dogberry. Kemp left the Lord Chamberlain's Men in 1599. The title page states that the play 'hath beene sundrie times publikely acted by the Right Honourable, the Lord Chamberlaine his seruants'.
1603	Death of Elizabeth I, accession of James VI and I.
1613	The play, according to a record of payment to John Heminges in May 1613, was performed as part of the celebrations of the marriage of James VI and I's daughter, Elizabeth, to Frederick, Elector Palatine.
1616	Shakespeare dies.
1623	*Much Ado* published in the Folio edition of Shakespeare's works.
1632	Second Folio, printed from the First Folio of Shakespeare's works.
1662	William Davenant's *The Law Against Lovers*, an adaptation of *Measure for Measure*, which features Benedick and Beatrice, first staged.
1748–1776	Benedick is played by David Garrick between the ages of 31 and 59. Benedick and King Lear were allegedly Garrick's favourite roles.
1862	The opera *Béatrice et Bénédict* by Hector Berlioz first performed at the Theatre der Stadt, Baden-Baden.
1882	Henry Irving and Ellen Terry open in *Much Ado About Nothing* at the Lyceum Theatre.
1898	The opera *Beaucoup de bruit pour rien* by Paul Puget, based on *Much Ado About Nothing*, is published.

1901	Charles Villiers Stanford's opera, *Much Ado About Nothing* premiered at the Royal Opera House, Covent Garden.
1959	John Gielgud and Margret Leighton, Peggy Ashcroft and Diana Wynyard performed the play on Broadway. Gielgud played Benedick between 1931 and 1959.
1965	Franco Zeffirelli directs Maggie Smith and Robert Stephens at the Old Vic.
1976	John Barton directs a Raj-inspired *Much Ado* at the Royal Shakespeare Company (RSC), starring Judi Dench and Donald Sinden.
1980	Terry Hands directs an RSC production with Sinead Cusack and Derek Jacobi.
1984	BBC Shakespeare *Much Ado About Nothing*, starring Cherie Lunghi and Robert Lindsay, directed by Stuart Burge. This production was featured in series seven of the BBC Shakespeare, created by Cedric Messina, which adapted thirty-seven plays between 1978 and 1985. *Much Ado About Nothing*, starring Michael York and Penelope Keith, was intended as the inaugural episode for the BBC series but was abandoned after shooting.
1993	*Much Ado About Nothing*, directed by Kenneth Branagh, starring Branagh and Emma Thompson (BBC Films). The film is notable for its mix of British and American actors, including Michael Keaton, Robert Sean Leonard, Denzel Washington, Keanu Reeves, Richard Briers, Brian Blessed and Kate Beckinsale. This was Branagh's second Shakespeare film, following *Henry V* (1989).
2001	*Di Chahta Hai*, Indian comedy-drama film and loose adaptation of *Much Ado About Nothing*, written and directed by Farhan Akhtar.
2005	BBC's ShakespeaRe-told *Much Ado*, directed by Brian Percival. This is a modern retelling of the story, written by David Nicholls and set in a

	television studio, starring Sarah Parish and Damian Lewis. Also featured in the 2005 series are *Macbeth*, *The Taming of the Shrew* and *A Midsummer Night's Dream*.
2007	Nicholas Hytner directs *Much Ado About Nothing*, starring Zoë Wanamaker and Simon Russell Beale. This production was notable for casting middle-aged actors in the roles of Beatrice and Benedick.
2011	*Much Ado About Nothing*, directed by Josie Rourke, starring Catherine Tate and David Tennant, at Wyndham's Theatre.
2012	Bollywood-style RSC *Much Ado About Nothing*, directed by Iqbal Khan, starring Meera Syal and Paul Bhattacharjee. The production was part of the World Shakespeare Festival.
2012/13	*Much Ado About Nothing*, directed by Joss Whedon, starring Alexis Denisof, Amy Acker and Fran Kranz (Bellwether Pictures). This a black-and-white film set in a contemporary California suburb, which opens with the backstory of Beatrice and Benedick, in which Benedick leaves Beatrice after a night spent together.
2013	*Much Ado About Nothing*, directed by Mark Rylance, starring Vanessa Redgrave and James Earl Jones. The production received largely negative reviews due to the apparent implausibility of senior citizens in the title roles, with Beatrice older than her uncle and Benedick inexplicably best friends with a youthful Claudio.
2014	Video blog series begins, *Nothing Much to Do*, set in a high school in New Zealand.
2014	Web series, *A Bit Much*, set in a summer camp.
2014	RSC production, *Love's Labour's Won*, directed by Christopher Luscombe. The play changed its name to *Much Ado About Nothing* when it moved to the Theatre Royal Haymarket in 2016.
2015	*Messina High*, teenpic film adaptation, directed by Owen Drake.

Introduction

Deborah Cartmell and Peter J. Smith

In *Much Ado About Nothing*, Shakespeare's characters are subject to the whims not of any outrageous fortune, but of each other's prejudices, attractions, affections, dislikes and long-standing grudges. Don John's malevolence has been rationalized by generations of literary critics and theatre directors but the playwright never bothers to explain it. Beatrice and Benedick's mutual adoration comes as a surprise – perhaps even to them; Shakespeare just lets it happen. Until Dogberry and Co. stumble across the conspiracy to defame the innocent Hero, there is a very good chance that Don John will get away with it. The brilliance of *Much Ado* is in its capacity to *appear* random. Its events are controlled only partially by its inhabitants, just as, in the world around us, unpredictability, chance meetings, accidents and unintentionality string together the events of any single life.

For Shakespeare's great eighteenth-century editor and commentator, Dr Johnson, the playwright's rejection of strictly circumscribed literary genres allowed his plays to exhibit 'the real state of sublunary nature, which partakes of good and evil, joy and sorrow'. Shakespeare's plays, Johnson goes on, express 'the course of the world [in which] many mischiefs and many benefits are done and hindered without design.'[1] Could a more accurate description of *Much Ado* be formulated? The *construction* of *Much Ado*, with its symmetries of marrying couples, its parallelisms between the gulling scenes or its ultimate poetic justice, is there all along. The play's brilliance, its delight, is in its capacity to disguise design in disorder.

W.H. Auden observed of *Much Ado About Nothing*, that the subplot of Beatrice and Benedick becomes the play's main focus and that of all of Shakespeare's couples, they seem the most 'equally matched'.[2] The play can be considered Shakespeare's 'Defence of Good Women' (to borrow Thomas Elyot's title of 1540), in its championing of both women misjudged by and equal to men: Hero, falsely accused of infidelity, and Beatrice proven to be equal – if not superior – to any of the men in the play. Beatrice offers, arguably, the best comic role for a woman in the Shakespearean canon. It is a play that attracts top performers who can play Beatrice as well as her male counterpart, Benedick, into old age. Possibly for these reasons, it is a play that has never gone of fashion in the theatre and one with a rich performance history (as this volume attests). The play stands apart from Shakespeare's other comedies in its extraordinary 'ordinariness', a play that shares with *Othello* a very recognizable world and one in which the audience leave the theatre, undoubtedly, on the side of the women.

Lacking battles, regicide, witches, ghosts, regime change or gory torture, *Othello* is often referred to as a 'domestic tragedy'. Its action is ordinary – not that its violence is not terrible – but it is, as Iago puts it, in comparison to the seismic political shifts of *Julius Caesar* or the woeful apocalypse of *King Lear*, for instance, 'small beer' (2.1.163). *Much Ado About Nothing* is to Shakespeare's comedies what *Othello* is to his tragedies. It has none of the vertiginous gender-bending double takes of *As You Like It* or *Twelfth Night*. It lacks the disturbing displays of racism found in *The Merchant of Venice* or the still troubling

stink of misogyny of *The Taming of the Shrew*. Its setting,
characters and situation are diurnal, ordinary and immediately
recognizable.

Stylistically, it is miles away from the sublime lyricism of
Twelfth Night or the metrical discipline of *A Midsummer
Night's Dream*. It is Shakespeare's most prose-y comedy and
just as its language is the spoken demotic of early modern
England, so its concerns are at once completely familiar and
entirely understandable – jealousy, resentment, infidelity,
gossip, vanity, fashion, cock-up and social one-upmanship. Its
focus is familial rather than political, its setting is limited to
one household rather than geographically spread (contrast
The Comedy of Errors or *Pericles*) and its misgivings are
readily solved by the fluky revelation of the conspiracy,
followed smoothly by the restoration of social stability through
the institution of marriage. All is – under the chaos of everyday
life – in the main, well, and it ends well.

This, along with *The Merry Wives of Windsor*, is
Shakespeare's most (to use an awful but currently fashionable
word) *relatable* play. *Merry Wives* is the only one of
Shakespeare's plays (excluding the histories) set in England
and although *Much Ado* is ostensibly taking place in the south
of Italy, its discourse, habitus and environment are as familiar
to its Southwark audience as the Thames or the Tower (see
Duncan Salkeld, Chapter 4 in this volume). The fictional
Messina of *Much Ado* is a version of the real capital city of
Elizabethan England with its revelling elite, masked for an
elaborate ball like today's Hooray Henrys spilling out of
Canary Warf office parties. After last orders, it becomes the
city of night, patrolled by its bumbling Watch who would
rather let the drunks sleep off their inebriation than have to
confront them – anything for a quiet life: 'We will rather sleep
than talk; we know what belongs to a watch' (3.3.37).[3]

Whereas *Merry Wives*' immediacy is comically overwhelmed
by the gargantuan Falstaff whose poetic comeuppance
transports us to a sylvan setting while he suffers a weird
Ovidian metamorphosis, *Much Ado* never turns its back on

the world of lived experience. It is a gritty, down-to-earth study of the desires and deceptions that drive ordinary people set in a world as Ewan Fernie describes that of *Romeo and Juliet*, portrayed in all its 'grainy shittiness'.[4] The plot flirts with the supernatural only to reject it. As the second Hero, Claudio's 'other wife' (5.4.60) is unveiled, the idea of resurrection is hinted at yet, lest we be seduced by this theatrical miracle, the play's most spiritual character, the friar, puts paid to any spiritual possibility: 'All this amazement can I qualify' (67). Secularity or, to put it another way, common sense will prevail: 'let wonder seem familiar' (70), so that instead of suspending our *dis*belief, the play, insistent on credibility, reinforces our *belief*.

Into this ordinary world, Shakespeare puts two extraordinary characters. Benedick and Beatrice, as the similarity of their names implies, are two sides of the same coin. Despite her withering rhetoric concerning Benedick, even Beatrice remarks upon their shared contempt for marriage: 'I am of your humour for that [i.e. as far as wishing to stay single is concerned]' (1.1.124). For his part, Benedick acknowledges Beatrice's physical attractiveness, describing to Claudio how much better looking than Hero she is: Beatrice 'exceeds [Hero] as much in beauty as the first of May doth the last of December' (1.1.182).

The speed with which the two Bs bat their banter to and fro anticipates the verbal tennis match which forces the two protagonists head to head in Stoppard's brilliantly comic *Rosencrantz and Guildenstern Are Dead*. Shakespeare (as always) has got there first and the complementarity of the two Bs' caustic remarks of, and to, one another is both a source of merriment among their spectators who egg them on with supportive high fives – 'You have put him down, lady, you have put him down' (2.1.260) – as well as a device that the play deploys to persuade its audience how paradoxically compatible they really are. As Leonato explains to the messenger in the opening scene, these two are on the same wave-length: 'They never meet but there's a skirmish of wit between them' (1.1.60). The explanation is designed not only to allay the messenger's anxieties but to quieten those of the audience. It is important that we know early on that this is bluster rather than substance and, though the needling may at times sound savage such as when Beatrice cruelly suggests that Benedick is ugly (1.1.130) or that Benedick refers to her as 'this harpy' (2.1.248), theirs is a rhetorical scuffle rather than a genuine confrontation.

In the second scene of *Richard III*, Gloucester shimmies round the verbal assaults of Lady Anne. While their stichomythia makes it sound as though they are on an equal footing, her petulant insults – 'diffused infection of a man . . . hedgehog' (1.2.78–102) and so on – are no match for his ingratiating fluency – 'Fairer than tongue can name thee' (81). Panicked to the point of speechlessness, she can only spit at him. He responds with oleaginous proficiency: 'Never came poison from so sweet a place' (146). Throughout their exchanges, he occupies the driver's seat and she is taken where he chooses. But the wrangles of Beatrice and Benedick are only superficially similar. While they echo each other in terms of individual words – 'my dear Lady Disdain! . . . Is it possible Disdain should die. . .' (1.1.112–14) – each interchange develops the logic of their joint conversation. In *Richard III*, the exchanges between Richard and Anne constitute the thrust and parry of hand-to-hand combat, a gladiatorial encounter of attrition; there can only be one winner. In *Much Ado*, by contrast, the individual contributions accumulate so that they complement each other even as their speakers deny each other compliment.

This love/hate relationship of Beatrice and Benedick is the overriding popular legacy of Shakespeare's *Much Ado About Nothing*. Probably first performed around 1598, it had been preceded in Shakespeare's canon by *The Taming of the Shrew*, around seven years earlier, a play concerned with a seemingly darker 'merry war' (1.1.58) between a man and woman as well as matrimonial concerns such as dowries, wedding services and post-marital obedience. Possible textual residues of *Shrew* may be found in Beatrice being accused of being 'so shrewd of thy tongue' by Leonato (2.1.17) and in Benedick's reference to her as 'Lady Tongue' (2.1.252). Beatrice's own resolution to reform is phrased in terms reminiscent of the earlier comedy: 'And Benedick, love on, I will requite thee, / Taming my wild heart to thy loving hand' (3.1.111–12). Pronouncing a woman a shrew, as Lynda E. Boose has reminded us, was no joke for an early modern audience. Being a shrew was one of the three most heinous crimes for a woman, following witchcraft and adultery.[5] As Hero is 'overheard' noting Benedick's alleged admiration for Beatrice, she remarks how the latter would set out to denigrate the most virtuous of men: 'I never yet saw man,' she says, 'But [Beatrice] would spell him backward' (3.1.59–61). Witches were supposed to summon their familiars by praying back to front. Hyperbolically, Hero accuses Beatrice's stubborn contempt for men as being a kind of witchcraft.

Indeed, as Mihoko Suzuki has argued in her discussion of the numerous cuckolding jokes in *Much Ado*, the play enacts the high cost of the men's jokes to the women in the play.[6] The distrust of women or the fear of cuckoldry that permeates the play, that a husband will almost inevitably be duped and grow horns, visualizing his emasculation, is proved unfounded but it is a paranoia that pervaded a culture which transmitted its reputation, estate and political power, generationally, to the eldest born son. Illegitimacy, as Alison Findlay has so powerfully shown, is the period's worst nightmare.[7] Edmund in *King Lear* is the walking representative of the bastard's evils, a lethal combination of Machiavellian self-interest, ruthlessness and betrayal. As the death of Desdemona and the denunciation of Innogen (in *Cymbeline*) demonstrate, the consequences of even an unproven whiff of infidelity could be catastrophic. However, for all Don John's malevolent design, Hero is eventually exonerated and in the comic world of *Much Ado*, in spite of a tirade of cuckold jokes (such as 'pluck off the bull's horns and set them in my forehead', 1.1.245), the women emerge as models of constancy.

While echoes of the earlier *Taming of the Shrew* can be detected in *Much Ado*, the Claudio and Hero plot contains traces of *Romeo and Juliet*. The suddenness of Claudio and

Hero's love for each other recalls the fatal attraction of Romeo and Juliet who seem to live by the aphorism coined by Christopher Marlowe in *Hero and Leander*: 'Who ever lov'd, that lov'd not at first sight?'[8] This poem probably inspired Shakespeare's choice of 'Hero' as a name and is recalled in Benedick's ironic model of the ill-fated lover in 'Leander the good swimmer' (5.2.30–1). In *As You Like It*, written around the same time, the pining Phoebe quotes Marlowe's line on the hopelessness of love at first sight (3.5.83), overcome as she is by the appearance of Ganymede. As if to illustrate the recklessness of such infatuation, Shakespeare has staged Ganymede as the external masculine disguise of the play's heroine, Rosalind. Usually, such unchecked impetuosity is a masculine shortcoming. *As You Like It*'s Orlando is just such a giddy youth and when Romeo sees Juliet across a crowded room, thoughts of his previous girlfriend, Rosaline, evaporate. In *Much Ado*, Shakespeare dwells on the intensity of such misguided passion so that Claudio's sudden fascination for Hero comes out of the blue: 'dost thou note the daughter of Signor Leonato?' (1.1.155). Nonetheless, even in this early part of the play, there is a hint of the incipient violence that will characterize the jilting at the altar. Claudio explains that the vehemence of his passion results from his experiences in battle. His marital enthusiasm has displaced his martial choler:

> But now I am returned [from war], and that war-thoughts
> Have left their places vacant, in their rooms
> Come thronging soft and delicate desires,
> All prompting me how fair young Hero is.
>
> (1.1.282–5)

The implication is that his attraction to her is as heedless as the heat of battle, a metaphor that finds its correlative in the 'merry war' of the two Bs. Lacking the devotion of Orlando, Claudio is gullible, readily accepting the allegations of Hero's inconstancy. Hero is wooed (oddly) by proxy, at Leonato's masque, Don Pedro standing in for Claudio. Subsequently,

Claudio is too quick to credit Don John's malicious rumour that Don Pedro intends to elbow Claudio's suit to one side: ''Tis certain so; the prince woos for himself' (2.1.159) and Claudio's sombre maxim is typical of his self-pitying narcissism: 'Friendship is constant in all other things, / Save in the office and affairs of love' (160–1). This early miscalculation, a combination of his vanity and his predisposition to mistrust others (Don Pedro and Hero), anticipates the more serious conspiracy, orchestrated by the villainous Don John and his accomplices, Borachio and Conrade, and adumbrates Claudio's inexplicable and perverse desire publicly to denigrate Hero at their wedding, throwing her back to her father as a 'rotten orange' (4.1.28). The two episodes are bound together by the reference to the citrus fruit. As Claudio laments Don Pedro's apparent appropriation of his intended, Beatrice mischievously describes him as 'civil as an orange, and something of that jealous complexion' (2.1.270). R.E.R. Madelaine notes that, 'the association between oranges and love or lust appears to have had some emblematic currency in the Elizabethan period.'[9]

Shakespeare makes Claudio, as Claire McEachern observes, 'far more of a cad'[10] than his literary predecessors. Leonato pleads with Claudio to make an honest woman of Hero if the two have already slept together, telling him, if you 'Have vanquished the resistance of her youth / And made defeat of her virginity–' (4.1.45–6). Similarly in *The Tempest*, Prospero is violently obsessed by the idea of his daughter's virginity remaining intact until marriage. He sets out the terrible consequences of premarital sex in a way designed to scare Ferdinand off:

If thou dost break her virgin-knot before
All sanctimonious ceremonies may
With full and holy rite be ministered,
No sweet aspersion shall the heavens let fall
To make this contract grow; but barren hate,
Sour-eyed disdain, and discord, shall bestrew

The union of your bed with weeds so loathly
That you shall hate it.

(Tem 4.1.15–22)

These examples illustrate the anxieties of patriarchal authority. When Leonato is persuaded – almost – of his daughter's iniquity, his denunciation of her is even more shocking than Claudio's stage management of it, especially to a modern audience:

> Could she here deny
> The story that is printed in her blood?
> Do not live, Hero; do not ope thine eyes!
> For did I think thou wouldst not quickly die,
> Thought I thy spirits were stronger than thy shames,
> Myself would on the rearward of reproaches
> Strike at thy life.

(MA 4.1.121–7)

Claudio stages a public humiliation of Hero and Leonato reacts by threatening to kill his own child.

Hero's only hope of survival, counselled by Friar Francis (in his trickery a kinsman of *Romeo*'s Friar Lawrence), is to pretend to be dead and hide away in a convent for an indefinite period. Ophelia too has been told to get to a nunnery, a byword in a period of proud Protestantism for a brothel. Although Hero survives the vicious dishonouring and disowning of her by both father and would-be husband, she becomes a victim of domestic abuse and as Claudio observes upon unknowingly being reunited with her on his second wedding, 'Another Hero!' (5.4.62). By the end of the play she is 'another Hero', no longer the optimistic and idealistic young woman of the first half but one who can never look at Claudio in the same way again. Even Beatrice changes after her submission to marriage. Her defiant behaviour, which climaxes in her most assertive outburst immediately following her declaration of love to Benedick, demanding he 'Kill Claudio' (4.1.287), is curtailed when her mouth is stopped (on the order of either Leonato or Benedick, depending on editorial choice) and she becomes the property of her husband. Uncomfortably, to modern audiences, the vociferous Beatrice, to quote Iago, '[f]rom this time forth . . . never will speak word' (*Oth* 5.2.301). The stage directions in the 1600 Quarto mysteriously include a wife for Leonato, 'Innogen' in 1.1 and 2.1, and her potential (albeit improbable) presence on stage as ignored and mute wife would give immense weight to Beatrice's unwillingness 'to hear tell of a husband' (2.1.321). As Peter J. Smith has pointed out, 'Marriage is a male institution wherein women are censored into nothing. The function of marriage at the conclusion of these [comic] plays is to render harmless the manipulative skills of Shakespeare's females. Paulina, Isabella, Viola, Rosalind and Beatrice are hurriedly married off to effect their ineffectiveness'.[11]

The unlikely and unsung heroes of the play are 'Keystone Kops' extras, the master constable, Dogberry, headborough (parish officer, one rank below constable), Verges and the members of the Watch, George Seacoal and Hugh Oatcake, who uncover the plot to discredit Hero, in spite of being mocked throughout the play for their bumbling behaviour, in particular Dogberry's inability to make himself understood by those of superior rank. Sneering at lower-status figures' inarticulacy, that of the Messenger, Margaret, Balthasar and, of course, Dogberry (originally played by Will Kemp, notorious for his ad-libbing in Shakespeare's company, The Chamberlain's Men), is a game repeatedly played by the higher ranked figures in the play, as McEachern observes (74–5), and one which keeps those at the bottom of the hierarchy firmly in their linguistic place. Even Hero, in the dressing scene (3.4) as R.H. McKeown has suggested, in his discussion of the play's civil conversations, 'actively polices Margaret's edgy attempts at repartee'.[12]

Although Shakespeare allows the Watch to solve the felony, a heroic outcome is resisted. The Watch is incapable of communicating the crime in a timely manner that would have prevented Hero's abuse. The play encourages laughter at the

Watch's expense, laughter that has become increasingly awkward in modern performances. For instance, Michael Keaton's adoption of an 'Irish' accent for Dogberry in Kenneth Branagh's 1993 film could be seen as thoughtlessly offensive (and not a little surprising given Branagh's own Belfast upbringing). In the RSC's 2014 production, set in the aftermath of the First World War, Dogberry's malapropisms and physical tics were implicitly attributed to shell shock and the 'comic' result was unintentionally unsettling:

> The tendency for the audience to find his twitching head, in particular, amusing was gratefully received by the production and Nick Haverson's performance prompts some intriguing questions about political correctness and laughing at disability. That the twitching was clearly shown to be the result of post-traumatic stress made it even more uncomfortable. It may seem inappropriate to censor such characterisations and, like it or not, some people find some disability to be a laughing matter, but to rely upon the Great War for the source of such comic effect is, at best, insensitive.[13]

While these accidental heroes (and especially their contemporary representations) are problematic, the play's anti-hero is equally so: as Geoffrey Bullough pithily puts it, 'Don John is a very small villain to cause so Much Ado.'[14] Don John has perplexed critics for his Iago-like lack of motivation. His malignity, the play seems to suggest, is simply attributable to his being born out of wedlock. The play survives in two editions: a Quarto of 1600 and the 1623 Folio based on a copy of the Quarto with some annotations. In the Quarto edition Don John's bastardy is present in the stage directions and speech prefixes but these would not be visible in performance unless Don John's appearance signified a bastard in some form. In *King Lear* and *King John* the plays' illegitimates are roundly labelled as such but Don John's bastardy is only casually mentioned and that not until well after he has made his escape (4.1.188).

However, as Angela Stock has observed, *Much Ado About Nothing* does not explicitly offer itself as a platform on which to debate gender transgression or racial exclusion, as we see in comedies such as *Twelfth Night*, *As You Like It* or *The Merchant of Venice*. Like *King Lear*'s Edmund, Don John's status as illegitimate is not related to 'any of the social, ethnic or religious minority groups that have attracted particular attention; he is no exotic intruder, enslaved colonial, puritan or Jew'.[15] But as Stock notes, as a bastard, he is one of the many 'nothings' in the play, significantly 'not of many words' (1.1.150), a product of extramarital infidelity and in direct contrast to the loose 'tongues' that surround him. As such, Don John embodies many of the issues that the play raises, summarized in the pun on 'nothing' in the play's title.

The meanings of the words 'nothing' – a void but more coarsely as slang for the female genitalia (i.e. no-thing where 'thing' means penis) – and 'noting' (as 'nothing' may well have been pronounced), signifying 'knowing' or 'noticing', have generated much of the play's criticism, concerned with themes of misogyny, eavesdropping, deception and the role of the onlooker. Claudio's fancy for Hero is phrased in such loaded terms as he asks Benedick, 'didst thou *note* the daughter of Signor Leonato?' (1.1.154, emphasis added). Benedick's response separates his observation from anything more salacious: 'I noted her not, but I looked on her.' The word's quibbling qualities cluster round the exchange between Don Pedro and the musician, Balthasar. As Don Pedro requests a song, the musician responds with a riddle that activates the polyvalent senses of the term:

DON PEDRO
    Nay, pray thee, come,
    Or if thou wilt hold longer argument,
    Do it in notes.
BALTHASAR   Note this before my notes:
    There's not a note of mine that's worth the noting.

DON PEDRO
Why, these are very crotchets that he speaks.
Note notes, forsooth, and nothing!

(2.3.50–5)

'Nothing' in its most nihilistic manifestation resonates through *King Lear* – a play where its meaning and tone offer, paradoxically, the only fixed point in a universe spiralling out of control. In *Much Ado*, by contrast, the word slips between its various senses and even, as the scales fall from the eyes of the two Bs, it figures within their clumsy declarations of mutual love:

BENEDICK
I do love nothing in the world so well as you. Is that
not strange?
BEATRICE
As strange as the thing I know not. It were as possible
for me to say I loved nothing so well as you. But
believe me not – and yet I lie not. I confess nothing,
nor I deny nothing.

(4.1.267–72)

For theatregoers, the most memorable scenes in the play are the gulling of Benedick and Beatrice (2.3 and 3.1) in which the two are fooled into thinking that their sparring partner is in love with them. Benedick's gulling is the longer of the two and mostly in prose whereas the tricking of Beatrice is in poetry, giving it a more formal or serious quality. In recent theatre productions, the tendency is to concentrate more on Benedick, with his attempts to conceal himself from Don Pedro, Claudio and Leonato made outrageously obvious to everyone but himself. Kenneth Branagh's Benedick in his film of 1993 tries unsuccessfully to make himself inconspicuous while noisily fumbling with a deck chair, David Tennant's Benedick in the 2011 Josie Rourke production accidentally covers himself in paint and in the 2014 RSC production, Edward Bennett as Benedick pops in and out of a giant Christmas tree. The quickness of Benedick's conversion to love attests to a latent desire for Beatrice, although his immediate concern is with how he will be perceived by the men.

In contrast, Beatrice is presented in her gulling scene as a sacrificial victim and the women take an almost sadistic pleasure in catching her like a fish that will 'greedily devour the treacherous bait' (3.1.28). In this scene, Hero, freed from male domination, becomes indeed 'another Hero'. Speaking in another voice (justifying Don John's previous assessment of her in 1.3.52 as 'a very forward March chick'), employing epic similes –

> Where honeysuckles ripened by the sun
> Forbid the sun to enter, like favourites
> Made proud by princes that advance their pride
> Against that power that bred it.

> (3.1.8–11)

– and drawing from Petrarchan conventions, she takes on the role of the masculine hunter in pursuit of the female prey. No punches are pulled in her character assassination of Beatrice who is accused of being 'self-endeared' (3.1.56), in love with her wit above all else. Picking up the imagery of wild birds from her accusers, Beatrice is quick to accept their harsh criticisms and, speaking in poetry for the first time in the play, vows to a future of self-effacement in which she will, in the conventional Petrarchan language of romantic surrender, tame her 'wild heart' for the sake of Benedick.[16] It is worth observing that Beatrice is subdued or even silenced, not by the men, but by the women. Although acting on behalf of the men, Hero's demolition of Beatrice can be seen as much an act of cruelty as of kindness. In the 2014 RSC production, Beatrice's gulling took a fraction of the time of Benedick's, perhaps reflecting a modern-day discomfort with seeing a woman, at the hands of other women, so effectively insulted and humbled.

New millennial productions of the play have moved away from concentrating on themes of wordplay, deception and misogyny, focusing on generational issues, with the ageing of Beatrice and Benedick at the core of the play with the parts taken by Zoë Wanamaker (aged 58) and Simon Russell Beale (46), directed by Nicholas Hytner in 2007 and Vanessa Redgrave (76) and James Earl Jones (82) directed by Mark Rylance in 2013 (see Chapter 5 by Elizabeth Schafer and Sara Reimers in this volume). Major British productions since 2000 attest to the play's popularity, especially with 'A-list' actors:

2006   Tamsin Greig and Joseph Millson, RSC, directed by
       Marianne Elliott
2007   Zoë Wanamaker and Simon Russell Beale, National
       Theatre, directed by Nicholas Hytner
2011   Eve Best and Charles Edwards, Shakespeare's Globe,
       directed by Jeremy Herrin
2011   Catherine Tate and David Tennant, Wyndham's
       Theatre, directed by Josie Rourke
2012   Meera Syal and Paul Bhattacharjee, RSC, directed by
       Iqbal Khan
2013   Vanessa Redgrave and James Earl Jones, The Old Vic,
       directed by Mark Rylance

Oddly, given the well-known Hollywood formula of beginning with an argumentative man and woman and ending with a made-for-each-other-couple, refined into what Stanley Cavell has dubbed the 'comedies of remarriage' (such as *Bringing up Baby*, directed by Howard Hawks, 1938, or *The Philadelphia Story*, directed by George Cukor, 1940),[17] the play was not made into a major film until 1993, directed by Kenneth Branagh. Compared to *Hamlet*, *King Lear*, *Macbeth* or *A Midsummer Night's Dream*, major screen adaptations of *Much Ado* are few and far between with BBC's ShakespeaRe-told's *Much Ado*, directed by Brian Percival, released in 2005 and a contemporary adaptation, directed by Joss Whedon, 2012, the most notable of these. But as we have suggested, the play is potentially the unacknowledged source for a range of films and novels employing the formula of a man and woman bickering at the outset and becoming a couple at the end, such as *It Happened One Night* (1934), *When Harry Met Sally* (1989), *Bridget Jones's Diary* (2001, based on the 1996 novel by Helen Fielding) or *La La Land* (2017). Jane Austen's *Pride and Prejudice* is a prime example of a book potentially inspired by Shakespeare's play with Benedick's definition of the perfect wife –

> Rich she shall be, that's certain; wise, or I'll none; virtuous, or I'll never cheapen her; mild, or come not near me; noble or not I for an angel. Of good discourse, an excellent musician, and her hair shall be of what colour it please God.
>
> (2.3.28–33)

– matched by Mr Darcy's notion of female perfection that so infuriates Elizabeth Bennet.[18] Like their counterparts, B and B, Elizabeth and Darcy end as a couple despite – or because of – their initial hostility to each other.

In 'The Critical Backstory', Alison Findlay examines three areas of the play – the Watch, the romance plot involving Hero and Claudio and the Beatrice–Benedick story. She notes across all three of these a 'critical tradition that simultaneously celebrates *Much Ado*'s display of clever wit' but at the same time is alert to 'the folly of those on stage and off who create much ado about nothing with both comic and potentially tragic consequences' (24). Findlay underlines the critical discontent with Claudio's (and the play's) treatment of Hero, a character who personifies 'women's vulnerability to male abuse' (27) but she also alerts us to the reservations characteristic of eighteenth- and nineteenth-century criticism about the outspokenness and immodesty of Beatrice.

Although appearing irregularly on screen, *Much Ado* has never been out of the theatre as Kathryn Prince observes in her chapter on the play's performance history. Prince highlights the habitual combination of the celebratory with the elegiac in productions of the play, which she describes as a 'generally conservative performance history' (63). Prince suggests that the popularity of the play is often a result of wallpapering over its cracks. Claudio's unbridled display of misogyny, for instance, is often made to be forgivable through casting Claudio as extremely young or in opting for a period setting or a hot climate with 'emotional volume' likewise 'turned up' (49), such as that of Iqbal Khan's RSC adaptation set in Delhi with a British Asian cast. However, this Bollywood-style production, while visually stunning, for Prince created its own set of problems. The 'intercultural ribbing' (61) and the 'experience of watching actors from the British Asian community depict contemporary Delhi-dwellers as objects of laughter was uncomfortable' (60).

In 'The State of the Art', Elinor Parsons observes how the darker side of the play has dominated criticism from the latter part of the twentieth century, reflecting on how the male characters are redeemed through editorial and performance decisions. And while theatre productions have been dominated by the performances of Beatrice and Benedick, critical attention has been placed on the figures of Hero and Claudio and editorial and performance decisions that affect the interpretation of gender, status and comedy.

Duncan Salkeld argues, in the next chapter, that Shakespeare evokes Italy through Italian poetic devices, particularly the ways in which Beatrice and Benedick are transformed into sonnet-writing Petrarchan lovers. While the play alludes to its Italian setting on a number of levels, topographical references place the drama firmly in London, in particular the lampooning of the Watch which Salkeld argues is almost certainly inspired by the London Watchmen, described in 1584 with the verbosity of a Dogberry: their function is to 'divide themselves into several companies and to apprehend all such suspect persons as they will find within their said wards and forthwith to search them for any dangerous and suspect things about them' (101).[19]

Reading Beatrice as a woman of 'a certain age' is tackled by Elizabeth Schafer and Sara Reimers in an analysis of Nicholas Hytner's 2007 National Theatre production, starring a middle-aged Zoë Wanamaker and Simon Russell Beale. While it is reasonable to deduce that Beatrice and Benedick are older than Hero and Claudio – as Leonato confirms that Benedick was a child at Hero's conception (1.1.102) – there is a tendency to extend the age gap in contemporary performances. Hytner's production dwelt on the backstory of Benedick and Beatrice with emphasis on Beatrice's 'I know you of old. . . .' (1.1.138–9) which Schafer and Reimers argue produced a more nuanced or novelistic Benedick and Beatrice in a production that seemed to be more resonant of Chekhov than Shakespeare.

In '*Much Ado* or *Love's Labour's Won*? Does It Matter Which?', Lois Potter also considers the backstory of Beatrice and Benedick and the significance of the war (from which the soldiers have just returned) with the possibility that the play is a sequel to *Love's Labour's Lost* with an original title to match. Potter reflects on the aftermath of the tantalizing appearance of *Love's Labour's Won* in Francis Meres's 1598 list of Shakespeare's comedies and looks at possible connections between *Love's Labour's* and *Much Ado*. She ends by looking at the plays within an evolution of an attitude to wit, from a somewhat confused attitude in *Love's Labour's* to one of complex interaction of the serious and the comic in *Much Ado*.

In the following chapter, Christy Desmet notes the influence of social media on Joss Whedon's 2012 film and the legacy of his *Much Ado* to contemporary internet productions, in particular, the 2014 adaptations, *Nothing Much to Do*, *SHAKES* and *A Bit Much*. Although the play's protagonists are a potential focus of empathy for a 'middle-aged' audience, as Schafer and Reimers have reminded us, Desmet's chapter reflects the appeal of the play to a younger, media-savvy fan base. She sees the emergence of social media presentations of *Much Ado* (and other Shakespeare plays) as witty, skilful and significant interventions in Shakespearean production and interpretation.

Finally, Brett Greatley-Hirsch and Sarah Neville, in 'Resources', consider recent print editions and online resources and suggest approaches for teaching the play. This chapter features annotated bibliographies on textual histories and sources, genre and language, sex and gender, music, performance history and dramaturgy and adaptations.

The enduring evolution of *Much Ado About Nothing* within the theatre, cinema and academy testifies to its popularity as well as its cultural significance. As the following chapters demonstrate, it is a play that continues to address contemporary concerns to do with the treatment of women, the magnitude of social rituals such as marriage and the malevolence and gravity of apparently innocent gossip. Yet for all its seriousness in terms of consequence, the world of the play is quite ordinary and its characters readily recognizable. Like *Othello* it may be only 'small beer' but, like *Othello*, it remains one of the most resonant and immediate plays in Shakespeare's canon.

1

The Critical Backstory

Alison Findlay

The earliest comment on *Much Ado* appears from one of the actors in Shakespeare's own company: Robert Armin, who took over the clownish role of Dogberry from William Kemp. Kemp's name appears in the speech prefixes to the 1600 Quarto, suggesting that the role was written with him in mind, but Armin, a very different kind of clown, had to step into Kemp's shoes. Armin's verse translation *The Italian Taylor and His Boy* (1609), which David Wiles notes is as much autobiography as popular romance,[1] comments explicitly on adopting the role of Dogberry, and implicitly draws attention to the type of comedy dramatized in *Much Ado*. Armin's dedications advertise his skill in morphing Kemp's style of grotesque buffoonery into his own deft, witty wordplay. Mimicking Dogberry, he asks his aristocratic dedicatees to excuse 'the boldnes of a Begger, who hath been writ downe for an Asse in his time, & pleades under *forma pauperis* in it still, not-withstanding his Contableship and Office' (A3). He reminds his 'invisible' readers that '*when the* Taylor *wants bombast, he will make Ragges fluffe out*' contrasting his own rhetorical skill, displayed in Dogberry's bombast, to the corpulence of Kemp, who had previously filled Dogberry's fine 'two gowns and everything handsome about him' (4.2.85–7).[2] Armin encourages readers to read more beneath the surface: '*will this meere foole, little learning, be so bould? why the wisest can do no more?*' implicitly suggesting that Dogberry is not altogether fool.

Dogberry and the Watch

Armin's incidental remarks are the first in a long critical tradition that recognizes the clownish figures of Dogberry and the Watch as witty constructions whose dialogue illuminates the serious concerns of *Much Ado*.

In 1664 Margaret Cavendish took up Armin's point and defended Shakespeare against the charge of writing scripts 'made up onely with Clowns, Fools, Watchmen and the like'. With a Dogberry-like wit of her own, she argues that Shakespeare's effective characterization of a Fool required more 'Witty, Wise, Judicious' and 'Ingenious' observation than scripting 'Sensible Discourses' since 'Tis Harder to express Nonsense than Sense'. Cavendish praised the powers of metamorphosis demonstrated in Shakespeare's composition of roles which suggest he 'was Really himself the Clown or Jester he feigns.'[3]

Critical admiration for the artful construction of Dogberry and the Watch continues, undaunted, throughout the eighteenth, nineteenth and twentieth centuries. Dogberry's appeal seems to be partly because he offers an indulgent image of our own folly. In 1774, Francis Gentleman saw the Watch as 'very whimsical characters, yet highly within the bounds of nature.' Although the cleverly constructed malapropisms were 'a little strained, yet we have met with instances in real life, not far behind.' Gentleman's view that the 'ignorant forwardness of fools in office . . . never fails to create a considerable degree of laughter'[4] is borne out by William Hazlitt's even sharper satiric perspective in 1817. He proposed that Dogberry and the Watch offer 'a standing record of that formal gravity of pretension and total want of common understanding which Shakespeare no doubt copied from real life, and which in the course of two hundred years appear to have ascended from the lowest to the highest offices in the state.'[5]

Looking back over the late twentieth century, Darl Larsen deftly compared Shakespeare's comic technique with that of the anarchic comedy team Monty Python. Both use incongruity to lampoon and then indulgently redeem authority figures:

> Dogberry and Verges not only speak what is not expected to be spoken, thereby disrupting a pattern, but they are also representatives of civil authority as they offer their gibberish. And the fact that Shakespeare then doubles back on expectations and allows these characters to figure so prominently in the successful resolution of the narrative is yet another incongruous element.[6]

Larsen's comparison to Python brings out an ambiguous quality in the comic scenes, and in the critical responses themselves. Critical superiority to Dogberry's idiotic pomposity is invariably balanced by an indulgent identification with his qualities and, moreover, with a sense of optimistic wonder that this foolish everyman is instrumental in creating the happy ending. The German critic Hermann Ulrici (1839) believed that Dogberry personifies 'the spirit and meaning of the whole' because his 'ever contradictory doings and resolves, thoughts and sayings' function as a microcosm of the play's preoccupation with the contradiction between 'subjective conception and objective reality.' In Ulrici's view, Dogberry 'who is so presumptuous and yet so modest; who looks at things with so correct an eye and yet pronounces such foolish judgements' embodies the paradoxical nature of *Much Ado* itself. While never allowing anyone to forget he is an ass, it is nevertheless he who 'is the very one to discover the *nothing* which is the cause of the *much ado*'.[7]

E.W. Sievers (1886) went further in arguing that Dogberry's sensitivity to the insult of 'ass' showed '*pathos*, in the fullest sense of the word.' Dogberry's curious combination of pride and vulnerability is a feature of common humanity in the play and beyond: 'Man, in spite of all his boast of freedom and independence is but the impotent creature of his temperament.'[8] John Allen's 1973 article 'Dogberry' draws on this tradition of reading the clown seriously as a 'comic everyman' whose egotistical folly reflects the play world. Allen argues that, as the 'nonpareil of beatific self-appreciation', Dogberry embodies the self-regarding tendencies of other characters in Messina, from the villain Don John to Beatrice and Benedick and the self-righteous Leonato. As such, he is 'the gross exemplar of an attitude which is endemic there', a short-sightedness and inflated sense of pride that threatens to plunge the play into tragedy. At the same time, Dogberry is responsible for illuminating truths through his nonsensical malapropisms and 'speaking some of the lines that lie at the satiric heart of *Much Ado*'.[9] More surprisingly, Allen proposes that Dogberry's transcendent self-assurance and his resolution of the plot makes him 'a special kind of *deus ex machina*', bearing comparison to noble figures such as Prospero in *The Tempest* or Duke Vincentio in *Measure for Measure*. While, on one hand, the play invests the everyman role with a mysterious wisdom, Dogberry's own prompt encourages everyone to 'forget not that I am an ass' (4.2.79–80). Allen thus shows how *Much Ado* invites our indulgence 'not only for Dogberry himself but for the Dogberry-like qualities of other characters in the play and even, by extension, in ourselves.'[10] The insights of Armin, who played Dogberry for the Lord Chamberlain's Men on how a fool's '*little learning*' might outdo '*the wisest*', thus inaugurate a critical tradition that simultaneously celebrates *Much Ado*'s display of clever wit and registers, with some uneasiness, the folly of those on stage and off who create much ado about nothing with both comic and potentially tragic consequences.

The Hero–Claudio plot: desire, death and genre

The romantic plot's proximity to tragedy has been an enduring issue for critics. Unease with the Hero–Claudio love plot may have influenced Davenant's decision to ignore it in his adaptation *The Law Against Lovers* (1662). The sudden, passionate turns in Hero and Claudio's romance were explicitly criticized for violating the rules of comedy and of probability in commentaries across the eighteenth century. Gildon's 'Critical Remarks on Shakespeare' in Rowe' s edition of 1709 identified tragic elements in all but three of Shakespeare's comedies, complaining 'that way of Trage-Comedy was the common Mistake of that Age.'[11] *Much Ado*'s generic hybridity was a case in point: 'This Play we must call a *Comedy*, tho' some of the Incidents and Discourse too are more in a Tragic Strain; and that of the Accusation of Hero is too shocking for either Tragedy or Comedy'. Claudio's conduct, 'to expose her in so barbarous a Manner and with so little Concern, and struggle and on such weak Grounds without a farther Examination in the Matter' was 'contrary to the very Nature of Love'. Charlotte Lennox's *Shakespear Illustrated* (1754), a pioneering, detailed study of Shakespeare's intertexts, concurred with this assessment. She roundly criticized Shakespeare for changing the circumstances of the romance 'for others, wholly inconsistent and ridiculous', with 'utter disregard to probability and contempt of Decorum'. In addition to altering perfectly good plots, Shakespeare was guilty of 'injudicious Change of the Characters', where he 'deviated from the Original [Ariosto's *Orlando Furioso*] to introduce his own wild Conceits' with a disastrous effect in the case of Claudio's role. Comparing it to Ariosto's Ariodante, Lennox observed: 'Claudio is mean, selfish, ungenerous and cruel: Qualities that are seldom found in the Heroe and Lover, and he is represented as both.'[12] James Miller's adaptation *The Universal Passion* (1737) addressed such concerns by staging a much more grief-stricken and repentant lover. The priest's idea that the image of Hero will return to Claudio's imagination 'More moving, delicate, and full of life', to make him 'wish he had not so accused her' (4.1.223–33) is dramatized in Miller's text. The romantic lead, Bellario, appropriates the priest's lines to address an idealized Lucilia who enters 'Into the Eye and Prospect of my Soul' and fills him with remorse. He is grief-stricken with guilt that her last pleas and tears were unable 'to quench my flaming Fury' or 'penetrate this base remorseless Breast.'[13] Miller rewrites Claudio using Valentine's lines from *Two Gentlemen of Verona* (3.1.170–81), as a passionate lover who feels he has been banished from himself in the 'fatal Banishment' from Lucilia:

> Unless *Lucilia's by me in the Night*
> *There is no* Mucick in the Nightingale,
> Unless I view *Lucilia* in the Day
> All Nature is a beamless Blank to me.

(72)

Bellario's vow to undertake 'solemn pentitential Rites, / To own my Rashness and her Innocence' (71) thus seems believable, though it is not staged. Miller gives more substance to the emotional attachment between the lovers by making Bellario reject a second marriage as 'Impossible' since it fills him with 'Horror' and his 'Nature shudders at the very Sound' (71). When faced with the veiled bride, Bellario can only remember 'my eternal Shame', and 'my pernicious, rash, distracted Folly' at the previous wedding (77). Miller's adaptation thus makes explicit the emotional unease often felt by critics and spectators with the second wedding that supposedly brings a harmonious conclusion to the romantic plot.

By expanding the role of Hero in the more spirited, witty Lucilia, Miller simultaneously registers scepticism about the happy ending. At the first wedding Lucilia admits her reluctance to marry since 'love of Freedom struggled in my Breast' (62) and when she takes off her veil at the second betrothal, Lucilia undercuts Bellario's hyperbolic apology that she is like 'a good Angel to a Wretch' by pointedly telling him 'You may again bring Wretchedness upon me', and refusing his embrace. Lucilia's unwillingness to risk her happiness again having 'once escaped the Wreck' is rendered entirely logical in her question 'Why should I prove the boisterous Main again?' (77). Her doubts about the adequacy of the play's ending are echoed by many actors and critics in the twentieth century.

Lucilia operates as an early feminist critical voice within the play, drawing attention to women's vulnerability to male abuse. Her lead is followed by Mrs Elizabeth Griffith, daughter of the manager of the Theatre Royal, Dublin, and an actor herself. Griffith's *Morality of Shakespeare's Drama Illustrated* (1775) saw the 'unhappy Hero' as a victim of slander, 'so very irksome a theme, that it disgusts me to dwell upon it.' She commended Beatrice's passionate attack on Claudio and the falsehood of men: 'There is a generous warmth of indignation in this speech which must certainly impress a female reader with the same sentiments upon such an occasion.' Beatrice was justified since 'there is nothing which a woman of virtue feels herself more offended at than defamation' and Antonio's contempt for 'the bragging profligates of those or, indeed, of any times' was likewise justified.[14]

Eighteenth-century concerns about the probability of the romantic plot began with Charles Gildon who complained that its 'Absurdities' of incidence were only redeemed by the 'admirably distinguish'd' villain Don John, without whose consistently 'sour, melancholly, saturnine, envious, selfish, malicious Temper' the events 'could not have gone on'. A sense of naturalness was also restored, for Gildon, by Leonato's passion.[15] Later critics seized on Leonato, Antonio and the Priest as figures whose sensibility and rational thought redeemed the play by eighteenth-century standards. These three figures had never received, and would never receive, more attention in commentaries. Francis Gentleman, writing in Bell's Shakespeare edition, argued that in Act 4 Scene 1 'there is a very nervous, beautiful strain of parental resentment and grief' in Leonato's speech 'and though we know *Hero's* innocence, we must strongly sympathize with the agitated father',[16] a view shared by Griffith. Gentleman criticized the Theatre Royal's decision to cut Leonato's further lamentations in Act 5 Scene 1 (even though he knows Hero is not dead), arguing that they express 'very strong reasoning in favour of those natural feelings which arrogant stoicism considers as weakness. We recommend these lines as well worthy of preservation, for speaking and perusal.' Gentleman likewise praised the Friar's lines, for 'much purity and fancy of expression.'[17] William Warburton was the first to notice the Priest's cleverness in asking Hero what man she was accused with as a means to test her innocence, arguing that the question showed him 'to be no fool'.[18] Elizabeth Griffith agreed the Priest showed 'a just knowledge of the world' and, in addition, noted his 'intimate acquaintance with the secret movements of the human heart' in his proposed plan to reform Claudio's misjudgement.[19] Even the (questionable) success of the Priest's plot did not redress dissatisfaction with the balance of justice at the end of the play, though. Gentleman believed that, even in a comedy, 'Shakespeare should have brought the *Bastard* to some disgrace or punishment for his villainy.'[20]

In striking contrast to these eighteenth-century complaints about inconsistency and tone, the late nineteenth-century critic Swinburne declared the play Shakespeare's 'most perfect comic masterpiece' praising its 'faultless balance and blameless rectitude of design' as evidence of the playwright's 'absolute power of composition'. Swinburne's acknowledgement that the second marriage between Hero and Claudio is a 'doubtfully desirable consummation' is telling. It forces him to argue that the demands of comedy make the marriage 'inevitable', and the play sustains belief in its appropriateness, in contrast to the 'tragic end' which characterizes *Measure for Measure*.[21] The tragicomic turn in the romantic plot had been re-evaluated with reference to Shakespeare's other work in 1877, by F.J. Furnivall. Inspired by Edward Dowden's campaign to study the development of Shakespeare's mind and art, Furnivall perceptively observed that the relationship between Claudio and Hero was a prototype for more mature craftsmanship in *The Winter's Tale*. He explained the 'cloud of darkness' in the play with reference to Shakespeare's expression of despair in Sonnet 146 but, nevertheless, confessed to 'a certain shock at the needless pain caused to Hero'.[22]

Kreyssig (1862) gave a relentless critique of Claudio as a 'spoiled fool of fortune' whose 'proud-swelling little heart' and complete gullibility cause Hero's suffering. Claudio's apparent insouciance following her supposed death further supports the 'unattractive features' that are 'part of Claudio's character'. In contrast to Gentleman's identification of Don John as the villain, Kreyssig credits Claudio's 'very ugly flaws' as lending necessary credibility to the plot. Faith in the turn from tragedy to comedy and in the redemption of Claudio is made possible, according to Kreyssig, because of the romantic hero's youth: 'Claudio is vain, arrogant, inconsiderate and fickle, but he is never vulgar; the canker of debauchery has not eaten away his bloom.' Claudio's 'errors' are given a 'certain license' by his youth, Kreyssig argues, noting (not altogether accurately) that 'the public verdict of three centuries' has hitherto largely excused him.[23] Mrs Inchbald, writing in *British Theatre* (1822), laid all blame on Don John, whose illegitimacy, a cause of social impropriety, inevitably marginalized him. Inchbald noted 'Shakespeare has given such an odious character of the bastard, John, in this play, and of the bastard, Edmund, in *King Lear*, that, had these dramas been written in the time of Charles the Second', it would not have furthered his popularity at court.[24]

More surprisingly, Hero, or rather the way in which she had been constructed by patriarchal society, was also the object of criticism in the late nineteenth century. The typical praise of Hero's 'modest, graceful excellence', her delicacy, her refusal to engage in vulgar repartee, given by critics like Henrietta Palmer in 1859,[25] was superseded in 1891 by Grace Latham's essay deploring submissive models of femininity in Shakespeare.

Latham remarked that, for Hero, 'discipline has been an exterior tyranny, not the lesson of self-government' and described her fate as an object lesson about the dangers of Victorian social education:

> Obedience and submission are duties to her, and have been instilled into her until they have become an instinctive habit. Gentle, modest and unassuming, she plays her part in society, with a quietness which is only saved from insipidity by its grace and good breeding. This short, brown creature is the ideal young lady of parents and teachers and in truth she is as perfect as her education will allow her to be; . . .
>
> But alas! Hero has lost any small power of self-assertion, or of independent action that she may ever have had. She can only open her lips when there is no fear of contradiction; a slave does not tell her desires lest they should be thwarted.[26]

Latham's striking comments look forward to later twentieth-century readings that focus on gender and on the social and sexual reasons for the success of Don John's tragic plot. Janice Hays's essay on *Much Ado* in the pioneering volume *The Woman's Part: Feminist Criticism of Shakespeare* (1980) considered Hero as a victim of the sexual distrust of women shared by the soldier-courtiers. Hero's function is to lead 'the male protagonist' beyond 'individualistic aspiration, assertiveness and narrow fictionality' that have been fostered by the all-male fighting community.[27] Carole McEwin (1980) paid attention to Shakespeare's dramatization of intimate conversations between women in Act 3 Scene 4,[28] and Elizabeth Schafer's *Ms-Directing Shakespeare* describes how this scene was staged by Helena Kaut-Howson, whose 1997 production featured Hero having a bath on stage which 'created a sense of women's space; open, relaxed but also fragile'.[29] Michael Friedman (1993) read the silencing of Beatrice and Hero as part of their preparation to become wives.[30] Carol Thomas Neely (1985) gave a definitive reading of how both plots climax in the broken nuptial.[31]

Focusing on the men rather than the women, Harry Berger drew attention to the power of male bonding in the play as a significant factor that drives the romantic plot away from a comic wedding and towards tragedy. He identifies a destructive potential in the 'excessive attachment to *machismo*' and 'fear of love and women' amongst the ex-soldiers and patriarchs of Messina. Hero and Don John are 'the play's two scapegoats' for the anxieties produced by the male community.[32] Richard A. Levin's *Love and Society in Shakespearean Comedy* (1985) presented Claudio as a mercenary wooer and Don Pedro as an increasingly isolated leader of the all-male community, whose repressed reluctance to surrender Claudio was possibly motivated by homosexual desires.[33] Celestino Deleyto (1997) pursues this line of enquiry in an analysis of Kenneth Branagh's film which deals 'at length with the threat that homosexual desire may pose to the central heterosexual romance'.[34]

Class issues are the focus of Elliot Krieger's interrogation of the social tensions that fuel Don John's plots, arguing that *Much Ado* scrutinizes 'the values of a society that refuses to question its values', namely those of a ruling class 'that attempts to mask the traditions and appearances that underlie its elitism'.[35] John Drakakis reads the ideological construction of the bastard Don John as demonstrating how the discursive practices of patriarchal ideology 'ensure the placing of individual subjects in relation to a state apparatus, one which masks, but would by no means exclude the exploitation of one class by another.'[36] Jean Howard (1994) analysed how the play's numerous staged shows, masquerades, interior dramatists and actors, are representations of theatrical practice that self-consciously produce and reproduce differences of gender and class.[37] Nova Myhill (1999) gave a perceptive analysis of how the staging of spectatorship self-consciously manipulates and educates its audiences, on and off stage, about the ways they watch.[38]

Late twentieth-century attention to intertexts and literary traditions further illuminates the Claudio–Hero plot. Charles Prouty's full-length study *The Sources of Much Ado About*

Nothing, published in 1950, defended Claudio as a young man following the proper conventions of early modern courtship and arranged marriage.[39] John Traugott (1982) analyses the influence of romance tradition and Laurie E. Osborne (1990) compares the staged nuptials to weddings in Italian novellas.[40] Martin Mueller's 'Shakespeare's Sleeping Beauties' compares Hero to other Shakespearean heroines who die and come back to life, deriving from Bandello's story of Timbreo and Fenicia.[41] Melinda Gough (1999) uses the discourses of epic romance and anti-theatricality to read Hero as a version of the beautiful enchantress exposed as a whorish hag, a type which can be traced back through Spenser's *Faerie Queene*, and Ariosto's tale of Ariodante and Genevra to the classical figure of Circe. Gough argues that Claudio's shaming of Hero demonstrates not only Shakespeare's 'critique of epic-romance violence' but an implicit critique of contemporary attacks on the theatre.[42] The play's juxtaposition of comic and tragic moods, noted by Gildon in 1709, has remained a critical preoccupation in the late twentieth century as shown in essays on the tensions in the comedy by D. Cook (1981), Marta Straznicky (1994) and Mihoko Suzuki (2000).[43]

The Hero–Claudio plot has provided a starting point for readings that have sought to credit *Much Ado About Nothing* as a serious comedy, in contrast to the apparent flippancy of its title. James Smith (1946) and A.P. Rossiter (1961) fruitfully suggested that the play was about misapprehensions, misprisions, misunderstandings, misinterpretations and misapplications, inspiring several articles on the fallibility of human perception.[44] Richard Henze contrasted destructive and positive modes of deception in the two intertwined plots of *Much Ado*.[45] Barbara Lewalski's essay 'Love, Appearance and Reality: Much Ado About Something' (1968), noted connections between the masquerade in the ball scene, the play-acting of Margaret as Hero and the gulling of Beatrice and Benedick as dramatic negotiations with Renaissance Neoplatonic discourses on love.[46] James McPeek (1960) perceptively reads the personified figure of 'Deformed', the 'vile thief' (3.3.122) identified by the Watch, as an 'inverse craftsman' who personifies the insights, deceptions and self-deceptions dramatized in the play.[47] David Lucking (1997) draws attention to the post-structuralist 'precariousness of the relation between sign and meaning' (8) which Deformed embodies as 'the presiding genius of the play, no less present for being absent' (23).[48] Deformed is, of course, Borachio's metaphor for fashion and the play's preoccupation with clothes, stage costume and sartorial imagery is addressed by David Ormerod (1972) and Michael Friedman (1993).[49]

The Beatrice and Benedick plot, wit and language

The witty couple of Beatrice and Benedick has received more attention than other figures or aspects of the play, and that critical tradition has been well documented, so this section offers a selection of varying responses across the centuries rather than a survey. Because both characters are reported as being 'sick' or 'well-nigh dead' for love of each other (5.4.80–1), it is appropriate that their earliest critical notice is in a medical book, the 1628 edition of Robert Burton's *Anatomy of Melancholy*. Burton's passing reference to *Benedict* and *Betteris* testifies to their popularity in the early seventeenth century. He cites them as an example of a couple who 'at first sight cannot fancie or affect each other, but are harsh and ready to disagree, offended with each others cariage', and 'finde many faults' in each other. Such an impasse can only be resolved by 'opportunity of living, or coming together'. Burton observes that 'ingresse, egresse and regresse; letters and commen fat[sh]ions may doe much'; that 'outward gestures and actions' can also help. However, it is close physical proximity 'when they come to live together in a house', like the domestic arena of Leonato's home, that kindles a conflagration of extreme affection.[50]

Leonard Digges's dedicatory verse to the 1640 *Poems of Mr William Shakespeare* singles out Beatrice and Benedick as crowd pleasers: 'let but *Beatrice* / And *Benedicke* by seene, loe in a trice / The Cockpit Galleries, Boxes, all are full'[51] The couple were admired by eighteenth-century critics for distinction of character, 'perfectly maintain'd' through the plot, in spite of their changing affections. Gildon judged them as 'two sprightly, witty, talkative' characters 'perfectly distinguish'd, and you have no need to read the names to know who speaks.'[52] Francis Gentleman thought they presented 'a very whimsical, but, at the same time, natural picture of love.'[53] Importantly for such critics, propriety was also maintained: Benedick had a more elevated discourse than the lewd Lucio of *Measure for Measure* according to Gildon.[54] Gentleman excused Benedick's indelicacy in the 'rather rude, and indelicate' cuckold joke (5.4.48–51) as a result of his disgruntled mood and remarked that 'Beatrice unfolds the archness of her character pleasantly, even on her first appearance'. Nevertheless, he recognized that in performance, the role demanded more than the 'general delicacy, without any extent of powers' needed to play Hero: '*Beatrice* requires peculiar vivacity of look, deportment and expression.'[55] Elizabeth Inchbald, part of the theatrical circle of John Philip Kemble and Sarah Siddons, thought Beatrice and Benedick's eavesdropping constituted a lack of 'perfect manners, or just notions of honour and delicacy' but felt their respectability was maintained since their witty, jocund demeanour made them 'so free from care, and yet so sensible of care in others'.[56]

Through the nineteenth century, critics and actors found difficulty in fitting the vocal Beatrice into the idealized model of femininity. G.G. Gervinus (1849) observed that the witty women of Shakespeare's second period, Beatrice included, 'are gifted to such a degree with intellectual and mental force' that 'seems to transcend the bounds of feminine capacity'.[57] At the end of the century, the actor Ellen Terry admitted to playing Beatrice 'more feminine and delicate than Shakespeare intended', reconstructing the role 'on a nineteenth-century plan'.[58] Nevertheless, she recognized the tragedy in Beatrice's sacrifice of her strong feminist values: 'Women who have fought the heart breaking battle against prejudice in any age do not need to be told what it is that "kills" Beatrice' in Act 4 Scene 1.[59]

Nineteenth-century critics responded variously to Beatrice's eccentricity and the likelihood of future happiness between the witty couple. Henry Cliff unreservedly lauded Beatrice as 'the *wit*' of the play, noting that 'Benedick is no match for Beatrice' since 'no man has her quickness, her pungency, her correct fluency of utterance, or her glistering weapons of imagery', but qualified this praise with sympathy for Benedick: 'Poor fellow!'[60] Women, who were finding their voices as critics and actors of Shakespeare, were just as equivocal. Anna Jameson labelled Beatrice as a 'termagant' but openly acknowledged the double cultural standard by which Benedick's 'gay manner of indifference of temper, the laughing defiance of love and marriage, the satirical freedom of expression' were judged differently as 'more becoming to the masculine than to the feminine character'. She argued that 'there is no doubt that Beatrice will make one of the best wives in the world'.[61] More negatively, Henrietta Palmer (1859) read Beatrice as a dangerously 'fast' woman, whose 'pert tongue' and 'vanity' made her affected, her speech but a 'dazzle of words'. Particularly opprobrious was her use of verbal wit 'for the discomforting of others', behaviour that was not in 'good taste'. Remarkably, Palmer dismissed Beatrice's love for Benedick as 'an experimental freak', without passion or romantic susceptibility. The emotional depth of Beatrice's soliloquy at the end of the garden scene was ignored by Palmer who focused instead on the opening line 'Stand I condemned for pride and scorn so much?' (3.2), as 'creditable alike' to Beatrice's 'heart and her good sense'. Palmer argued that while 'gratuitous impertinence and unseemly forwardness of Beatrice may jar with one's fine ideas of a lady', her spirited defence of Hero in the church nobly redeemed her.[62]

It did not redeem Beatrice for Thomas Campbell, who declared her 'an odious woman', and disagreed with Jameson's view that Beatrice and Benedick would enjoy a happy future beyond the play's ending. 'I have no such hope,' he wrote, 'my final anticipation in reading the play is that Beatrice will provoke her Benedick to give her much and just conjugal castigation.'[63] In a counter-attack reminiscent of the play itself, Andrew Lang proposed that it was 'absurd, indeed idiotic' to call Beatrice 'odious' and that her wit 'is of her own time' and 'the wit combats must be judged historically'.[64] Helena Faucit, Lady Martin, used her experience of playing the role to argue that 'we shall not do Beatrice justice unless we form some idea of the relations that existed between her and Benedick before the play opens'.[65] Faucit did not go as far as to note Beatrice's remark that Benedick had previously won her heart with 'false dice', but she did suggest that Beatrice missed him significantly. Twentieth-century critics have developed analysis of a pre-play relationship. For example, Stephen Dobranski's close reading of the play's imagery of sex, pregnancy and loss argues that these fragments evoke the illusion of a past sexual relationship between Beatrice and Benedick, whose sense of pain and loss is replayed in the potentially tragic Hero–Claudio plot.[66]

Modern actresses' opinions on the role were collected by Penny Gay in a survey of productions from 1949 to 1990. In 1950, Peggy Ashcroft, according to John Gielgud, chose to reject the traditional Beatrice of grand sartorial style and 'wore much simpler dresses and created a cheeky character who means well but drops bricks'.[67] Maggie Steed, who played the role in Di Trevis's 1988 RSC production, saw Beatrice as being trapped in the role of the clown or family entertainer in Leonato's household 'still the outsider, "singing for her supper"'.[68] Sinead Cusack's 1982 performance had explored 'A Beatrice who gets very angry. A woman who has been damaged by society.'[69]

Beatrice and Benedick's social eccentricity in resisting romance and marriage has continued to preoccupy critics. Michael Taylor's article '*Much Ado About Nothing*: The Individual in Society' (1973) reads Beatrice and Benedick's powerful sense of self-interest as reflecting a wider lack of social cooperation in

Messina that ultimately threatens the social order and points to a world which will not be peopled.[70] Steven Rose (1970) likewise identified a disturbingly powerful element of self-love as well as love in the protagonists' speech while Barbara Everett analysed the play as an 'unsociable comedy' (1994).[71]

Critics in the twentieth century have revisited the play's sparkling display of 'wit', expanding their focus beyond Beatrice and Benedick to include the Hero–Claudio plot. William G. McCollom (1968), for example, reads wit as a rhetorical strategy depending on tension, linked to the mix of comic and tragic effects in the play, and argues that the play's final witty joke is on Claudio.[72] Carl Dennis's 1973 article on wit and wisdom charts a journey from 'wit' that relies on the sceptical assessment of sensory evidence to a more mature system of 'belief' which 'entails giving up the outer eye of reason for the inner eye of faith'.[73] The play's use of language has been taken up by several critics. R.G. White first noted the pun on 'nothing' and 'noting', which were pronounced alike in early modern England, and its pertinence to a text where all the characters 'are constantly engaged in noting or watching each other'.[74] Barish (1974) considers the patterns of prose while Hunt (2000) looks at how the play redeems language.[75] Lynne Magnusson argues that it is everyday language of courtesy that draws the plots and characters of the play together and, indeed, enacts the rituals of social maintenance and repair that prevent the plot from plunging into tragedy. The slander of Hero is a speech action: 'words are spoken that should not have been spoken' but the play's comic logic treats this 'as one more social mistake that can be repaired', when Claudio admits his error. The 'controlled punning' of witty exchanges of Beatrice and Benedick is a conscious mistake-making that demonstrates the plenitude of language. Ultimately, it is Dogberry who 'offers insights into the psychology of politeness' as 'the most peaceable way' to resolve problems.[76] Robert Armin's initial assessment that '*the wisest can do no more*' than '*this meere foole, little learning*', seems to have stood the test of time.

2

Performance History

Landmarks, Tendencies, Outliers, Recursions and Riffs in the Performance History of *Much Ado About Nothing*

Kathryn Prince

Much Ado About Nothing is one of Shakespeare's most enduringly festive comedies, repeatedly conscripted to lend a celebratory tone to momentous occasions and to offset the riskier elements of a company's season by providing a reliable crowd-pleaser that has earned its reputation as a virtually director-proof play. While *Much Ado* had already been 'sundrie times acted' before 1600 according to the Quarto published that year, its first recorded performance was at the wedding festivities of King James's daughter, Princess Elizabeth, in 1613. It has been associated with times of celebration ever since, and has never fallen out of the repertory. The earliest surviving comment on its popularity, made by Leonard Digges in his 1640 preface to Shakespeare's poems, is as true today as it was then:

> . . . let but Beatrice
> and Benedicke be seene, loe in a trice
> The Cockpit, Galleries, Boxes, all are full.[1]

The great eighteenth-century Shakespearean actor David Garrick commemorated the end of his bachelorhood with a production at Drury Lane in 1748, interrupted for his wedding and honeymoon, cheekily capitalizing on his depiction of 'Benedick the married man', a role he would continue to perform until 1776. Helen Faucit came out of retirement for one night in 1879, at the age of 65, to perform Beatrice opposite Barry Sullivan's Benedick for the Shakespeare Memorial Theatre's grand opening.[2] In 1978, the BBC and Time planned to launch their Complete Works series with *Much Ado*, and even brought its stars to New York on the Concorde for a promotional tour, but the completed film was blocked under mysterious circumstances having to do, it was rumoured, with internal BBC politics.[3] In 2005, the BBC launched its ShakespeaRe-told television series with David Nicholls's modernized version set, metatheatrically, in a television station, with Sarah Parish and Damian Lewis as feuding onscreen talent and Billie Piper as the weathergirl. *Much Ado* was one of four adaptations commissioned by the Royal Shakespeare Company for its Complete Works festival in 2007, along with *The Tempest*, *A Midsummer Night's Dream* and *Julius Caesar*. Only *Hamlet* rivals *Much Ado* as a play to inaugurate great projects, and no play, even *A Midsummer Night's Dream*, exceeds it in celebrating the power of performance to effect change within its fictional world and, by extension, in the real world.

Always a reliable seat-filler and a favourite vehicle for celebrity casting, *Much Ado* has, until recently, resisted the modern tendency to darken, deepen and complicate Shakespeare's comedies to reflect the perspectives of political criticism. *Much Ado* does begin with a party and end with a wedding, but the sense of celebration thus created is always bittersweet and precarious: after all, the party is marred by mischief and misunderstandings, and the wedding, when it does finally take place, is a second attempt staged under false pretences, with a groom coerced into marrying a replacement bride as form of restitution for his role in the death of the first. Highlighting these bittersweet elements, productions often invoke notions of elegy and nostalgia, of autumn and last chances, to capture this sense that the happiness at the play's close is somehow fleeting, evasive, nearly missed and precarious. This tone is often achieved by resituating the play not in Shakespeare's Messina but rather in some real, exotic society on the brink of upheaval, whether colonial India in John Barton's 1976 production, Cuba on the eve of revolution in Marianne Elliott's in 2006, the last days of the Empire of Brazil in Christopher Newton's in 2012, or even small-town America, chastened by the First World War but still unschooled in the lessons that would soon come from the Great Depression, in A.J. Antoon's in 1972. A recent tendency to depict Beatrice and Benedick as older lovers, careworn, lovelorn and too jaded to experience Hero and Claudio's more naive sort of love is another variation on this autumnal theme, epitomized in Zoë Wanamaker and Simon Russell Beale's middle-aged lovers in Nicolas Hytner's 2007 production (see Chapter 5 by Schafer and Reimers in this volume) and pushed well into winter in Mark Rylance's coldly received 2013 production starring Vanessa Redgrave and James Earl Jones. While Beatrice and Benedick have traditionally represented opportunities for actors of advancing years, this emphasis on the characters' age, rather than a certain flexibility in casting, is new.

Rylance's wintry production, and its chilly critical reception, is a notable outlier, one of a few that, like Di Trevis's bitter,

Brechtian 1988 production for the Royal Shakespeare Company, could be characterized as a critical failure. What the main body of theatre history reveals, in both its celebratory and its elegiac productions, is a determined attempt at idealization and universality, either the glorification of a lost past or, more smugly, of a modern age that has erased the kinds of impediments that complicated the course of true love in less enlightened times. An inventory of such productions would certainly include John Barton's 'Raj' production for the RSC in 1976, in which Judi Dench and Donald Sinden's high-stakes battle of the sexes took place within the context of a richly detailed setting vivid with stiff upper lips and Victorian proprieties wilting only slightly in the Indian heat. This interpretation of the play, set among the British inhabitants of colonial India, was widely adored, but in retrospect it raises troubling questions about colonialism and racism that detract from its glowing critical reception and calls into question elements that reviewers at the time seem to have accepted at face value, not least John Woodvine's Dogberry, whose mangled English and eagerness to please were handily explained by his status as a local hire. Though very much in keeping with a tendency to situate the play in a past just on the brink of yielding to modern ideas about romance, it was also, perhaps only in retrospect, fuelled by a self-regarding style of Englishness associated with colonialism and now also UKIP and Brexit. Its polar opposite, Trevis's 1988 RSC production, was as critically reviled as Barton's was admired, significant because it reveals the boundaries of what reviewers at the time would countenance. Her darker vision of the play, highlighting its inequalities of class and gender, coincides with trends in both Shakespeare criticism and the wider culture in the 1980s, but she was accused of distorting the play for political or, worse, it seems, intellectual ends. If a glance in the rear-view mirror casts a darker light on Barton's production, the reverse is true of Trevis's: it does not seem to warrant the outraged reviews that it received, and the evidence on the archival video suggests that while the critics may have been outraged, the audience found much to admire. Between these are legions of celebratory, comfortable productions endorsing a modern, liberal humanism associated with Shakespeare's supposed universality. *Much Ado*'s filmography certainly reflects this, in Kenneth Branagh's lush 1993 Tuscan idyll and Joss Whedon's effervescent 2012 Hollywood house party, or even the grittier 2010 documentary *Much Ado in Mostar* that positions Shakespeare's play as a beacon of hope and a mechanism for reconciliation in the aftermath of the Bosnian civil war.

Landmarks

Film and television productions help to shape a larger public's sense of what a play means. As Joseph Papp observed in his introduction to the 1973 television broadcast of the New York Shakespeare Festival's production, now rereleased on DVD, in one evening more people would watch *Much Ado* on CBS than had seen it during its Festival run, its Broadway transfer or, indeed, its entire history of stage performance from Shakespeare's time to that moment. The same might be said of Branagh's and Whedon's films with their wide distribution and enthusiastic publicity, and to a lesser extent of those stage productions that, like Josie Rourke's at Wyndham's Theatre and Jeremy Herrin's at the Globe, both in 2011, were broadcast by digital relay to cinemas or filmed for later release. The legacy of these television and film versions is often apparent in subsequent stage productions, even, because of their persistence in digital form, decades later: the lesser-known East German film, Martin Hellberg's 1964 *Viel Lärm um nichts*, is one of the intertexts for Marius von Mayenburg's 2013 production at Berlin's Schaubühne, which borrows from numerous cult and popular cinematic genres for its stage effects.

The BBC-Time Complete Works film broadcast in 1984 is certainly part of this category of influential productions, the introduction to the play for the pre-Branagh generation of students. This film is haunted by the ghost of an earlier one, the 'lost' tape of 1978 rediscovered at the British Film Institute in 2008.[4] Donald McWhinnie's *Much Ado*, starring Michael York and Penelope Keith, was supposed to be the first play broadcast in this ambitious project to produce all of Shakespeare's works for television. In 1978, McWhinnie's *Much Ado* was taped, edited and publicized, but, for some reason never explained even to the actors involved, it was never broadcast. There were rumours of difficulties with Dogberry and the other nightwatchmen, or with accents, or with personality clashes within the BBC's administration.

Both versions are important, the 1984 because it was widely disseminated and the 1978 because even though it never found an audience it demonstrates that the BBC had initially turned to *Much Ado* to launch this major cultural project; the corporation did so once again in November 2005 to launch an innovative series of four modernized Shakespeare plays in a controversial season of experimentation. The BBC supported its ShakespeaRe-told series with a variety of digital resources designed to appeal to the technology-savvy youth market and, therefore, to the same educational market that the Complete Works series had targeted a generation earlier. Nobody at the BBC seems to have been claiming that ShakespeaRe-told was this generation's answer to the Complete Works but, as the BBC's investment in experimental digital resources for it demonstrates, a great deal of effort went into surrounding ShakespeaRe-told with materials that emphasized its status as a funny, undemanding way into a more serious engagement with Shakespeare's works.

The television critic David Liddiment, writing in the *Guardian*, interpreted ShakespeaRe-told in light of a review of the BBC's subsidy, one component of an institutional strategy to demonstrate that it was both fulfilling its cultural mandate and also attracting impressive numbers of viewers to its programming. Like the *Bleak House* of that season, reimagined as a soap opera, or the scandalous, sexed-up *Rome*, Shakespeare as sitcom has a devious sort of logic to it, especially broadcast in a coveted time slot, just after *East Enders*. As

Liddiment notes, that slot also pitted *Much Ado* against *Coronation Street*, so the fact that the BBC managed to attract some 4.6 million viewers for *Much Ado*, the first show of the series, is especially impressive. Unlike critics who bemoaned the sexing up and dumbing down of the BBC that season, Liddiment saw the season's schedule as a cunning response to what he called the station's 'double bind: damned if it attracts large audiences (too commercial), damned if it attracts small audiences (bad value for licence payers)'.[5] *Much Ado* was a safe bet for the series opener, finding a substantial audience and hitting the sweet spot between edification and entertainment.

As a plea for the value of the BBC, *Much Ado* is an intriguing choice. The play is a festive comedy about the bumpy but ultimately happy course of true love, but it is also one of Shakespeare's most convincing statements about the transformative power of performance. Stage-managed by the benevolent Don Pedro and the Friar, the malevolent Don John and Borachio, and the bumbling Dogberry, characters in the play are brought to believe things that are not, or at least not overtly, true, but should be. Love, reconciliation and justice (also shame, suffering and apparent death) are brought about through scenes crafted for various audiences. The celebratory mood of *Much Ado* depends on maintaining the contrast between the benevolent trickeries in the play – the two gulling scenes that bring Beatrice and Benedick together, the ostensibly punitive second wedding scene that unites Hero and Claudio happily ever after – against the deception, deliberately unstaged by Shakespeare, which convinces Don Pedro and Claudio that they have witnessed Hero's infidelity on the eve of her wedding. When directors choose instead to underscore the inherent similarities of these and other performances in the play, by staging an incident that Shakespeare left unscripted or playing up the family resemblance between Don Pedro and Don John, they risk raising troubling questions about the nature of deception and the value of performance that can resonate far beyond the play world of Messina.

Perhaps the strong celebratory elements of this play allow it to sidestep critical contentiousness. The fact that *Much Ado* has been selected to launch significant projects is indicative of an important aspect of the play, its capacity to generate a mood of purposeful celebration. Just as *Henry V* is a play often associated with times of war, *Much Ado* is a play that has been used to mark occasions of significance. There are certainly dark elements in the play, which in some productions almost overshadow the merry war between Beatrice and Benedick. Where Shakespeare barely sketches the villain Don John and his henchmen, for example, directors have provided a plausible context for their plot to derail Hero and Claudio's wedding. Don John was a Che Guevara-like figure in Marianne Elliott's 2006 production, fighting against a social system that reifies the privilege of the main characters. The programme's precise dating of the action suggests, rather interestingly, that he is on what will ultimately be the winning side of the Cuban revolution. This production dwelt, as many do, on modernity in the act of becoming, not least in Beatrice's modern pencil skirts and mannish shirts that signalled her distance from the full-skirted frocks of the other women. Dogberry's blooming romance with Verges hinted at another emerging modernity, more optimistically than another production with similar themes, Helena Kaut-Howson's 1997 production at Manchester's Royal Exchange, in which Don John was a gay man damaged by Messina's toxic masculinity and enforced heterosexuality. Toxic masculinity is a theme that can be traced back to Bill Alexander's 1990 production, an outlier in the performance history because of its focus on male relationships of all kinds.

Tendencies

Unlike Shakespeare's other comedies, *Much Ado* is rarely subverted or ironized in order to score political points; nor has it been supplanted in the repertory by an adaptation the way that Nahum Tate's *King Lear* replaced the Shakespearean original in Restoration and eighteenth-century productions. The Restoration adaptation of *Much Ado*, William Davenant's 1662 Lincoln's Inn Fields play *The Law Against Lovers*, is more accurately described as an adaptation of the much less popular and darker comedy *Measure for Measure*, with about 100 lines of Beatrice and Benedick's merry war incorporated for comic relief. It seems to have been performed only three times, even less, that is, than *The Universal Passion*, the Reverend James Miller's eighteenth-century adaptation, which was performed ten times when it was new in 1737 and revived once in 1740. Miller combined *Much Ado* with Moliere's *La Princesse Élide* to create a sentimental, romantic comedy along neoclassical lines, reflecting the eighteenth century's sensibilities. For possibly the only time in *Much Ado*'s entire performance history, in *The Universal Passion* Hero and Claudio emerge from Beatrice and Benedick's shadow to become the focus of dramatic interest, borrowing some aspects of these latter characters' wit in the process. More typically, adaptations, including Berlioz's opera *Béatrice et Bénédict* or Rolin Jones and Billie Joe Armstrong's 2015 rock opera *These Paper Bullets*, for example, diminish Hero and Claudio or even omit them altogether.

While Beatrice and Benedick are not, structurally speaking, the main characters of this play, these are the roles that have attracted each period's most talented actors, some like David Garrick over and over again from 1748 to 1776, or John Gielgud from 1931 to 1959, including a production that ran for ten years at the Royal Shakespeare Company, analysed in a chapter of Pamela Mason's *Text and Performance: Much Ado About Nothing*.[6] While earlier ages were willing to indulge a certain degree of latitude in terms of age-appropriate casting, these career-long Benedicks underscore a significant directorial choice to be made. In recent productions, both Nicholas Hytner and Mark Rylance chose to illustrate the effects that can be achieved by using age meaningfully, Hytner with the middle-aged Zoë Wanamaker and Simon Russell Beale,

Rylance (himself an award-winning Benedick in Matthew Warchus's 1994 production) with the elderly Vanessa Redgrave and James Earl Jones.

Shakespearean comedy often works towards a process of regeneration in which elderly figures of authority, usually strict fathers and dictatorial dukes, are resisted until eventually the forces of youth lead to marriage, reconciliation and a sense of society renewing itself. *As You Like It*, with its improbable resolution in which the blocking figures find themselves in the forest of Arden with a more amenable attitude, and *A Midsummer Night's Dream*, with fairy magic facilitating the comic resolution, are two examples of Shakespeare's regenerative comedies. If Beatrice and Benedick are young lovers this regeneration works fairly unproblematically, ending in one wedding and the promise of another, sealed with a kiss. Older lovers complicate this model, though depicting Beatrice and Benedick as visibly older than Hero and Claudio does have some significant advantages, suggesting that her insipidity and his callousness might improve with maturity. One of the most pleasing aspects of the cancelled BBC Complete Works version is a Hero (Ciaran Madden) with some spirit.

The reconciliation between Hero and Claudio is a sticking point in this play's production history, one that has led to a great deal of directorial ingenuity. Casting a painfully young Claudio is one frequent solution, giving him the excuse of youth and naivety, but a change of scene is another. The quest for a setting in which Claudio's violent rejection of Hero at the altar can be understood and forgiven, by both her and the audience, has often meant a turn to cultures and periods in which extreme forms of patriarchy and the unbridled expression of emotion are expected. A 'period' setting can certainly amount to no more than an opportunity to create arresting visual images and a richly detailed imaginary world, perhaps the case in Antoon's 1973 production with its ragtime soundscape, Roosevelt-era roughriders and Keystone Kops, or it can be a more fully fledged scaffolding that explains the characters and their actions. The distinction between an aesthetic and a semiotic use of setting is not always clear cut nor immediately apparent even to professional reviewers, or to theatre historians seeking to reconstruct past performances through these reviews. To Michael Dobson, for example, Greg Doran's choice of 1930s Sicily for his 2002 RSC production seemed purely aesthetic, contributing 'elegance and clarity but little more' and even undermining relevance by situating the play within a 'poignant escapism, spared any uncomfortable contemporary references'.[7] The setting does function as effective semiotic scaffolding, however, according to Jami Rogers's more sustained analysis of the production, situating the extreme actions and heightened emotions of the characters within a palpably patriarchal onstage world.[8]

A setting that gives a modern audience what Shakespeare's choice of Sicily gave his spectators, an instant sense of characters operating with the emotional volume turned up, is often used to make sense of the extreme reaction to Hero's supposed infidelity. A second motive for changing the setting relates to the tantalizingly underwritten relationship between Don Pedro and his brother, Don John. As an illegitimate son and malcontent, Don John perhaps anticipates that more fully developed bad brother, Edmund in *King Lear*, in much the same way that Leonato, the misguided and suffering father, can be seen as an early hint of Gloucester or even Lear himself. Arguably, the basic fact of Don John's illegitimacy would have been a sufficiently strong signal to Shakespeare's audience that he is a villain, obviating the need for any further explanation of the feud between the brothers, although Shakespeare's bastards are not always villainous. Faulconbridge, the character referred to as the Bastard in *King John*, for example, is sympathetic. However, Don John is neither sympathetic like Faulconbridge nor fully developed like Edmund. If comprehensible character motivation is the goal, for contemporary audiences the source of Don John's malignity, and the cause of the rift between the brothers, is underdeveloped. Shakespeare barely hints at a rebellion that has pitted Don John against his more powerful legitimate brother; perhaps, but not necessarily, this is the very skirmish from which Don Pedro's soldiers are returning triumphantly as the play opens, dragging Don John with them as a vanquished but pardoned foe.

The setting of Marianne Elliott's 2006 RSC production, on the cusp of the Cuban revolution, provides a meaningful context for that rebellion and a clear source of the friction between the brothers. Don John emerges as a Che Guevara figure, despising the decadent characters of Leonato's and Don Pedro's entourages and eventually arming himself against them. The social order that is restored at the end of the play is shown to be fragile and fleeting, lending this production a bittersweet quality. As with Doran's production, reviewers were divided on the relevance of this setting. Charles Spencer, in the *Telegraph*, saw this as an inspired choice, even if it missed creating a political connection: 'It is, for instance, a terrific idea to set the action in the pre-Revolutionary Cuba of the 1950s – not for any great political reason, but simply because it creates exactly the right atmosphere of heat-drenched languor, battered elegance and macho values.'[9] Michael Billington, in the *Guardian*, saw the same choice as gratuitous:

Why Cuba circa 1953? One is tempted to ask, Why not? Given that I've seen the play set in British India, Renaissance England, and even, on one daring occasion, in Sicily where it takes place, Latin America seems as good a choice as any. What it offers is a plausible military context, a raffish glamour, and endless opportunities, gloriously seized by Olly Fox's score, for rumbas, sambas and congas. It is a touch gratuitous to suggest that the villainous Don John, who precipitates Hero's disgrace, should turn into a rifle-toting revolutionary.[10]

Outliers

As Billington's inventory of settings suggests, because of *Much Ado*'s ubiquity in the repertory many productions receive unenthusiastic, underwhelmed or mixed reviews comparing them to other, better ones the reviewer remembers fondly or even suggesting, as Robert Crew does about Richard Rose's 2015 production, that 'There comes a time when you think you have seen enough versions of a particular play, and Shakespeare's *Much Ado About Nothing* would be high on my list.'[11] 'Every director thinks they know what they are dealing with when they tackle *Much Ado About Nothing*, and every theatre critic too', Michael Dobson asserts in his review of two 2011 productions, Josie Rourke's at Wyndham's and Jeremy Herrin's at the Globe.[12] It would be reasonable to see Bill Alexander's 1990 RSC production as an attempt to say something new about an overdone play by transforming it from a romantic comedy into an exploration of male camaraderie and its toxic antithesis, or even as a timely reflection on modern masculinity in the wake of second-wave feminism and the rise of Margaret Thatcher. Although the influence of this production's lush set designed by Kit Surrey to provide an array of garden seats and bowers can be seen in Branagh's film and stage productions including Nicholas Hytner's, in other respects Alexander's is very much an outlier. His production gains its alternative readings largely at the expense of Beatrice (Susan Fleetwood) and her relationship with Benedick (Roger Allam), a loss too heavy for the production to sustain.[13] While Fleetwood was a powerful, intelligent Beatrice, the production 'seemed unwilling to allow her' a 'genuine weight and seriousness', Peter Holland has suggested, to the extent that her plea 'O that I were a man' (4.1.304) sounded, he says, 'like a rational ambition' in this man's world.[14] As Alison Findlay rightly observes, in its focus on male relationships the production 'never really knew what to do with Fleetwood's assertive Beatrice'.[15] The solution was, too often, to isolate and humiliate her; in this production, Beatrice's gulling came closest to a shrew-taming. A revealing detail, noted by Findlay, is the promptbook's repeated reference to 'the girls' of the cast as a single entity, reflecting a pre-feminist view of women for which the production seems, in

some ways, to long.[16] The backlash, against feminism and
Thatcher, was also a repositioning of the RSC following Di
Trevis's controversial production two years earlier.

While Trevis's 1988 RSC production is unquestionably
another outlier in the play's history, it is very much at home
among the political plays produced in 1980s Britain.[17] At the
Glasgow Citizens' Theatre, where Trevis had trained as an actor,
the connection between politics and theatre was inescapable;
her training there, and her experience performing and directing
the plays of Brecht, gave her the tools to reinvent *Much Ado
About Nothing* as a protest play. Trevis nailed her colours to the
mast, not least in her casting choices. Critics could not stretch
their imaginations to believe that there could be any chemistry
between her Beatrice, a tall, rather masculine Maggie Steed who
reminded critics of Margaret Thatcher, and the smaller,
deliberately cowering Clive Merrison. The casting of Merrison
offers further evidence about Trevis's intentions: he had played
Don Pedro in Howard Davies's 1980 production for the RSC's
Warehouse, depicting this character as an arrogant, unpleasant
manipulator whose exclusion from the final merriment seemed
absolutely fitting. Together, Merrison and Steed created an
awkward, mismatched but nevertheless deeply compatible
couple within their shallow, materialistic, crass and selfish
society: Thatcher's Britain transferred to a slightly warmer
climate.[18] Trevis's production inhabited a world in which wealth,
power and beauty are interdependent currencies, each providing
access to the other. Beatrice, doubly hampered by her economic
status as a poor relation living off the largesse of her
conspicuously wealthy uncle and by her lack of physical appeal,
is apparently inescapably marginalized, living by her wits.
Benedick, slight, stooped and balding, has neither the economic
clout nor the charm to win a trophy wife like his shallow friend
Claudio's superficially impeccable Hero. Meeting at the bottom
of the social pecking order, Beatrice and Benedick are an odd
couple who seem, paradoxically, to be made for each other.

Like many directors, Trevis consciously and systematically
uses the actors' bodies to create striking stage images, and

while some of these were noticed by reviewers they were not understood as components of an overall directorial vision and technique. One reason that Trevis's production of *Much Ado* would be seriously underestimated by the critics is that the critical discourse surrounding Shakespeare productions lacked the vocabulary to articulate, or even to properly understand, quite what the reviewers were witnessing. Trevis's *Being a Director* articulates a directorial vision forged over the course of a career that was only beginning when she directed *Much Ado*.[19] As such, it explains an approach that matured and developed beyond what she would have been attempting in 1988, but it sheds light on some elements of the production that have not been well understood by theatre history and that were certainly ignored at the time, even though *Much Ado* is a play that Trevis chooses to ignore in her book, almost as though avoiding it there could erase the experience from her memory.

Her Brechtian reading of the play emphasized power relations, and the arrangement of the actors on stage repeatedly conveyed those power relations in visible ways. There was a strong visual connection between three varieties of humiliation, for example, first Hero collapsing into her wedding dress and being consumed by it as she falls to the floor, then Margaret scrubbing that floor on her hands and knees after the abortive wedding, and finally Claudio kneeling painfully as he articulates his penitence. Claudio and Hero standing stiffly at a rather impersonal distance from each other suggested a formality and lack of ease with their supposedly romantic relationship, strongly juxtaposed with the physical ease and proximity between Beatrice and Benedick. Don Pedro, Don John and Leonato, relegated at various points to the periphery of tightly gathered clusters, signalled their shared status as outsiders.

Another clearly Brechtian slant resulted in something unusual about the laughter in this production, which, as Robert Smallwood's review perceptively notes, seems always to be at Beatrice and Benedick's expense rather than shared with them.[20] Instead of a merry and amusing battle of wits,

Trevis presented two rather unattractive people whose antics were ridiculous, not endearing, making them socially awkward, not, as other productions often suggest, anachronistically modern. Casting was certainly one component, but that was only the first in a series of consistent directorial choices that as a whole circumvented the creation of empathy, preventing the more typical narrowing of the emotional distance between these actors and the audience, favouring instead a sustained distance that allowed them to remain ridiculous right to the end. Critics responded to this choice as an aesthetic failure, expecting to find their affection for Beatrice and Benedick fostered.

Trevis effectively used visual elements to convey her subversive interpretation. Costume and setting, not textual cuts, systematically undermined the potential for a straightforwardly celebratory experience. As in the productions of James Edmondson at the Oregon Shakespeare Festival in 1976 and Terry Hands at the RSC in 1982, the elaborate artifice of the production's visual elements contributed to a critique of the culture's superficiality. Like many directors of *Much Ado*, Trevis was unable fully to integrate all aspects of what is very much a play of discrete parts, dark and light; one explanation for this 'failure' is that her approach favoured the Brechtian epic and, not incidentally, the episodic dramaturgy typical of early modern drama as well. Her production is unusual for having absorbed the strange, dark tone of the nightwatchmen's scenes and allowed it to permeate the rest of the play, rather than the more customary approach of trying to play these scenes for sheer comedy. From this perspective, at least, Trevis achieved an interesting and successful experiment.

Mark Rylance's 2013 Old Vic production was also a clear attempt to push the limits of this overly familiar play, reshaping it as an exploration of new love in old age. Part of the problem with this unsuccessful production was the age of the two leads, Vanessa Redgrave (76) and James Earl Jones (82), particularly the latter, whose laborious delivery, 'palpable sense of effort' and apparent physical fatigue distracted critic Charles Spencer with concerns about whether the casting constituted 'cruel and unusual punishment'.[21] Jones remained seated throughout most of his performance, due to apparent infirmity, and appeared at times to struggle to remember and deliver his lines. Michael Billington suggested, in his *Guardian* review, that with this production 'the great and noble cause of age-blind casting suffers a setback', a sentiment echoed in Paul Taylor's review for the *Independent*.[22] The larger problem was not only the age of the actors, but also the fact that this was not, as Billington and Taylor seem to suggest, an age-blind production. The actors were not, like Helen Faucit or David Garrick, playing characters decades younger than themselves and asking the audience to wink at the illusion. For both Spencer and Billington, a sticking point was the premise, nonsensical in this production, that Beatrice and Benedick might go on to have children: Benedick 'must have a pretty special IVF clinic in mind' when he opines that the 'world must be peopled', Spencer cruelly remarks.[23] The peopling of the world, a traditional goal of festive comedy, was sacrificed in this production that went well beyond autumnal. While age-blind casting is a respected tradition in Shakespearean production not likely to be scuppered by Rylance's experiment, his attempt to test the upper limit of Beatrice and Benedick's apparent ages seems to suggest that there is one. Distracted by this single overwhelming flaw, critics generally failed to attend to other interesting choices: by setting the action among American GIs billeted in an English village, Rylance heightened the sense of a clash of cultures within Leonato's home, particularly by including African American soldiers. Though this aspect of the production was eclipsed by the ages of its two stars, and perhaps not fully developed, it suggests a comparison with A.J. Antoon's production and, in its interracial central relationship, a positive element that worked precisely because it absorbed so little attention. In a slightly perverse way, by distracting audiences and critics with the advanced ages of his stars Rylance may have helped the Shakespearean stage to take a step forward in regards to race.

Rylance's critics were bemused or disappointed by his experiment, just as Bill Alexander's had been about his exploration of masculinity, but these responses are respectful compared to the critical mauling meted out to Trevis. Rylance and Alexander had pushed the limits of *Much Ado* and, apparently, at least according to the reviewers, transgressed them. Trevis, in contrast, met with a 'chorus of disapproval of quite unusual unanimity' that was personal, as Robert Smallwood observed in his retrospective assessment of the RSC's season. She was warned to stay away from Shakespearean comedy forever, on the grounds that she obviously lacked a sense of humour.[24]

Trevis's reviled production along with Bill Alexander's and Mark Rylance's are the exceptions that prove the rule: this play is, the critical response shows, not quite director-proof, but perhaps nearly so. One reason is that its darker elements are largely contained, sequestered from the main action in contrast to comedies in which the darkness and the light are more mingled, like Shakespeare's problem comedies, or those which have become problematic for audiences with modern sensibilities, like *The Merchant of Venice* and *The Taming of the Shrew*. In *Much Ado*, the villain, Don John, is two-dimensional, with forty speeches consisting almost entirely of brief remarks one or two lines long, barely sufficient to serve his function as the blocking figure characteristic of Shakespearean comedy; he is functionally aligned with Malvolio and Shylock, but, in contrast to them, he is, as he himself expresses it, a man 'not of many words' (1.1.150). Compared to the obsessively self-explanatory Richard III and Iago, whose soliloquies tell the audience precisely what they are planning to do and why, Don John is no more than a sketch, so much so that his blocking role is sometimes shifted onto Don Pedro, who becomes a brooding, solitary presence among the merry pairings of the final scene, as in Peter Hall's 2005 production. Don John's plot, apparently hatched in a moment, is explained simply as the result of a dislike for Don Pedro and Claudio, the 'young start-up' who 'hath all the glory of my overthrow' (1.3.62). From its inception, it is a vulnerable plan: Margaret need only reject Borachio's advances to prevent it, or come clean about her dalliance in order to exonerate her mistress once the accusation of infidelity has been made. Productions sometimes highlight the sense that the broken wedding scene is almost a comedy, with a happy outcome narrowly averted. They accomplish this by including Margaret among the wedding guests, where she would be able to dispel the tension with the confession that she chooses not to provide. The scene so vividly conjured for Claudio and his friends is written to take place offstage, although here, again, directors are often tempted to stage it for two audiences, the deceived onstage spectators and the wiser ones offstage. These are two examples of moments in which directors seem determined to mingle elements that Shakespeare has kept separate, heightening the sense of darkness lapping at the edges of the comedy. Alexander and Rylance, in their experiments, left this darkness on the periphery; without altering the text in this way, Trevis allowed it to seep into the entire world of the play, eventually overwhelming it.

One of the payoffs of Trevis's approach is that in her search for darkness she paid close attention to the play's minor characters, and was repaid with insights. The weak points of many productions are Don John, an exceptionally underwritten villain, Margaret, whose failure to save Hero with a confession begs explication and, most glaringly, Dogberry, whose antics often fall flat in performance. By focusing on the class elements inherent in this play, Trevis, without altering the text, lent some welcome depth and purpose to these characters, who emerged as a particular kind of underclass, outsiders to the privileged society inhabited by the main characters. Trevis highlighted the elements of class struggle already present within the play, instantly providing a source for the illegitimate Don John's otherwise motiveless malignity and eliminating any incentive for the exploited Margaret to incriminate herself for the benefit of her shallow mistress. The superstructure of Brecht was sometimes occluded by the non-Brechtian acting: in the

archival video Margaret does seem strongly affected by the
disaster she witnesses, the picture of shame as she slips away
from the circle of women surrounding the prostrate Hero, but
she chooses, nevertheless, to remain silent. Trevis's consistent
approach was to allow the actors to use the techniques of
psychological realism to seek audience sympathy, but to use
the production's superstructure to withhold that sympathy
from them.

Recursions

Sympathy was certainly a feature of Iqbal Khan's warm-
hearted, well-received, but not unproblematic 'Indian'
production at the RSC in 2012 that makes light of, and even
perhaps reifies, precisely the kinds of inequalities that Trevis
was highlighting and that productions set firmly in exotic
lands or the distant past manage to sidestep. Described as a
'big, fat, Punjabi wedding',[25] Khan's production is in some
ways a retort to John Barton's for the RSC in 1976, set in India
during the dying days of the British Raj, though in other ways
it is recursive, only serving to underscore how little progress
the RSC has made in the intervening decades when it comes to
some of these inequalities.

   Khan's exotic Indian setting was explicitly chosen to situate
the more extreme actions within a plausible context. As he told
the *Indian Express*: '*Much Ado* deals with family honour,
interrogation of marriage, subordinate role of women,
masculinity, comically shambolic servants and amateur police
force. In India, social hierarchies are still clearly present. On a
recent visit to Delhi, I encountered a place very much like what
I imagined Elizabethan England to have been.'[26] The difficulty
with this is that the actors cast in Khan's production are British,
not Indian, though they hail from the British Asian community.
The production's Beatrice, Meera Syal, is a well-known figure
in British culture with an MBE for her accomplishments as an
actor and author. She is best known for her roles in *Goodness*

Gracious Me and *The Kumars at No. 42*, and frequently comments on issues such as the typecasting of what the UK calls 'Asian' actors (in North America, 'East Indian' or 'Indian,' even when they are Pakistani, Canadian, American or British). Although some comments from the RSC suggested that Khan was hoping to cast a Bollywood actor opposite her, eventually RSC regular Paul Bhattacharjee, another British Asian actor, was announced as the production's Benedick.

The production seems, initially, to contrast with Barton's, one of the most critically acclaimed modern stagings of *Much Ado*. Like Khan, Barton had seen India as a plausible context for the play's action. Judi Dench, at 42, transformed the contemporary understanding of Beatrice. While the performance history reflects the earlier casting of older actors as Beatrice, notably Helen Faucit at 62, Dench departed from tradition by portraying Beatrice as middle-aged rather than relying on the audience's willing suspension of disbelief, as Faucit did. Dench's Beatrice was knowing and wise, neither Lady Disdain nor a 'merry heart', but rather a sensitive, damaged woman, giving emphasis to Beatrice's hints that Benedick has hurt her in the past and using that pain as a motive for much of her wit. Like Beatrice, Benedick, played by Donald Sinden, had a sensitive, intelligent side that emerged as the behaviour of his superficial, fun-loving companions became intolerable. In contrast to productions that attempt to soften Claudio and Don Pedro by eliminating their insensitive jokes after the broken wedding, this production used the lines to show the limitations of these characters and emphasize Benedick's moral superiority. Unlike Benedick, Claudio and Don Pedro were perfectly willing to make Hero the butt of their jokes, just as Leonato had no apparent qualms about mocking Dogberry. The notion of chivalry or noblesse oblige was lost on most of the characters in this production, making Beatrice and Benedick all the more inevitably right for each other.

Barton's production fits perfectly into the tendency that I have suggested is typical of this play's performance history, with Beatrice and Benedick demonstrating more modern qualities than the other characters. A disregarded political angle that might have furthered the production's celebration of modern values was raised by Barton's decision to depict the Watch as native recruits to the colonial army, comical in their attempts to imitate the behaviour and language of the English soldiers. Dogberry, played by John Woodvine, was an Indian sergeant, his malapropisms transformed into a sometimes-poignant attempt to fit in with the colonizers.

In general, reviewers at the time failed to register any objection to Barton's treatment of the Watch. Harold Hobson, writing for the *Sunday Times*, is one notable exception:

> Mr Barton's premise is that a coloured man is funny merely by being coloured. Ridicule his salaams, comic ways of sitting down, and too precise forms of speech, and you have something that sends audiences into paroxysms of delight. Personally, I found this racial joke offensive, but it clearly filled the theatre with a comforting sense that if the British have lost an empire they can at least jeer at those who have gained it.[27]

The same might be said for Khan's production, in which the laughter at Dogberry's expense in Barton's production permeates the entire play. Like Barton's reviewers, Khan's were generally charmed, though for me the experience of watching actors from the British Asian community depict contemporary Delhi-dwellers as objects of laughter was uncomfortable. Richard Rose's 2015 Tarragon production, set in the Indian-Canadian enclave of Brampton, Ontario, struck me as a more successful version of the same premise, without the queasiness inherent in actors from one culture mocking another. The blue berets of Don Pedro's soldiers in Khan's version might have distinguished his UN peacekeepers from Barton's colonial army, but some of the attitudes about what is funny seemed not to have evolved much from the patently racist humour of 1970s Britain. Kate Rumbold noted in her review of Khan's production that, especially when considered alongside another contribution to the Cultural Olympiad, the Globe-to-Globe festival welcoming productions from around the world, this quasi-Indianness seemed 'pseudo-international, even inauthentic'.[28] Rose's production, with its warm-hearted exploration of a local culture depicted by members of that culture, offered many of the advantages of Khan's, including a welcome opportunity for numerous actors of colour to perform Shakespeare in a mainstage production, but without the intercultural ribbing that, though well-intentioned, marred Khan's, however delightful the singing, dancing and spectacle.

Riffs

Thanks to *Much Ado*'s opportunities for singing, dancing and spectacle, productions almost invariably use music to create an exotic fictional world, whether the 'rumbas, sambas and congas' Michael Billington noted in Marianne Elliott's Cuba or the Bollywood-inspired tunes of Khan's Delhi and Rose's Brampton. In addition to this, the play has been adapted for musical performance since Hector Berlioz's opera *Béatrice et Bénédict*, first performed at the newly completed Theater der Stadt at Baden-Baden in 1862 – another celebratory performance – and at Weimar the following year. As the title suggests, Berlioz's interest is primarily in the musical potential of the merry war between his two protagonists, distancing the opera from outmoded melodrama inherent in the play's main plot and embracing the more modern *opéra-comique* – another way of suggesting that the play is about the triumph of modern values.

A few notable recent projects have dwelt on the play's martial, as much as or more than its marital, aspects. These include the American Music Theatre Project's 2006 musical *The Boys Are Coming Home*, later renamed *One Step Forward*, which focuses on American soldiers returning from the Second World War; Roy Williams's 2007 *Days of Significance*, which follows young British soldiers into Iraq; Steve Nemsick's 2010 documentary *Much Ado in Mostar*, which observes Muslim and Catholic actors rehearsing a production against the backdrop of a city ravaged by the civil war that had pitted them against each other; and Christopher Luscombe's 2014 RSC production that pairs *Much Ado* with *Love's Labour's Lost* to depict soldiers on the eve of, and at the end of, the First World War. While it may seem that these productions undermine my overall argument that *Much Ado* is a play for times of celebration, with no discernible shift in its performance history, a closer look tells a different story. The American Music Theater Project is housed within Northwestern University's Communications Department, and *The Boys are Coming Home* was produced as the grand finale of the project's inaugural year. Its emphasis is not on wartime, but on the soldiers' troubled adjustment to peace. *Days of Significance*, though darker, was one of four new plays commissioned for the Royal Shakespeare Company's Complete Works festival. *Much Ado in Mostar* emphasizes the healing power of Shakespeare and, specifically, of this play. Finally, Luscombe's production renames the play *Love's Labour's Won*, thereby both proposing a handy solution to the mystery of a lost Shakespearean play and providing a satisfying conclusion to *Love's Labour's Lost*, an answer to its cliffhanger about whether the couples formed over the course of the play will indeed live happily ever after (on the play's variant titles see Chapter 6 by Lois Potter in this volume).[29]

Together, these projects suggest that *Much Ado* may be ripe for revision as a play about the lasting effects of war on the soldiers who fought in it, on the civilians left behind and on the society that they forge together in peace. This would make Bill Alexander's rather problematic 1990 production, currently an outlier, a vanguard in its obsession with masculinity and male interactions. Another tendency in recent productions that take both Beatrice and Benedick past maturity, like Nicholas Hytner's and Mark Rylance's, is to make space for explorations of mature love beyond *Antony and Cleopatra*, a strand of performance history that begins with Judi Dench's Beatrice in 1976.

The theatre has often served as a site in which questions perplexing a society are explored, though, as I have suggested, productions of *Much Ado* seem to do this with the deck stacked, by selecting settings in which these perplexing issues are fully resolved with the benefit of hindsight and geographical privilege, confirming that Shakespeare, the director and the audience share unthreatening, liberal humanist values. Di Trevis's Brechtian disaster, Bill Alexander's uneven exploration of toxic masculinity and Mark Rylance's derided experiment with elderly actors are three exceptions to a generally conservative performance history. Alongside the glorious, festive, comfortable productions that serve to confirm *Much Ado*'s reputation as a celebratory play, these outliers hint at its more subversive potential.

Productions cited

1748   Drury Lane, perf. Hannah Pritchard, David Garrick

1862   *Béatrice et Bénédict* (opera) by Hector Berlioz, Theater der Stadt, Baden-Baden, perf. Anne-Arsène Charton-Demeur, Achille-Félix Montaubry

1879   Shakespeare Memorial Theatre, dir. Barry Sullivan, perf. Helen Faucit and Barry Sullivan

1964   film, *Viel Lärm um nichts*, dir. Martin Hellberg, perf. Christel Bodenstein, Rolf Ludwig

1965   National Theatre, dir. Franco Zeffirelli, perf. Maggie Smith, Robert Stephens

1967   BBC (television; version of the 1965 stage production), dir. Franco Zeffirelli, perf. Maggie Smith, Robert Stephens

1973   CBS (television; version of the 1972 stage production), dir. A.J. Antoon, perf. Kathleen Widdoes, Sam Waterston

1976   Royal Shakespeare Company, dir. John Barton, perf. Judi Dench, Donald Sinden

1978   BBC-Time Complete Works, dir. Donald McWhinnie, perf. Penelope Keith and Michael York

1984   BBC-Time Complete Works, dir. Stuart Burge, perf. Cherie Lunghi, Robert Lindsay

1988   Royal Shakespeare Company, dir. Di Trevis, perf. Maggie Steed, Clive Merrison

1990   Royal Shakespeare Company, dir. Bill Alexander, perf. Susan Fleetwood, Roger Allam

1993   film, dir. Kenneth Branagh, perf. Emma Thompson, Kenneth Branagh

1997   Manchester Royal Exchange, dir. Helena Kaut-Howson, perf. Josie Lawrence, Michael Mueller

2002   Royal Shakespeare Company, dir. Gregory Doran, perf. Harriet Walter, Nicholas le Prevost

2005   BBC, ShakespeaRe-told adaptation by David Nicholls, perf. Sarah Parish, Damian Lewis

2006   Royal Shakespeare Company, dir. Marianne Elliott, perf. Tamsin Greig, Joseph Millson

2006   *The Boys are Coming Home* (musical) by Leslie Arden and Berni Stapleton, American Music Theater Project, dir. Gary Griffin

2007   National Theatre, dir. Nicholas Hytner, perf. Zoë Wanamaker, Simon Russell Beale

2007   *Days of Significance* (adaptation) by Roy Williams, Royal Shakespeare Company, dir. Maria Aberg, perf. Pippa Nixon, Jamie Davis

2010   *Much Ado in Mostar*, documentary by Steve Nemsick

2011   Donmar Warehouse at Wyndham's Theatre, dir. Josie Rourke, perf. Catherine Tate, David Tennant

2011   Globe, dir. Jeremy Herrin, perf. Eve Best, Charles Edwards

2012   Royal Shakespeare Company, dir. Iqbal Khan, perf. Meera Syal, Paul Bhattacharjee

2012   Stratford Festival, dir. Christopher Newton, perf. Deborah Hay, Ben Carlson

2012 film, dir. Joss Whedon, perf. Amy Acker, Alexis
      Denisof
2013 Old Vic, dir. Mark Rylance, perf. Vanessa Redgrave,
      James Earl Jones
2013 *Viel Lärm um nichts*, Schaubühne, trans. and dir.
      Marius von Mayenburg, perf. Eva Meckbach,
      Sebastian Schwarz
2014 Royal Shakespeare Company, dir. Christopher
      Luscombe's RSC (as *Love's Labour's Won*), perf.
      Michelle Terry, Edward Bennett
2015 Tarragon, dir. Richard Rose, perf. Anusree Roy, Alon
      Nashman

3

The State of the Art

Elinor Parsons

In her introduction to the 2001 New Casebooks collection of essays Marion Wynne-Davies records that criticism on *Much Ado* shifted during the latter part of the twentieth century from an engagement with the play's light-hearted mirth to consider its status as a 'dark and problematic comedy'.[1] Extracts from articles by Harry Berger, Jr, S.P. Cerasano, Barbara Everett, Penny Gay and Jean E. Howard are taken as representative of the interrogation of the play. The two most recent articles are Everett's and Howard's (both first published in 1994) and whilst they acknowledge the superficial pleasures of the play there is a balance between engagement with the play's historical context and analysis of its characters and construction. Howard's perspective is particularly open to the way that the play accommodates shifting perspectives. Wynne-Davies acknowledges that the critical revision of the play emulates a process that is integral to theatrical productions, yet the essays in the collection concentrate on the play on the page and, when the stage is considered, it is within an early modern context rather than that of the modern theatre and screen.

The collection pairs *Much Ado* with *The Taming of the Shrew*, contrasting with the pattern of the earlier casebook edited by John Russell Brown where *Much Ado* and *As You Like It* shared a volume. Wynne-Davies suggests that the connection between *Much Ado* and *Shrew* lies in the latter play's 'cultural construction of gender hierarchies and the way in which the text's own self-referential allusions undercut the sense of a mirror-like representation of reality'.[2] The *Much Ado* essays are placed first because Wynne-Davies suggests that the play is 'far more popular, being produced and taught more often than the early comedies as a whole'.[3] Production on screen is implicitly excluded here because, as Diana Henderson's essay on *Shrew* makes clear, one distinctive feature of *The Taming of the Shrew* is the number of screen versions that it has inspired. In contrast, Branagh's 1993 feature film of *Much Ado About Nothing* is somewhat isolated. The play's presence on television and film has increased since the beginning of the twenty-first century (with the BBC's 2005 ShakespeaRe-told series and Joss Whedon's 2012 feature film) but it remains a text that has a greater profile theatrically.

Positioning the play

Acute theatrical awareness characterizes Leah Marcus's fiercely illuminating essay: 'The Shrew as Editor/Editing Shrews'. The article may seem an unlikely source for critical perspectives on *Much Ado* but its interrogation of the continuing influence of male-oriented editorial traditions implicitly connects with key concerns of recent *Much Ado* criticism. Marcus suggests that the preference for *Much Ado* is 'based on implicit hierarchies of taste and gender sensitivity'.[4] Scholarly traditions are challenged on the basis that 'even for the Elizabethans order and hierarchy were not unitary, essential categories, but rather sites of contestation in which different models competed for cultural authority'.[5]

In 2004 an all-female production of *Much Ado About Nothing* was directed by Tamara Harvey as a follow-up to the success of Phyllida Lloyd's all-female production of *The*

Taming of the Shrew in the previous year. In 2014 the Royal Shakespeare Company affirmed *Much Ado*'s maturity when pairing *Love's Labour's Lost* with *Much Ado* retitled as *Love's Labour's Won*. Those productions were revived at Chichester in its 2016 summer festival and subsequently transferred to the Haymarket Theatre in London's West End. The creative team for those productions will in 2017 produce *Twelfth Night* for the RSC which secures a sense of chronological progression.

The work of three scholars in 2000 – Mihoko Suzuki, Pamela Mason and Deborah Cartmell – helps lay the pathways for debates about approaches to *Much Ado* during the twenty-first century.

Hero and Claudio – gender, class and comedy

Suzuki continues an established critical tradition of focusing on the Hero and Claudio plot strand. Her emphasis contrasts with the way in which, in performance, it is Beatrice and Benedick's relationship which demands the greater attention. Suzuki situates *Much Ado* within the context of three other plays which span a ten-year time frame. By setting *Much Ado* (1598) alongside the later comedy of *Twelfth Night* (1601) the argument contrasts the methods of those plays with two anonymously written tragedies, *Arden of Faversham* (1591) and *A Warning for Fair Women* (1599). The four plays are connected by the way they all 'dramatize the convergence of an anxiety about shifts in class relations with an anxiety about instability in gender relations'.[6] The two tragedies are what Suzuki defines as 'domestic tragedies' and both 'displace blame for social dislocation and disorder from upstart males onto wives'.[7] In contrast, she asserts that Shakespeare's comedies 'reverse this process to scapegoat upstart males in place of transgressive females'.[8] Fundamentally, both *Much Ado* and *Twelfth Night* 'negotiate the twin issues of social mobility and volatile gender relations'.[9] The two areas of interest are interconnected. Suzuki identifies Don John and Borachio as male scapegoats in the play and considers how their involvement in the plot exposes parallel anxieties about gender and class relations.

Her argument is developed by granting sustained attention to Shakespeare's sources. In addition to Bandello and Ariosto, Suzuki gives space to Marlowe and Chapman's *Hero and Leander*. In focusing on the way Shakespeare departs from these materials, attention is drawn to Leonato's reaction to Claudio's defamation of his daughter. Leonato's conviction that his daughter is guilty deviates from Bandello where Timbreo's accusation persuades no one. The characterizations of Beatrice and Benedick both take attributes from Ariosto's Rinaldo by jointly taking on the challenger role in seeking to vindicate the heroine's honour. The way that Claudio diverges from Ariosto's Ariodante and adopts what Suzuki identifies to be, with comparative reference to Troilus, 'the ubiquitous strategy of Shakespearean heroes to construct women as promiscuous and duplicitous',[10] means that the accusation carries greater weight. In identifying the 'boldness' of Hero's namesake in Ovid and Marlowe, Suzuki challenges the received critical opinion of a compliant and reticent Hero and draws attention to the way 'she orchestrates the eavesdropping scene to ensnare Beatrice in III.i'.[11]

Suzuki links Hero and Margaret to suggest that 'the play's critics as well as its characters attempt to relegate Hero to the role of passive object of exchange ... so they make similar efforts to contain the role of Margaret'.[12] Close engagement with Margaret's appearances in the play prompts a more complex interpretation of her character. The banter with Benedick and Balthasar in Act 2, the role she plays in the masquerade and her flirtatious conversation with Benedick in the final act all serve to support the idea that she 'displays disquieting abilities to transgress gender as well as class divisions'.[13] At the conclusion of the play, Suzuki suggests that Margaret and Ursula might be seen to disrupt the endorsement of patriarchy with the promised double marriage for the single women by the way that they 'remain masked and undomesticated, emblems of the opacity and potential unruliness of women'.[14]

Suzuki frames her essay by reflecting upon Elizabeth's position on the throne and suggests that her unmarried state is open to reproach in the example set by the comedies where marriage is indicative of social harmony. Ultimately Suzuki suggests that *Much Ado* is critical of its aristocracy but its coherence is not fundamentally questioned, though one exception is the way that Don John's illegitimacy excludes him from privilege. Particular attention is paid to cuckoldry jokes which connect women's sexuality and agency and Suzuki suggests that the way the action of *Much Ado* interrogates these jokes marks it as distinct from other Shakespeare comedies where 'the cuckolding jokes appear harmless enough'.[15] She argues that the play dramatizes what the jokes 'cost to women – how they serve as instruments of patriarchy to discipline and subjugate women'.[16]

An examination of a particular aspect of the Hero/Claudio narrative strand appears in Ewan Fernie's exploration of *Shame in Shakespeare*. He suggests that 'Shakespeare first fully explored the gendered dimension of shame in *Much Ado About Nothing*'[17] and he provides a careful reading of the play to support his contention that, rather than expose Hero's shame, 'something like a homosocial virus of shame has been triggered by the mere idea of a contaminated woman'.[18] His reading contrasts with that of Lynda E. Boose and Gail Kern Paster, for whom 'shame is a Foucauldian resource of power, used especially for the repression of women; a female sense of shame is prescribed by patriarchy in order to proscribe sexual revolution'.[19] Fernie argues that this is a partial account of shame and attends to 'Shakespeare's interest in shame as a psychological, an ethical and a ritual experience, a transforming moment extraordinary to behold on stage, which may motivate or complete a dramatic action, sending ripples of more or less vicarious shame through the theatre and thereby perhaps having a more positive ethical and political effect outside it'.[20]

By focusing upon *Much Ado*, Fernie suggests that 'Leonato's shame, like Claudio's, is a form of pathological concern with self'.[21] Fernie's emphasis on the male characters prompts him to argue that 'it is really Claudio who has been reborn from within'[22] and in this respect the play can be seen as a precursor to the tragedies to which Fernie dedicates his core chapters (*Hamlet*, *Othello*, *King Lear*, *Antony and Cleopatra* and *Coriolanus*). The pattern in *Much Ado* can be seen as anticipating the way that Shakespeare's tragic heroes 'are routinely driven by fear of shame to self-assertion, before learning the priority of a more moral or spiritual sense of shame as, ironically, it is exemplified by their own daughters and wives'.[23] Fundamentally, 'the climactic shame finally accepted by the fallen men spells a timely end for the corrupting illusions of male pride'.[24]

Benedick – text and performance

The thrust of Pamela Mason's article on *Much Ado* is in sympathy with Suzuki's argument about female suppression but Mason challenges the established critical interest in Hero and Claudio by focusing instead on Benedick. The premise of her argument concurs with Leah Marcus's concerns about a male-oriented tradition and precise attention is given to generally accepted editorial intervention which simplifies the misprision in the masked ball. At the core of the argument is a questioning of 'the motives that lie behind the conviction that change is required'.[25] It is critically a matter of the reassignment of lines which are, in the Quarto and Folio texts, given to Benedick:

BENEDICK
    Well, I would you did like me.
MARGARET
    So would not I, for your own sake, for I have many
    ill qualities.

BENEDICK
  Which is one?
MARGARET
  I say my prayers aloud
BENEDICK
  I love you the better; the hearers may cry amen!
MARGARET
  God match me with a good dancer.
BALTHASAR
  Amen!

(2.1.92–97)

Twentieth-century editorial tradition has intervened either by granting Balthasar the whole sequence with Margaret (Claire McEachern's Arden edition does this) or by including Borachio. The only editor within the past century to trust the Quarto and Folio readings is David L. Stevenson in the Signet edition (1964) and his decision accords with the sparring between Benedick and Margaret in 5.2.

Terry Hands' 1982 Royal Shakespeare Company production adhered to the speech prefixes as originally printed. Mason suggests that the decision to reassign owes a great deal to editors' 'convictions about character ... emendation here creates a constancy in Benedick which better suits editors' preconceptions and possibly their sense of masculine solidarity'.[26] The editorial solidarity that Mason notes has been matched in the theatre by the cuts to Benedick's overhearing scene where Don Pedro's searingly critical comments have often been removed. Restoring the edges to Benedick's character makes it more possible for him to experience a 'radical change' which is exemplified in 5.2 when 'he is accommodated by the women and is accommodating to the women'.[27] In positioning Benedick as someone who is redefining his identity, Mason draws attention to a further example of a near-consensus in editing. In the closing movement of the play an introspective subclause has been cut for most Benedicks in performance: 'Therefore it is most expedient for the wise, if Don Worm – his conscience – find no impediment to the contrary, to be the trumpet of his own virtues' (5.2.76–9). That emendation aids the characterization of one who is 'confident, even arrogant, and certainly robust in his self-confidence'.[28] If, however, the statement is delivered in full it adds sensitivity to Benedick's character and there is a wider implication that his bond of allegiance and friendship to Don Pedro have been replaced by Don Worm, his conscience.

The shift in register during Benedick's speech towards the end of the play is also noted at the beginning of the twentieth century by Maurice Hunt in his detailed examination of language. Speech 'often becomes disjointed from meaning'.[29] Although the attention to the Watch is comparatively brief, Hunt's piece stands apart from other critical assessments by seeking to balance his consideration of characters across the play's narrative strands. The Friar is, Hunt suggests, isolated because he is the 'least caught up in the power games that distort and falsify what is said and heard'.[30] Hunt concludes by giving sustained attention to Benedick's progression in the play towards a simpler form of expression. Hunt attributes Benedick's 'halting sonnet' (5.4.87) to the effect of love and suggests that it has greater value accordingly. A secondary meaning of Bene-Dic suggested by Hunt is 'speak well' and that notion is fulfilled in his 'relatively unadorned, direct speech' at the end of the play.[31]

The conclusion to Mason's argument provides one further example of editorial meddling. In the Quarto and Folio texts – 'Peace, I will stop your mouth' – is spoken by Leonato but some modern editions reassign the line to Benedick 'to effect a more conventionally acceptable romantic tableau'.[32] In addition to giving the line to Benedick, an inserted stage direction frequently compounds the push towards sentimentality. Mason suggests that Leonato retains the line then there is a range of possibilities, such as Leonato castigating Beatrice, warning her to concede the debate, or relinquishing his control of Beatrice to Benedick. The potential the moment has for an uneasy note in the resolution prompts Mason to draw connections with the relationships in *Measure for Measure* as Davenant did in his adaptation, *The Law Against Lovers* (1662), which couples these two plays. In interrogating editorial and theatrical practice, Mason offers a conclusion that usefully connects with Suzuki's piece, despite a different nuance in what was explicitly a historical contextualization of the play. Both critics would seem to concur with the recognition that it is 'cuckoldry that has been a mainstay of the play's verbal energy and its plot'.[33]

Sexuality on film

Deborah Cartmell's detailed examination of Kenneth Branagh's 1993 film of *Much Ado About Nothing* appears in her monograph, *Interpreting Shakespeare on Screen*. Cartmell sets Branagh's film alongside Zeffirelli's 1968 film of *Romeo and Juliet* (with some attention granted to Luhrmann's 1996 film too). The films are yoked together by their engagement with sexuality. Cartmell notes the gap between popular conception of Shakespeare's *Romeo and Juliet* and the cultural work it is asked to perform. She draws a contrast between the daring representation of homoeroticism in Zeffirelli's film and Luhrmann's far more conservative presentation and that accords with the attention that is given to the earlier 1990s film of *Much Ado About Nothing* which, she suggests, demonstrates a move towards more conservative interpretations on screen. Cartmell traces its choices in order to reveal its portrayal of a seemingly uncomplicated celebration of heterosexuality: 'a so-called positive image of sexuality'.[34] The film 'stresses maturity over youth and authoritarianism over rebellion' and Cartmell draws attention to the age gap of about ten years between Beatrice and Benedick and the more junior Hero and Claudio.[35] The rearrangement of the final three scenes means that Don Pedro and Claudio appearing in front of the monument precedes Benedick's meeting with Beatrice thereby granting the older couple greater attention. The more restrained, chaste note at the end of the film (in contrast with its lusty opening) is compounded by the validation of Beatrice and Benedick's love by the older generation. The casting of older actors as Leonato and Antonio helps ensure a sense of gravitas and adherence to tradition. Particular attention is paid to the reshaping of the text. Cartmell usefully includes an edited transcript of the final scene and notes the cuts and transpositions made by the film. The method connects with Mason's approach and, indeed, Mason's article gave some attention to the decisions taken by Branagh. Both Mason and Cartmell observe that nearly half the play is cut in the film. There is, of course, the recognition that adaptation for the new medium needs to take place but both draw attention to the ideological implications of the choices. Branagh's screenplay offers commentary on some of the decisions which reinforces the sense for both critics that the 'various modifications . . . let the men . . . off the hook'.[36]

A few years later, Judith Buchanan notes Branagh's intertextuality and makes a case for it interpretatively. For example, the initial appearance of the men is akin to that of John Sturges' *The Magnificent Seven* (1960) and 'These are men who, like Sturges' gun-toting posse, feel keenly their separation from the world of domestic attachment and responsibility'.[37] Opening with Balthasar's song being spoken by Emma Thompson's Beatrice adds to an initial suggestion that these gendered roles might be interrogated but ultimately it is 'the film's uncompromising comic vision' which means the glimpses of tensions and complications dissipate.[38] There is an echo of Mason's frustrations when Buchanan observes in relation to the casting of Don Pedro (Denzel Washington), Claudio (Robert Sean Leonard) and Leonato (Richard Briers) that 'Individually and collectively, these three actors seem born to be let off the hook'.[39] Whilst Philippa Sheppard also observes that 'through editing, Branagh has diminished the motif of men betraying women', her article focuses on the film's interpretation of the song, 'Sigh no more ladies', as 'the only significant representative of the play's darker commentary on heterosexual relationships that is left intact in the film'.[40]

Cartmell records that the film's final impression of Beatrice is of her being silenced when her mouth is stopped with a kiss. The potential for a challenging and unsettling resolution that has been noted by Suzuki and Mason is ignored in Branagh's film with the way it embraces the romantic ending. Cartmell suggests that during the kiss, Branagh 'allows [Emma Thompson as Beatrice] to speak through her gestures' which accommodates Thompson's assertion that they are therefore 'total equals'.[41] Cartmell's engagement with the film is balanced across both plot strands and she notes the inevitability of the resolution: 'For the play to be formally comic, Beatrice must marry Benedick as Hero must marry Claudio. But it is "another Hero" who marries Claudio, a crestfallen, humiliated automaton who can only do what she is told'.[42]

Reading *Much Ado*

A revised edition of F.H. Mares's 1988 New Cambridge text was published in 2003 and the key addition is Angela Stock's inserted section in the introduction examining 'Recent Stage, Film and Critical Interpretations'. She identifies how the play 'confronts the director with the almost impossible task of probing the comedy's dark side while also fulfilling the expectation that it will be funny, enchanting, vibrant, heart-warming, exuberant and romantic'.[43] The stage history focuses on English theatre productions since 1988 and, despite the substantial cuts in the subsequent film, Stock notes how 'the genial atmosphere' in Judi Dench's Renaissance Theatre Company production influenced Kenneth Branagh's 1993 film (in which he reprised the role of Benedick). Stock pays particular attention to Beatrice's age in productions (see Chapter 5 by Schafer and Reimers in this volume) and Stock observes that 'the play is tipped far more dangerously towards tragicomedy if Beatrice's challenge to "Kill Claudio!" and Benedick's subsequent exchanges with his prince and his friend are delivered not by impetuous youngsters but by adults who fully grasp the implications of their words'.[44]

In assessing criticism, Stock asserts that '*Much Ado* is an oddity . . . in that theatre audiences inevitably prefer the merry couple . . . while literary critics and cultural historians generally find more grist to their various mills in the plot of the near-tragic youngsters led astray by the princely brothers'.[45] Stock suggests that the most rewarding scholarly discussions draw the two puns in the title together, so on one hand 'the themes of sexuality, gender relations and misogyny' and on the other 'eavesdropping and deception' and the 'most fruitful contributions follow the play in interlinking these two fields of discourse'.[46] Her summary concludes with the idea that 'Misogynist fears appear to be justified: women, and more dangerously, the woman's part in men, threaten the very foundations of patriarchal order, in effect, they turn men into rebels against authority.'[47]

The Arden series has brought a female editor to the play. Claire McEachern's Arden 3 text of *Much Ado* (2006, revised in 2016) frames its engagement with the text in terms of oppositions. The pairs of lovers are set against one another: 'One pair have been the darlings of the theatre, the other, a target of scholarly scrutiny.'[48] The play is seen accordingly to contain light and dark, qualities which are allied loosely to that which is theatrical and that which is scholarly and the sympathies of the editor are towards the latter: 'This edition treats the play as a literary text, not a script'.[49] That ambition paradoxically perhaps seems to provide context for the weight of editorial stage directions which may help a reader imagine the physical dimension of each scene but it seems to be at odds with the critical context of a widening of interpretative possibilities. For example, in 3.1 it is suggested that Hero and Ursula '[*approach Beatrice's hiding place.*]' (3.1.33) and in 4.2, it is suggested that the '[*Watch lead Borachio and Conrade forward, then step back.*]' (4.2.10).

Pamela Mason may be pleased to note that McEachern seeks to put a stop to editorial tradition by assigning to Leonato 'Peace! I'll stop your mouth' (5.4.97). McEachern suggests that Leonato's instruction is 'in keeping with his characteristic attempts to stage-manage this scene' and that it 'provides for a more egalitarian accommodation between the lovers than would Benedick's own declaration of intent to silence Beatrice'.[50] Indeed, it is in Hunt's examination of speech in the play that he describes Leonato as a 'linguistic autocrat'.[51] It is perhaps surprising that whilst McEachern seeks to open out interpretative possibilities in assigning the line to Leonato, these choices are guided by the insertion of two stage directions: 'Peace! [to Beatrice] I will stop your mouth. [Hands her to Benedick.]' (5.4.97). McEachern is clearly seeking to avoid instructing that a kiss necessarily takes place and instead the dominant idea is one of patriarchal control 'in handing Beatrice over to Benedick . . . he will silence her merely by getting her a husband'.[52] The absence of any speech or stage directions for Beatrice means that the challenge of interpreting her silence is now in the context of strong gestures and speech from her uncle and her husband-to-be.

The addition to the introduction in the revised edition reflects on the connection between scholarly attention to the more sombre aspects of the play and production choices with McEachern even finding 'the darker themes of sexual betrayal'[53] present in what she admits is a lighter touch overall in the BBC's 2005 ShakespeaRe-told version. McEachern grants greater space, however, to recent critical interest in cultural history, and in particular to the impact of the Reformation. The resonance that cuckoldry may have had for the play's first audiences is considered with an extended analysis of Moses' metamorphosis as a horned man. The horns initially had positive connotations of strength and power but they became a mark of shame too: 'To be horned is not so much to be cuckolded as it is to believe the wrong thing'.[54] McEachern rejects the idea that the image of Moses is one that Renaissance audiences would have summoned when cuckoldry is mentioned but 'the story of mistaken belief corrected . . . was a particularly charged one for Reformation audiences'.[55] Ultimately McEachern seeks to suggest that rather than the pairs of lovers being linked in tragic terms they might be connected in a more joyful way if there is openness to the perception that they 'undergo conversion experiences in which former prejudices are cast off, false beliefs are exchanged for true ones, as the parties concerned feel themselves recognized for who they truly are'.[56]

Hearing and *Much Ado*

In addition to paying attention to Benedick, Maurice Hunt, in his article on language in the play, also gave attention to Hero. He suggests that when she whispers in Claudio's ear in the final scene 'her silence, which had become a sign of patriarchal oppression in playgoers' minds, acquires positive value'.[57] Diana Henderson seeks to read Hero positively and she works hard to unsettle the deep-seated 'cultural assumption that equates speech with activity'.[58] Her premise is that 'Nowhere is the play of confusion among sight, sound, and word more overt than in *Much Ado About Nothing*' and her piece pays compelling attention to Hero.[59] Henderson makes much of the sound of Hero's name suggesting that the 'h' connects aurally for an audience with Beatrice's 'H' (aitch/ache) in 3.4. In drawing attention to that letter, Henderson suggests that 'The "h," marking the difference between noticing and not, between merely having ears and using them to hear, stands well for the dramatic character whose name begins with that character: the often silent but highly significant Hero'.[60] Fundamentally, Henderson seeks to identify the interpretative range that Hero offers. She notes the potential for Beatrice to upstage her cousin and suggests that 'It is up to the director and performer to decide whether Hero's silence indicated complaisance in her given role or others' patronizing presumptuousness (or both), yet it seems worth noting that if Hero is anything, she is no fool'.[61] Henderson's analysis argues connections with Emilia and Hermione which usefully depart from the more common alliance with *Shrew*'s Bianca, a female character who has tended to be contained interpretatively. Henderson draws attention to Hero's more active role in the play's female-only scenes but cautions how this has drawn critics towards interpretation of Hero as duplicitous. Drawing on Howard Felperin's deconstructionist approach Henderson dissects Hero's role. In defending what might be seen as a retrograde step in the employment of a critical framework from decades ago, Henderson questions a contemporary tendency to value only the apparatus that has developed in more recent years.

Henderson pulls together her ideas by examining Hero on screen. She sets Branagh's film alongside two earlier television versions: Stuart Burge's 1984 BBC's Complete Works version and Nick Havinga's PBS Theater in America 1973 television recording of a studio presentation of the Joseph Papp stage production. Henderson defends her decision to assess the effect of the cuts made by the versions, showing her wish not to seem unresponsive to the necessity of adapting the text to suit the shift in medium. She highlights the way that the cuts are symptomatic of a reshaping – in particular in the Branagh film – which compounds the way that Hero's role is minimized. In contrast, both television versions demonstrate more subtle choices and 'allow more variety, tension and awareness of the social contexts shaping the women's behaviour'.[62] Crucially, Henderson suggests that Branagh's film looks *at* Hero rather than *through* Hero's eyes. Both Henderson and Cartmell seek to strengthen the pedagogical engagement with a text such as *Much Ado* through an analysis of the films.

A key dimension of the Blackwell Companion series is its wish to cater for the needs of undergraduate students. Mihoko Suzuki's essay appeared in the *Feminist Companion to Shakespeare* (2000) and two other volumes grant sustained attention to *Much Ado*. The third volume of *Shakespeare's Works* on *The Comedies* (2003) includes Alison Findlay's essay on the play which will be considered later in this chapter. Perhaps more surprisingly, the Companion dedicated to *Shakespeare's Sonnets* (2007) has an essay which concentrates on *Much Ado*.

Patrick Cheney's chapter marks itself as unique in the collection by choosing to focus upon the text of one of

Shakespeare's plays. Indeed, the piece questions the boundary placed by scholarship between the plays and the poems and concludes by emphatically defining Shakespeare as a 'poet-playwright' which, Cheney suggests, is 'Shakespeare's . . . own compound form of authorship'.[63] Cheney is explicitly seeking to refocus the lens through which critical perspectives on the play are formed. In considering the structure of the play, he notes its 'two scenes of revelation: the first (more famous) about theater; the second (less discussed) about sonneteering'.[64] He argues that the sonnets written by Benedick and Beatrice which Claudio and Hero pluck from their friends' pockets (5.4) are crucial to the play's conclusion. The idea that the revelation of the sonnets in the final scene suggests the play 'might also be processing a professional dynamic of authorship between . . . poetry and theater; sonneteering and playwriting'.[65] Benedick shifts between these forms during the course of the play. He begins the play as a 'Prince's jester', a 'consummate theatrical man' and then in 3.2 it is Claudio who notes that Benedick has undergone 'a decisive . . . character change': 'Nay, but his jesting spirit, which is now crept into a lute-string and now governed by stops' (3.2.53–4).[66] For Cheney, Benedick's shift to 'lutenist' can be read alongside his instruction in 2.3 to the Boy to give him a book during which 'Benedick turns from stage to page'.[67]

He establishes Benedick's overhearing scene as pivotal in the play because of its position 'at the structural midpoint'.[68] Cheney seeks to move beyond a reading which emphasizes a patriarchal conflict between the two brothers in terms of an emphasis upon Don Pedro's theatrical action as one where he 'uses theater to bring about a marriage' in contrast with Don John's use of 'theater to break marriage up'.[69] Cheney pays particular attention to nuances of Balthasar's song 'Sigh no more, ladies . . .' (2.3.60–75) for which Cheney suggests there is 'a surprising dearth of commentary'.[70] He commends it as 'one of the most remarkable in Shakespeare's theatrical canon'.[71] The absence of any 'ladies' onstage to whom the song might be addressed 'takes the song out of the fiction to ladies in the theater audience'.[72] Cheney claims that it now becomes a '*lyric manifesto*, critiquing masculine theater for its *deceptive agency* . . . and its *unfaithful desire* . . .'.[73] The concluding sentiment of 'Hey nonny nonny' encourages women to be vocally independent and to adopt a register which is distinct from the dominant masculine mode. More usually, it is through a focus on female characters that a female-centred response to the play is formed.

The final sequence of Cheney's argument focuses on the responses to Hero in the wedding scene and a contrast is drawn between the literal interpretation made by Leonato of Hero's blushing cheeks, affirming, as he sees it, her guilt. The nuances of the Friar's response lead Cheney to suggest through his careful 'noting' of Hero's face that he 'witnesses nothing less than a religious epiphany occurring in the face of an unconscious girl: a dramatic metaphysical action beyond human agency'.[74] The moment signals Shakespeare's 'deep commitment to print culture'.[75] Two other poetic moments are considered: Claudio's epitaph in which 'the artistic quality of his lyric lends access to a more profound interiority than we might initially have imagined' and the contentious song in the final act which some editors follow Capell in assigning to Balthasar.[76] McEachern suggests this would be a 'plausible choice' but the Arden edition keeps the possibilities open with: 'one or more singers [*Sing.*] Pardon, goddess of the night . . .' (5.3.12).[77] Cheney's enthusiasm for the 'stunning poem' is justified by the way that 'this religious lyric confronts darkness head-on' and so he commends its structural function in terms of the way its position draws attention to the play's doubled interest in poetry and theatre.[78] Fundamentally, Cheney suggests that *Much Ado*'s conclusion is 'validating the art of the sonnet as an important cultural institution for individual identity and social relationships'.[79]

Watching and *Much Ado*

Alison Findlay's 2003 article for the *Blackwell Companion to Shakespeare's Works III: The Comedies* reads the play within a delicately woven tapestry of critical and performance contexts. Findlay unfurls the key image in her analysis with Margaret's description of Hero's wedding dress (3.4.16–20). The moment establishes various strands in Findlay's approach: historical contextualization (in relation to Beatrice d'Este, Duchess of Milan 1491–1497), an interest in material properties, interrogation of the idea of fashion and consideration of social hierarchies and aspiration. Fundamentally Findlay argues for *Much Ado*'s 'profound exploration of identity in which gender and religious politics create a mingled yarn of meanings about inwardness'.[80] Several moments of communal dressing up are identified – the masked ball (2.1), the planned wedding (4.1), the cloaked ritual of mourning (5.3) which is closely followed by the promise of another masked ball and wedding – and the question Findlay poses is 'what power have clothes to shape identity'.[81] In noting a correlation with the favour-changing in *Love's Labour's Lost*, Findlay suggests that the men's exchange of favours in *Much Ado* ultimately 'marks a reaffirmation of identity ... rather than a questioning of it'.[82] That idea does not minimize the significance of the space granted to the analysis of the masked ball. Paying attention towards the journey for Beatrice and Benedick places emphasis upon the danger that their independence poses to society, for their 'witty solipsism threatens to pull Messina apart at the seams just as surely as Don John's villainous plots'.[83]

In 2012 Findlay returned to *Much Ado About Nothing* in her journal article for *Shakespeare*: 'A Day to Remember: Wedding Ceremony and Cultural Change'. The piece strikes its keynote with the way Hero frames her anticipation of when she will be married: 'Why, every day, tomorrow' (3.1.101). Her words point attention towards an 'acute consciousness of past, present and future which converge on the event'.[84] In addition to close engagement with the intricacies of the ceremony as it is contained in *The Form and Solemnizacion of Matrimonie*, Findlay also examines details of the Sarum script – the rite established by the Bishop of Salisbury in the eleventh century – and considers the way that the early modern ceremony taken from *The Book of Common Prayer* (1549) is influenced by medieval practices. She draws attention to local differences and the uncertain status of the marriage ceremony. Unlike baptism it could not be classified as a sacrament because it was not instituted by Christ nor outlined in the Bible and this explains some of the Church's divided disposition in relation to weddings. A weighting towards the negative sense of the ceremony might be explained in the way that whilst it was seen as 'an incarnation of the divine union between Christ and the Church' it had the capacity to be demonic in character with its papish rites and as 'a revival of medieval decadence'.[85] Findlay argues that the context here heightens an awareness of Shakespeare's politically inflected representations of weddings. The Italian setting made Catholic practice logical and she sets *Much Ado* alongside *Shrew* and considers the subversive qualities in the way Petruchio behaves in his Act 3 wedding to Katherine. She feels that the broken nuptial ceremonies in *Much Ado* have a more complicated relationship with the religious debates. The preparations are for a big community wedding but it is Leonato's suggestion that it should be the 'plain form of marriage' which breaks with these traditions and that disruption is then amplified by Claudio's actions which signal 'an angry attack on the ancient ceremony'.[86]

   Findlay then considers the affective power of marriages and provides a framework by engaging with the philosophical approaches of Maurice Halbwachs and Paul Connerton. Her interest is in the extent to which collective memory is produced for the onstage community and how those watching might be embraced within it. Ultimately Findlay suggests that there is a division between male and female behaviours and suggests that 'women identify with each other as objects of desire'.[87] The extent to which marriage conventions today – with the insistent 'day to remember' rhetoric – are so closely mirroring the style of presentation adopted in previous centuries asserts the 'power of marriage ceremonies as liminal, affective events'.[88]

   An interest in collective action extends beyond the events within the play to more recent performance contexts in

Douglas Lanier's analysis of Joss Whedon's 2012 film of *Much Ado*. Lanier seeks to contextualize Whedon's choices with reference to Branagh's earlier film. He identifies in the work of both directors a shared emphasis upon the community of performers but in contrast to Branagh's escapist location and lush filmography, Whedon's filming took place in his own home with handheld digital cameras. Whedon creates a visual connection with screwball comedies by deciding to film in black-and-white, but the association that Lanier prioritizes is with the aesthetic of documentary film. The film's metacinematic qualities are deepened by the associations with Whedon's distinctive directorial style. Indeed, Lanier notes that the photographer in the film (who, at one moment, looks directly at the camera) might be read as a surrogate for the director as 'the one who makes the private public through a visual medium'.[89] A more straightforward distancing device is offered by the casting of actors who will be easily recognizable to followers of Whedon's directorial work. Lanier notes an emerging critical tradition examining 'the Whedonverse' (see Chapter 8 by Greatley-Hirsch and Neville in this volume). The much publicized narrative surrounding the film that it is following on from Whedon's play-reading sessions with friends helps accentuate the sense of a blurring of personal and professional relationships between the cast. Fundamentally, Lanier suggests that Whedon manages to resist wholeheartedly embracing a 'Hollywood ending' with the film's 'darker-hued portrayal of small-group dynamics in Messina and early twenty-first century America'.[90]

My chapter began with the suggestion of a movement in the critical tradition towards an emphasis upon the darker aspects of *Much Ado About Nothing*. In reflecting on twenty-first century publications, it seems that by complicating received opinion about the integrity of the edited text, about gender, status, comedy and performance choices, critical responses have been keen to emphasize the play's deep and rich value. Several writers have drawn attention towards what they define as the play's equivocal dimensions. Mihoko Suzuki engages with the 'equivocal' interpretative ideas about Margaret, suggesting that 'the play nevertheless attempts to repress this anxiety about Margaret, by repeatedly – if equivocally – exonerating her'.[91] Findlay considers 'the equivocal nature of clothes' in the play.[92] Judith Buchanan suggests that Branagh's casting in *Much Ado* of the senior male figures softens the play by 'putting unquestionably benign forces in places where the text may be read more equivocally'.[93] These observations serve to highlight the potential that remains for *Much Ado* to be revived and reinterpreted.

4

New Directions

Letting Wonder Seem Familiar – Italy and London in *Much Ado About Nothing*

Duncan Salkeld

This chapter focuses on the mix of continental and English elements in *Much Ado About Nothing*. It argues that while the play seems to depict an Italianate romance in which true love meets adversity but wins out in the end, its more unsavoury elements are decidedly local. In certain respects, this Sicily is England, and its Messina is London, although we may not initially think so. Near the end of the play, the Friar declares, 'Let wonder seem familiar' (5.4.70), and Shakespeare clearly wanted to cultivate a sense of wondrous unfamiliarity in retaining the story's faraway setting. The character names 'Don Pedro' and 'Conrade' add to the continental atmosphere. Martin Wiggins has suggested that, 'the war which has just finished could be that of the Sicilian Vespers of 1282, which

put Pedro III of Aragon on the Sicilian throne'.[1] Conrad IV's
coronation as king of Sicily in 1250 may have prompted
Shakespeare's use of that name too. But the play makes wonder
seem familiar by fusing contradictions, giving its audience
simultaneously yet contrary visions of the same society. The first
sees a settlement based upon trust, courtship and romantic
fulfilment; the second envisions only lies, betrayal and deceit.
Granted that the play is a comedy, the first of these must
serve for the denouement. Yet in sailing so close to tragedy,
the play vividly stages the possibility of the second. Early
modern audiences filing out of the Curtain in Shoreditch, or
the Southwark Globe, might have wondered which of these
outlooks had in fact been the more realistic.

    Critical opinion has long been concerned with the play's more
unsettling aspects. Claire McEachern's Arden edition of the play
devotes a section to its critical history and finds the question of
realism a recurring preoccupation. She notes that Charles
Gildon, in 1709, found the play's treatment of Hero shocking.
That she should eventually marry her slanderer seemed to him
'degrading'. For Gildon, Shakespeare draws men and women so
perfectly that we believe 'that the discourse is real and no fiction'.
William Hazlitt, in 1817, was convinced that Shakespeare drew
the blundering absurdities of Dogberry and Verges 'from real
life'. Noting that Anna Brownell Jameson found in Beatrice
'a spirited and faithful portrait of the fine lady', McEachern
argues that this concern for psychological plausibility is filtered
through contemporary attitudes regarding 'appropriate female
behaviour'. The poet Thomas Campbell was not so admiring. Of
Benedick and Beatrice, he wrote, 'I once knew such a pair: the
lady was a perfect Beatrice; she railed hypocritically at wedlock
before marriage and with bitter sincerity after it. She and her
Benedick now live apart . . . each devoutly wishing that the other
may soon pass into a better world'. Barbara Everett, in the
twentieth century, felt that, in this play, Shakespeare achieves 'a
novelistic sense of the real'.[2] Taking a partially new historicist
approach, Jean Howard has argued that the play's dramatization
of lies responds to real-world anti-theatrical pressure exerted by

city Puritans. Lorna Hutson, in *The Invention of Suspicion: Law and Mimesis in Shakespeare and Renaissance Drama*, suggests that Dogberry's malapropisms create a parallel effect in articulating 'the inherently preposterous working of suspicion itself'.[3] Early modern London was a suspicious place. In a richly detailed study, Lena Cowen Orlin has shown that Elizabethans worried that privacy might foster illicit behaviour.[4] It is worth asking whether audiences might have noted a degree of realism in the play. Would early English audiences have regarded Shakespeare's Messina as reassuringly alien or worryingly familiar? How might we read the play in terms of its local, London context? In order to begin to answer these questions, this chapter considers three aspects of *Much Ado about Nothing*: its inception as a printed text, its construction of Italy and its apparent connections with contemporary London life.

Printing

Much Ado About Nothing was first printed in quarto in 1597 by London printer Valentine Simmes, and published by Andrew Wise and William Aspley. Since 1594, Simmes had printed works for a variety of publishers. His first play-text, Shakespeare's *Richard II*, was issued in 1597 in quarto. It evidently sold well because he put out a second quarto in the same year, and a third in 1598. Subsequently, he undertook to print *Richard III*, *1 and 2 Henry IV* and *Much Ado About Nothing*. Altogether, Simmes had a hand in half of the eighteen Shakespeare quartos published before 1616, five of which were published with Andrew Wise. The broader story of Wise and Simmes's work, collaborations and interest in Shakespeare has yet to be told.[5] It is likely that Simmes printed the manuscript of *Much Ado About Nothing* much as he received it, although his compositors did introduce slips or errors of their own. In certain respects, these errors are fortunate because they inform us further about the play's connections to early modern London.

At the start of 4.2, Dogberry and his neighbours appear on stage for the second time and prepare to examine their prisoners. In the earliest printed versions of the text – the 1600 Quarto and the 1623 Folio – the speech prefixes at this moment have the names of the actors rather than the characters. Dogberry is given as 'Kemp', and Verges as 'Couley'.[6] These prefixes refer to Will Kemp, the leading comedian in the Lord Chamberlain's Men, and Richard Cowley, usually a player of minor roles. It used to be thought that these slips were Shakespeare's, a sign of his so-called 'foul papers', but, as Paul Werstine has argued, the concept of 'foul papers' is itself misleading, and there is evidence to think that such errors were introduced by a scribe or book-keeper rather than the author.[7] The mistake of 'Kemp' for Dogberry is fortunate because it helps us to date the play. Kemp left the company for Worcester's Men in 1599. So the play must pre-date 1599. Francis Meres' 1598 list of Shakespeare's plays in *Palladis Tamia* omits *Much Ado About Nothing*. If the play was written shortly before the printing of *Palladis Tamia* (entered on the Stationers' Register on 7 September 1598), this may have been too close for Meres to include it. Lukas Erne has suggested that Shakespeare's company had something akin to a policy of publishing plays approximately two years after composition and performance. Since the play first appeared in print in the 1600 quarto, a composition date (on Erne's terms) may be set in or around the latter half of 1598.[8]

A further complication arises from the fact that, as *Much Ado About Nothing* was being prepared for publication, its progress was temporarily halted by means of a 'staying order'. Together with *As You Like It*, *Henry V* and Ben Jonson's *Every Man in His Humour*, the play was listed in the Stationers' Register as among a group of books 'to be staied'.[9] No one knows precisely why printing was delayed but consensus has centred around the idea that the playing company, or the publishers, might have wanted to avoid unauthorized publication. It seems possible that the 1600 Quarto of *Henry V* was not sanctioned by the company but simply a version cobbled together for print purposes only, and Wise and Aspley may have wanted to ensure that they were not responsible for the output of a garbled text. As Sonia Massai has shown, Wise had an interest in textual accuracy, and took care to correct the second and third quarto editions of *Richard II*, *Richard III* and *1 Henry IV* between 1598 and 1602.[10]

Also significant is the relationship between the play's two earliest versions, the 1600 Quarto and 1623 Folio texts. It is customarily supposed that the compositors of the Folio set their text broadly speaking from the Quarto, even duplicating some of its errors. Additionally, they must have had access to knowledge of how the play was performed, or to an independent manuscript.[11] The Folio shares the Quarto's error of including the actors' surnames as speech prefixes at the start of 4.2. But it is more exact about the bearing of drums onstage before the masque, the precise moment when music should play for the dance in Act 2 (TLN 561).[12] There are further hints in the Quarto text that it was, at least in part, set from dictation. In both the Quarto and Folio texts, the Friar tells Leonato, 'Your daughter here the princess (left for dead) / Let her awhile be secretly kept in' (TLN 1866–7). But Hero is not a princess and the only prince in the play is Don Pedro. The line may preserve a mishearing from Simmes's printing house. To clear up the confusion, all modern editions adopt Lewis Theobald's eighteenth-century emendation of the line to, 'Your daughter here the princes left for dead. / Let her awhile be secretly kept in' (4.1.202–3).[13]

Another possible aural error directs our attention to contemporary London rather than to Sicily. The character of Don John is not developed in any great detail in the play. His motive for ruining Hero's marriage is never properly made clear, and he describes himself simply as 'a plain-dealing villain' (1.3.29–30). This lack of complexity is apparent in other characters as well, including Margaret, Conrade and Borachio. We might attribute a motive of some sort to Don John in that slandering Hero as a 'contaminated stale' (2.2.23) depicts her as the kind of woman his mother (by implication) was alleged to have been. But this is to lend a degree of psychological complexity to a character who, as a self-confessed 'villain', is little more than a sketch or cipher. Near the start of the second act, he is introduced in both Quarto and Folio stage directions as 'dumb John' (2.1.75, Q sig. B4, TLN 492). This mistake is most plausibly a mishearing of 'Don John' by Simmes's compositor. We do not know of any Londoners nicknamed 'dumb John' but we do know of a 'Deaf John', a poor man living in Bridewell Hospital. In 1600, he is recorded as 'Comon about the howse', and allowed portions of bread, beef, porridge and beer twice a day. 'Deaf John' owned virtually nothing until, at Easter 1603, he was given a hat, band, doublet, breeches, garters, shoes, points and a shirt. By May 1606, he was dead and his chamber given over to Murrey, the hospital beadle.[14] Ben Jonson memorialized him in a quarrel at the start of *The Alchemist*, where Subtle tells Face that, but for him, Face would have remained in utter obscurity, a low-life in 'an alehouse darker than Deaf John's' (1.1.85). Murrey brewed beer for Bridewell, a place with a particularly dark reputation for cruelty and Jonson evidently presumes that some of his audience will get the joke. 'Dumb John' remains a printing-house mistake, either a mental confusion with 'Deaf John', or – more likely – a simple mishearing on the part of the play's earliest compositor.

Italy

Hutson's term 'preposterous' might well describe much of the play's action, but this is much as it should be for a work drawn mainly from literary sources. The Hero–Claudio storyline derives from Ariosto's epic poem *Orlando Furioso* (1516). In strong iambic rhythms, the fifth canto narrates the story of Genevra and Ariodante (the Hero and Claudio figures in Shakespeare's comedy). Polynesso, a rival suitor for Genevra, persuades Dalinda, a handmaid who loves him, to impersonate her, and receive him – by means of a rope ladder at her balcony – in her chamber. Ariodante watches the event unfold with his brother Lurcanio, and is later rumoured to have thrown himself from a cliff into the sea. Lurcanio condemns Genevra publicly and has her placed under sentence of death. In the event, Ariodante dives, and being a lusty swimmer, he comes back as though from the dead, convinced of Genevra's innocence. He defeats Polynesso in knightly combat, and hears the evildoer's confession before he dies.[15]

Ariosto's version is the play's earliest known precursor. Shakespeare drew more substantially from the version of this story told by Matteo Bandello, included in his collection of *Novelle* (1554). In Bandello's tale, the play's violent prehistory is given more substance. In a popular uprising, Sicilians mercilessly slaughter all French occupying forces and any native woman made pregnant by them. Supported by a papal force, King Piero of Aragon restores order by invading and declaring himself King of Sicily. He defeats an attack by the King of Naples's ships, and in celebration of this great military success, jousts and tournaments are held in Messina. One of the knights contending in the lists, Sir Timbreo di Cardona, falls ardently in love with Fenicia, daughter to Messer Lionato de Leonati, and sets about courting her. According to Bandello, Don Timbreo had 'carried himself nobly in the recent campaigns'.[16] The parallels with Shakespeare are quite evident. Piero of Aragon becomes Don Pedro, also of Aragon. Claudio, a Florentine who has done 'in the figure of a lamb the feats of a lion' (1.1.14–15), is based upon Bandello's Timbreo. Leonato is, in Bandello, a man 'loved as one who sought to hurt nobody'. His character largely transfers to the play, where we find him a genial, likeable host. The heroine of Bandello's tale, Fenicia, is renamed by Shakespeare after the female protagonist in Marlowe's poem *Hero and Leander*, published in 1598, the year in which Shakespeare's play seems to have been written.

The villain in Bandello is Timbreo's treacherous friend, Sir Girondo, a man who has 'proved himself most doughty in the wars'. He arranges for an ambitious young courtier to tell Sir Timbreo that a 'friend' of his 'goes often twice or three times a week to sleep with Fenicia and enjoys her love'. The courtier informs Timbreo that his friend 'is going there as usual this very evening and I shall accompany him as I have done on other occasions'. Girondo disguises himself as the 'friend' and climbs up a ladder to a window in Lionato's house and enters 'as if he had a mistress within'.[17] The parallels with Shakespeare's play will be clear, except that, in Bandello, Timbreo witnesses the event, while Claudio plans to see it but the scene is not in fact staged. Instead Shakespeare cuts from Claudio's initial reaction to hearing that his betrothed is 'every man's Hero' (3.2.95–6) to Borachio's report of the events to Conrade in 3.3.138–56. We next encounter Claudio when he rejects Hero at the friary or church at the start of Act 4.

It is worth tracing the events of Bandello's version a little further since they have a bearing both on the start and end of Shakespeare's play. It seems that Shakespeare began this play with some uncertainty as to how it would progress. His inclusion of Leonato's wife 'Innogen' in the opening stage direction may be one sign of this indecision. Another might be Balthasar's appearance in the stage direction at 1.1.90, even though he first speaks rather later in the masked dance at 2.1.89. It is also possible that Benedick was initially planned as the villain of the play. Beatrice mocks him as 'a disease' and 'a pernicious suitor' (1.1.81, 123). Casually referring to Hero, Benedick asks Claudio, 'Would you buy her that you inquire after?' (1.1.170), a question with seemingly lurid implications. He afterwards jokes that he might make a good brothel-house sign (1.1.236). In the second act, Beatrice refers to Benedick as a man practised 'in devising impossible slanders', surrounded by 'libertines' who commend 'his villainy' (2.1.126–8). These lines are inconsistent with the character that gradually emerges but entirely in line with Bandello's Sir Girondo. Shakespeare's Beatrice, a refined version of the unruly Kate in *The Taming of the Shrew*, could hardly marry a villain, and so, we might conjecture, Don John was invented, leaving Benedick free to become her romantic and comic counterpart.

Bandello's tale also underlies Shakespeare's denouement. Timbreo publicly casts Fenicia off after he has espied her supposed liaison. Fenicia (whose name derives from the Italian for 'phoenix', the bird of resurrection) swoons as though dead and her apparently lifeless body is laid out for interment. Just as her body is being washed before burial, she awakens and, overjoyed at this miraculous recovery, her parents hasten to her uncle's house to proceed with a mock funeral designed to bury any public shame that might yet attach to her. However unsatisfactory the events at the end of Shakespeare's play may seem, they broadly follow Bandello. Now convinced that Fenicia is dead, Sir Girondo is struck with guilt, believing himself to have been her assassin. He confesses his deceit and magnanimously offers to kill himself. Sir Timbreo – who knows nothing of Fenicia's recovery – forgives him, but instructs him to restore the good name of his beloved. Two years later, Sir Timbreo visits Lionato's brother and finds a girl residing there equally as beautiful as his Fenicia – a girl named Lucilla, and who is, of course, Lionato's 'buried' daughter. Believing that he is marrying Lucilla, Timbreo's eyes fill with tears when asked by the priest if he has ever loved another. Lionato then discloses the truth of Fenicia's recovery, and her secret life as Lucilla. Overjoyed, Timbreo embraces the long-lost Lucilla-Fenicia as his bride. The King and Queen of Sicily are so impressed with the story that they shower the couple with riches: 'All this,' writes Bandello, 'befell Sir Timbreo because of his faithful love: the evil that Sir Girondo tried to do was turned to good'.[18]

Shakespeare establishes the Italian setting of his play early on, with Leonato's anticipation of young male visitors to Messina. We learn that Claudio originally comes from Florence, Benedick from Padua, and Don Pedro and (presumably) his brother from Aragon in Spain. Brief allusions to Messina, Venice and the Duchess of Milan sustain the continental topography for the rest of the play. But the European influence persists through the lively verbal games the characters play. Beatrice says of Claudio: 'The Count is neither sad, nor sick, nor merry, nor well – but civil count, civil as an orange, and something of that jealous complexion' (2.1.269–71). Beatrice's pun 'civil as an orange' conceals a reference to Seville, but also anatomizes Claudio in terms that Don Pedro recognizes as a 'blazon'. The 'blazon' was a familiar Petrarchan device in which the physical beauties of the adored person are described. Don Pedro replies, 'I'faith, lady, I think your blazon to be true; though I'll be sworn if he be so his conceit is false' (2.1.272–3). The conceit is another Italianate poetic device in which a central metaphor governs the detail of a poem. Moreover, once Benedick has turned adoring lover to his disdainful lady (a familiar Petrarchan motif), he begins to write sonnets. This playful approach to Renaissance poetry at times leads to innuendo. When Leonato and Claudio trick Benedick into believing their amiable lies, Leonato describes Beatrice as penning declarations of her love: 'O, when she had writ it, and was reading it over, she found "Benedick" and "Beatrice" between the sheet?' Claudio, noting the implication, replies simply, 'That' (2.3.136–8).

These poetic Italianate references are continued in the fifth act when Benedick tries his hand at poetry with Margaret. He finds creative writing a frustrating experience, managing only to rhyme 'baby' with 'lady', 'scorn' for 'horn' and 'school' for 'fool', none of which bodes well for his attempts at impressing Beatrice (5.2.35–40). Shakespeare seems always to have had his earlier Italianate comedy *The Taming of the Shrew* in mind when writing this play. Not only is Beatrice described as 'shrewd' and 'too curst' by Leonato and Antonio (2.1.17–18), but when she comes to believe that Benedick loves her, she speaks of his love 'Taming my wild heart to thy loving hand' (3.1.112). Both she and Kate speak a line about leading apes into hell (*TS* 2.1.34; *MA* 2.1.35). A moment near the end of the play also seems to echo the earlier comedy: Benedick asks, 'Sweet Beatrice, wouldst thou come when I called thee?' and Beatrice responds, 'Yea, signor, and depart when you bid me' (5.2.41–2). The lines recall the husbands' wager at the end of *The Taming of the Shrew* as to whose wife will come when called. By the end of *Much Ado About Nothing*, both Beatrice and Benedick have become Petrarchan lovers.

Claudio waves a piece of paper before the assembled company with a 'halting sonnet' from Benedick '[f]ashioned to Beatrice'. Hero has another, from Beatrice 'containing her affection unto Benedick' (5.4.86–90). By these tokens, the Italianicity of the play is established. But the world of early modern London is never far away.

London

For all its romance, wit and intrigue, *Much Ado About Nothing* has elements that would remind a contemporary audience of a world closer to home. Near the end of the play, Benedick no longer minds being teased about marriage. He declares that, 'a college of wit-crackers cannot flout me out of my humour' (5.4.99–100). In the 1623 Folio text of the play, the word 'college' is capitalized, indicating, it would seem, that either Heminges and Condell, or perhaps the printing-house compositors, understood a proper noun to have been intended. Whittington College stood on the eastern side of St Michael's Church, north of Thames Street. It was established by means of a legacy after the death of mayor Richard Whittington for the training of priests, and supported a nearby almshouse. After the dissolution of the monasteries in 1536–1540, the College was ransacked, but the almshouse retained its name.[19] If, as seems possible, Benedick's reference to a 'College' of wit-crackers is a passing allusion to this London locus, it is little more than a slight and witty play on words, and yet it confirms that elements in this play had local implications.

A more striking topographical reference seems to occur just before the masked ball that takes place near the start of the second act. Stage directions in the Folio text suggest how the action of this scene should take place. Masquers enter 'with a drum' as a prelude before music begins for the dance (signalled by a stage direction in the Folio, but not in the Quarto). During this prelude, Beatrice encounters Benedick and pretends not to recognize him. She then goes on to describe Benedick as 'the

Prince's Jester, a very dull fool', a man given to creating ridiculous slanders, who keeps company with libertines, practises villainy and is mocked and beaten by those around him. She adds, 'I am sure he is in the fleet' (2.1.130). Both the Quarto and Folio texts capitalize the word 'fleet' ('Fleete' in Q, 'Fleet' in F). Again, the printing-house compositor seems to have understood that a proper noun was intended. The line may refer either to the London River Fleet or the Fleet prison situated nearby. The River Fleet separated Bridewell Hospital from Blackfriars. It ran from the north-western suburb of Clerkenwell, under Holborn Bridge and due south to the Thames. Barely a river and sometimes described as a ditch, it was renowned especially for its stench and filth. The Fleet prison was situated south of Holborn Bridge on the river's eastern bank, and was used mainly for the incarceration of debtors. Either way, Beatrice's words bear local implications, a mocking reference to the river, or perhaps the gaol, or possibly to both. This kind of specific topographical reference is rare in Shakespeare, but it would have reminded an audience of the much less exotic, metropolitan world to which the actors belonged. The play hints that this world of bastards and jilted lovers, represented in Don John and Hero, lay a good deal closer to home.

Perhaps the most obviously English elements in *Much Ado About Nothing* are the members of the Watch. The leading members of this group all seem to have relatively English-sounding names – Dogberry, Verges, George Seacoal and Hugh Oatcake. These are the 'honest neighbour[s]' of Messina, a distinctly English bunch of playhouse buffoons (3.5.1). This company of blunderers is essentially a reworking of Petruccio's servants in *The Taming of the Shrew*, or of Peter Quince and the mechanicals in *A Midsummer Night's Dream*. Quite by accident, they manage to expose the conspiracies of Don John and his henchmen, Borachio and Conrade. Dogberry and his friends are lovable in their foolishness, yet they also lend the comedy a satirical edge, aimed not just at the amateurish, lower-levels of City authority, but by implication at the metropolitan ruling elite. Making fun of the Watch could be a whipping offence. John Franck was taken into Bridewell on 23 August 1561, 'for that he is a common quareller and fighter and that he railed upon the constable in his watch and calling him & his companye gowneslaves and other like words'.[20] On 22 May 1602, Thomas Lewis, a 'cobbler' was brought in for being drunk in the streets at midnight and fighting with the Watch.[21]

Watches had been maintained in London throughout the sixteenth century. But they could easily lapse. In February 1584, the court of aldermen reiterated the importance of holding a 'good & substantial Watch' each night in a number of London wards or districts. The Watch should consist of 'choice and sufficient inhabitants' who were 'well and orderly weaponed'. They should patrol the streets 'every night . . . at nine of the clock and continue until five of the clock in the morning and not to sleep in the meantime.' The order added further instructions: they were to

> divide themselves into several companies and to apprehend all such suspect persons as they will find within their said wards and forthwith to search them for any dangerous and suspect things about them, and then to commit them to ward into one of the Counters of this city there to remain until the Lord Mayor be ~~satisfyed~~ certified of their names and several offences.[22]

The wording of this order chimes with Shakespeare's parody of the Watch in his comedy. If a version of it was ever posted on a public bill, he might well have read and mimicked it. The aldermen even got their words wrong in recording it – 'satisfied' for 'certified'. The mistake reminds us of Dogberry's malapropisms. He informs his sturdy neighbours that the Watch's job is 'to comprehend all vagrom men' (3.3.25). Bringing on stage the constable Dogberry, headborough Verges, Hugh Oatcake and George Seacoal – every one of them good men and true, though none of them terribly bright – Shakespeare gives his audience the kind of character they might easily recognize from their street or quarter, squeezing every possible bit of fun out of their ineptitude. The Watchmen seem rather uncertain of their duties and ask what they should do if an offender doesn't come quietly. Dogberry gives them helpful instruction: let him go, make no noise, sleep on duty, leave drunks alone till they sober up, let thieves escape, and, above all, stay no man against his will (3.3.26–80).

Having arrested Don John's men, Borachio and Conrade, Dogberry and the Watch arrange to meet at the prison with pen and inkhorn to set down their 'excommunication' (Dogberry's mistake for 'examination') (3.5.59). The gaol in which they gather is not just any kind of court-house. It is a place for petty criminals run by the lowest levels of City authority, the constables and men of the Watch. These smaller gaols were the 'Counter' prisons named in the 1584 order for keeping nightly watches. London had three Counters, two in north London, in Wood Street and the Poultry, and the third in Southwark. The Wood Street Counter had a cell called 'the hole', presumably the worst part of the gaol. Falstaff alludes to the terrible smell to be caught when passing by the Poultry Counter gate. He tells Mistress Ford she smells as sweet as the fragrances of Bucklersbury, but complains (just as Mistress Page enters) that Meg Page stinks like a prison entrance: 'Thou might'st as well say I love to walk by the Counter gate, which is as hateful to me as the reek of a lime-kiln' (MW 3.3.71–4). Editors propose that this topical allusion must refer to the Southwark Counter, adding that its environs would have been particularly unpleasant. But there is no real evidence to support this claim, and the strong likelihood is that Shakespeare had in mind the Counter in the Poultry, since the Poultry lay only a few steps north of Bucklersbury.[23]

We know a little about the layout of the Southwark Counter from a surviving ground plan of its structure. The building burnt down in a fire of 1675 and was rebuilt in 1685. A design of it made in 1686 depicts the new building but is likely to reproduce the footprint of the first. The plan shows eight private dwellings on the east side facing out on to the main thoroughfare, Borough High Street, and the King's Arms tavern on the west side with stairs leading to a court room above. The Counter itself was a relatively small space consisting of three rooms, a parlour with hearth (15 ft × 15 ft), a kitchen with a hearth (15 ft × 20 ft) and an adjacent common room (20 ft × 25 ft) with a small yard outside (10 ft × 20 ft).[24] The illustration may be a guide to London's other 'Compters' north of the Thames, in the Poultry and Wood Street, the latter having a fearsome reputation. Every year, the London authorities appointed or confirmed a 'clerk to the compters', plus a keeper for each of them, and listed their duties. These petty officers, accountable to a London Sheriff, presided over the smaller local gaols. Many of them were not only wide open to low-level corruption but also nearly illiterate. We do not normally think of a scene in *Much Ado* being set in a prison, especially one so grim, but a contemporary audience watching 4.2 was likely to have brought a 'compter' to mind. This low-level bureaucracy in charge of the 'compters' was distinguished by its livery. A stage direction at the beginning of the scene states that the constables and sexton are wearing 'gowns', and Dogberry closes the scene boasting he is 'one that hath two gowns' (4.2.86–7). We may recall John Franck's contemptuous denunciation of London's minor officers as 'gowneslaves'.

The Bridewell archives occasionally list the names of constables who patrolled London's streets. An entry for 16 March 1574/5, notes parishioners of Islington who served in the Watch: Robert Biggins, William Spakeman, William Gardener, constable Thomas Lyllie, John Campion, Martin Beckett, constable John Cantie, John Nicholas and constables Richard Jackson and Nicholas Rochester.[25] The historian Joan Kent has challenged the idea that members of the Watch and local Master-Constables were as inept as Shakespeare makes them out to be.[26] But given that crime detection and notions of justice were so rudimentary at the time, it should not come as any surprise to learn that patrols were easily evaded, and broadly incapable of suppressing or containing most low-level

criminal activity. In 1602, London's aldermen felt the need to
reiterate in the strongest possible terms the need for Watches
to be effective and carried out conscientiously – a clear
indication that they were not:

Tuesday the 2 of November 1602

Forasmuch as it daily appeareth that the constables of
London by reason of their remissness and negligent
carelessness in the due and true operation of their several
offices and places whereunto they are sworn, are a great
cause that the statute for the restraint of the poor lately
made to so good an end is almost utterly frustrated and the
intent thereof well now utterly disappointed to the great
Privy Council's and the discredit of this city and the
government thereof. For the better remedying and redress
of all which abuses it is now ordered that suit shall be made
to the right ho[nourable] the Lord Mayor and Court of
Aldermen that they may be pleased to appoint a special man
to be an overseer of the said constables to be careful to see
them perform their offices according to the Statute in that
behalf lately made. The neglect whereof may be conceived
to be the cause of so many vagrant persons abounding in
this city without punishment or contradiction.[27]

The 1602 order makes clear that the constables' failure to
carry out their duties means that the processes of 'restraint' are
'utterly frustrated' and 'disappointed' to the 'discredit' of the
City. Low-level ineptitude reflected badly upon the aldermen
and lord mayor. With this degree of incompetence, perhaps
Dogberry's entertaining malapropisms were not quite so
far-fetched: 'exhibition' for commission, 'excommunication'
for examination, 'burglary' for perjury, 'redemption' for
damnation, 'opinioned' for pinioned, and 'suspect' for respect.
In the midst of this distant Sicilian tale, clumsy English
constables make for incongruous but topical comedy. There is
some reason to believe that in 1598, when *Much Ado About*

Nothing was probably written, City night watches were still not fulfilling their appointed duties. Prosecutions for petty crime at Bridewell Hospital in that year rarely mention them. By contrast, prosecutions in 1604–1605 frequently cite 'the Watch' as an arresting body. Of course, watches were not limited to London. It was the late seventeenth-century note-taker John Aubrey who recorded a tale that the character of Dogberry had indeed been based upon a real person – a constable Shakespeare encountered at Grendon Underwood, near Aylesbury, Buckinghamshire:

> The Humour of the Constable in Midsomernight's Dreame, he happened to take at Grendon, in Bucks (I think it was Midsomer night that he happened to lye there) which is the roade from London to Stratford, and there was living that Constable about 1642, when I first came to Oxon.

Aylesbury lay on the route between Stratford on London. It was there that the famous son of Stratford, Sir Hugh Clopton, had constructed 'a way three miles from Aylesbury towards London' for travellers to and from the Midlands.[28] Aubrey's story is inaccurate in at least one key respect – he mistakes the name of the play. Yet in other ways, it seems sufficiently contingent and specific to be quite plausible.

It is worth bearing in mind that some members of Shakespeare's audience may well have been Italian. We know that the Venetian Ambassador Antonio Foscarini visited the Curtain and Fortune playhouses.[29] The registers for St Leonard's, Shoreditch, the parish church that served the community in and around the Curtain theatre, show a number of 'strangers' living in the vicinity, mainly French and Italians: Katherine Winkell, Beatrix Saintclere, Francis Leyfranke, Sapio Burhone and Edward Bassano. The Bassanos were a large family of musicians who lived in Shoreditch and Bishopsgate. Other strangers, apparently Italians, included Patrice Ubaldino, Boone Provoio (a widow) and 'John, an Italian'.[30] These were still a minority since most parishioners were native English people. Yet some Italians in London were hugely powerful and influential. Horatio Palavicino was one of the wealthiest merchants in England. Dealing mainly in products associated with dyeing fabrics, he held a virtual monopoly that gave him such wealth that he was able to lend substantial sums of money to the Crown. He took out naturalization in 1585 and was knighted in 1587. A close associate of his, Benedict Spinola, held a licence to trade in wine and wool, and lived for most of his life in Fenchurch Street, London. Palavicino and Spinola were surrounded by coteries of influential Italian merchants and members of the English aristocracy. The Earl of Leicester, Robert Dudley, described Spinola as 'my dear friend and the best Italian I know in England'.[31] But both of these men were also involved in the illicit world of London prostitution. The play's blend of nobility and lechery, and its fusion of Italian and English elements, bears a certain realism when considered in light of criminal intercultural exchanges that were taking place across all of north London.

Together with his uncle, Alessandro, Palavicino sought out those aspects of London life that chimed with Don John's vision of the world. Gregorius Legrande, a 'stranger', stood charged on 19 January 1576 with allowing 'much whoredom' to take place in his house. Apparently, some of his serving-maids were now with child by 'diverse Italians', one of whom was 'Oratio Pallavasina', who got his steward, 'Gregorie Defrancko', to make arrangements for the child's immediate care, and stand as its godfather.[32] On 16 March 1578, Gilbert Pereman, former servant to 'Oratio Palafasyne', was interrogated concerning his master's activities. He testified that Palavicino had met a friend, one Christopher Demonte, at Barking, and asked Pereman to arrange 'wine and good cheer' and some women for them. He did so but it seems the women had the good sense not to turn up. Benedict Spinola was named, in January 1577, as a 'cashere' who had 'had the use of Mistress Mewtas at Bermondsey Street'. He had given her forty shillings and a gold ring worth twelve shillings. She had sent him in return a pair of gloves. On another occasion, he slept with one Mary Patman in his chamber and at the Ship at Temple Bar. A notorious pimp named William Mekyns told the court that, 'He promised her a gown of clothes and Giles Keys brought it, and about a year past he lay with Mary Patman at the Ship at Temple Bar'. Mekyns added that one of Spinola's serving-men had slept with Elizabeth Cooper at the house of a well-known brothel owner, Mistress Esgrigge, in Whitefriars.[33] Rose Flower ran another bawdy house 'in a lane by Mr Spinaloes garden' and welcomes 'every folk', with 'one or 2 hores for all that come'.[34]

These details illustrate the fact that Italians and Londoners mixed at both the highest and the lowest social levels. Broadly speaking, London was a very divided society: the aristocracy kept large houses in Westminster and along the Strand, set away from the crowded City of London, hemmed in by its historic walls. Merchant-strangers seem to have lived around the City's peripheries. Palavicino had a house in St Dunstan's in the East, and later in Bishopsgate. Spinola resided in Fenchurch Street, and London's Lombard Street was famous for housing Italian goldsmiths – hence its name. Spinola's children settled in Bishopsgate and Shoreditch, not far from the Curtain and Theatre playhouses. It was in this north London suburb, in fields by the Curtain playhouse, that an English maid-servant encountered a stranger named 'Master Benedick' in the spring of 1601.

On 15 March 1601, Margery Copeland stood in court and testified that she was a servant in the household of Master David Lewis, in Old Fish Street near London Bridge. She was about the age of 24 and brought into Bridewell to give her account of events that had taken place about ten days earlier. Copeland had been walking on a Tuesday night between 7.00 pm and 8.00 pm on the southern side of Cheapside, a main London thoroughfare near St Paul's, when she was encountered by a merchant-stranger. He led her northwards through the streets towards Shoreditch. She confessed that he 'drew her alonge into the fcildes towards the Curtaine in Holloway' and there he 'had the use' of her body. This reference looks very much like an allusion to the Curtain playhouse which was situated just south-west of Shoreditch, near Moorfields to the south and Finsbury Fields to the west. John Stow, writing in 1603, observed that the Curtain stood 'on the Southwest side towards the field'.[35] The Curtain, evidently a landmark in the area, was not, as C.L. Kingsford writes, pulled down in 1600, but continued to show plays until the end of James VI and I's reign.[36]

The case gives further details about how the crime was supposed to have remained hidden. Afterwards, having no English, he signalled that he kept no money about him, but took a knife and cut the gold chain with a jewel from around his neck, insisting she take it. He then led her back into central London, explaining that he needed to talk with a French merchant 'about [near] the Exchange'. Arriving there at the Royal Exchange, he knocked at the door and talked with a scrivener, instructing him that he should buy goods from Copeland. He then asked her to go with him to his lodgings in Whitecross Street, near the Fortune theatre, and there hid her in his chamber. He bade Copeland creep under the table so that she might not be seen, and she later lay under his bed in a little trundle-bed. In her testimony, she explains that, the merchant 'had the use of her body twice that night'. In the morning, at 7 o'clock, he let her out 'unseen of anybody in the howse'.

It is just possible that a 'Master Benedick' living near the Fortune or Curtain playhouse might have prompted Shakespeare's idea of a 'Signor Benedick' in the play and lent it further topicality. The encounter with Copeland post-dates the play by four years, and Master Benedick may well have been French and not Italian. Yet the web of ruses, presumptions and stratagems involved in the case suggests some of the more local and contemporary ways in which the play may have been understood by audiences at the Curtain. To all appearances, the courtly, witty world of Messina seems so very different from London, but only so long as we ignore Don John's construction of it. From her testimony, Copeland seems perhaps to have been easily led, and a man in the position of Master Benedick promised financial and social advantages. At her prosecution, Copeland was already a prisoner, while Master Benedick seems to have remained at large. We know why Hero is sequestered in a mock-death at the end of the play. It is what happens to Fenicia in Bandello, and Shakespeare evidently followed his source material, ensuring, as the Friar says, that Hero be 'secretly kept in' (4.1.203). The Italianate fiction of *Much Ado About Nothing* touched on familiar local anxieties in late sixteenth-century London. For, as Copeland's case shows, a woman like Hero finding herself so accused or utterly compromised, might well wish to remain hidden or depart unseen. Audiences at the Curtain, observing the play's tale of gender inequality, slander and apparent shame, may have seen beyond a world of Sicilian 'wonder' to a more 'familiar' substratum of predation, suspicion and betrayal.

5

New Directions

Much Ado – Women (and Men) of a Certain Age

Elizabeth Schafer and Sara Reimers

Much Ado About Nothing identifies several men – Leonato, Antonio, Verges – as 'old';[1] and Claudio as a 'young Florentine' (1.1.10), but the ages of the lead roles, Beatrice and Benedick, are less certain. Beatrice's familial relationships might indicate her age: she is Leonato's niece and uncles are, generally, older than their nieces. Benedick's line 'the world must be peopled' (2.3.233), if taken seriously, might indicate Beatrice is premenopausal. As Benedick is part of a victorious army, it is likely he is physically vigorous. Leonato states that Benedick was a child when Hero was conceived (1.1.102), so he is probably between 20 and 40 years of age. However, as soon as any production of *Much Ado* is cast, the ages of all the characters become defined, limited by the age range that the performers can represent, especially in a production committed to a realistic aesthetic. The relative ages of Beatrice and Benedick have a particular impact on the play's capacity to generate meaning and the 'three-dimensional literary criticism' – the phrase is Simon Russell Beale's[2] – that is embodied by production choices. At a time when complaints about the paucity of roles for women of a certain age, especially in Shakespeare, are rife,[3] Beatrice is one Shakespearian role that women 'of a certain age' have managed to lay claim to. But what happens to *Much Ado* when Beatrice is presented realistically, and in a realistic context, as being 'of a certain age'?

Perceptions of the category 'of a certain age', usually understood as 'middle-aged', will vary and the twenty-five-year age gap between the two writers of this chapter means we perceive 'middle age' differently.[4] Audience reactions to any *Much Ado* positioning Beatrice as middle-aged will also vary in relation to prevailing cultural, historical and staging norms: daylight, candlelight, gaslight or the searchlight of electrical lighting will all affect the appearance of a character's, or a performer's, age as will, for example, costume, posture, gait and prevailing fashions for light, or heavy, stage make-up. In fact many Beatrices and Benedicks have been far from youthful,[5] but a love-amongst-the-seniors *Much Ado* might be particularly strategic now when subscriber audiences are often dominated by ageing baby boomers. Richard Monette had such a hit at Stratford, Ontario, in 1998, with a *Much Ado* which cast Martha Henry (60) as Beatrice and Brian Bedford (63) as Benedick, that the production transferred to Broadway. In 2007–2008, at London's National Theatre, Nicholas Hytner (51) also achieved great critical and box office success with a *Much Ado*, starring Zoë Wanamaker (58) and Simon Russell Beale (46).[6] Because it was committed to thoughtful, thorough realism, and was not an age-blind production – indeed, the perceived age of Beatrice and Benedick had crucial semiotic significance – Hytner's production offers a valuable instance of 'three-dimensional literary criticism' in relation to age and *Much Ado*.

Reviewers frequently commented on the age of Wanamaker and Beale, plus Hytner's commitment to the backstory of a previous, unsuccessful relationship between Beatrice and Benedick.[7] In interviews, Wanamaker (ZW) and Beale (SRB) explained:

> ZW We think it's a complete misunderstanding. Something quick happened, where he opened up but not enough, or they opened up to each other and then they closed up again.
>
> SRB I think Benedick's a commitment-phobe in the classic sense. But also that it was one barb too many from Beatrice as well. So it wasn't just 'I don't want to marry.' It was also 'I can't marry you because you drive me f***ing mad, my Lady Tongue.' We didn't sleep together, did we?
>
> ZW I don't think so.

This subtext of love gone wrong certainly powered through the production.

Wanamaker's Beatrice could have read as younger than the actor's 58 years, but as a public figure, well-known for screen as well as stage appearances, the performer's actual age haunted her performance. Charles Spencer commented:

> Russell Beale is 46, Wanamaker is – but no, gallantry forbids. Let's just say that her 50th birthday probably now seems a distant memory.[8]

Spencer's coyness reflects gendered ageism, implying that a woman should not own her age, as well as pointing to the perceived gap between Wanamaker's apparent and actual age. However, for Wanamaker, Beatrice's age was significant. On being offered the part, her first question to Hytner was 'Aren't I a bit old?'[9] and:

> ZW [. . .]It came as a complete surprise to be asked to do it. But it sort of makes sense. Speaking as a woman, when

you get to your late thirties you know that the clock is ticking. You also begin to know that your perfect partner ain't going to happen unless you make a compromise of some kind. The difference between their relationship and that of Hero and Claudio is young love and older love. It's a much wiser combination.

SRB It's two people who don't necessarily fall in love at first sight but grow to love each other. They're not going to have children. The one thing you do know is that at the end of the play, they are the ones who are going to be together. I don't hold out huge hopes for Claudio and Hero.

Beale and Wanamaker's discussion is grounded in age-related subtext which, in this realist *Much Ado*, was created to explain the characters' motivations.

As a consequence of this backstory, Wanamaker's Beatrice started the play damaged, despairing and drinking to forget. The production lingered over lines that suggested an earlier relationship between Beatrice and Benedick, with Beatrice, on 'hearing the approach of the soldiers', becoming flustered and having 'to hide to compose herself'.[10] The sequence leading to Beatrice's reproach to Benedick, 'I know you of old. . . .' (1.1.138–9) was reconfigured so that this short speech became a bitter solo with Hytner's choreography creating a focus on Beatrice's aching loneliness. Firstly, at 1.1.106, Leonato, his household and his visitors drifted upstage, dissipating the effect of the crowded scene Shakespeare's text suggests. Having established focus on Beatrice and Benedick alone downstage together, Hytner then had Benedick walk upstage after 'I have done' (1.1.137). Consequently Beatrice's 'You always end with a jade's trick' (1.1.138) was addressed to Benedick's departing back, and for 'I know you of old . . .' Beatrice was left, totally alone, downstage; the implication was that Benedick had walked out on her before. The melancholy mood was then broken as everyone came bustling back downstage, even though most characters had to leave again a few lines later

(153 s.d.). The slightly frantic choreography contrasted starkly with the stillness of, and the sense of abandonment conveyed in, Beatrice's lonely solo.

While Hytner paced the action so that the audience must hear the pain as Beatrice talked of Benedick lending her his heart for a while (2.1.255–8), Beale played Benedick as more resilient and Christopher Hart suggested 'it is much easier, and less unkind, to laugh at a middle-aged bachelor than at a middle-aged spinster'; Hart saw Wanamaker's Beatrice as 'a poignant and unhappy sight', a woman 'haunted by her own childlessness'.[11] In addition, the ache in Wanamaker's voice made Leonato appear insensitive and unobservant when he commented 'There's little of the melancholy element in her, my lord. She is never sad but when she sleeps' (2.1.316–17); this suggested, as Hart argued, 'just how little [Leonato] and the other men understand the mournful root of [Beatrice's] ceaseless wit and raillery.' With a more youthful, emotionally robust Beatrice, the scenario might have seemed less bleak.

Pausing, and precise, almost musical, timing, were also used to elaborate Benedick's share of the backstory[12] and Beale used significant pauses to hint that Benedick is still in love with Beatrice: 'There's her cousin, . . .[pause]. . . an she were not possessed with a fury, exceeds her as much in beauty as the first of May doth the last of December' (1.1.180–2).

The most spectacular example of this rewriting-by-means-of-pausing, however, came in Benedick's eavesdropping scene, 2.3. After jumping into a plunge pool to avoid being discovered, Beale peered over the side of the pool, and in a moment that typifies his creative, critical repositioning of Benedick, he changed 'love me? Why, it must be requited' (2.3.216–17) into 'love me? Why?????? [huge pause] . . . It must be requited'. This moment was much noticed and commended in reviews,[13] and it made plausible, appealing sense in relation to Beale's Benedick, who was characterized as cracking jokes to cover his insecurities, a bookish soldier, middle-aged and, despite the recent military action, physically out of condition.

A logical repercussion of playing Beatrice and Benedick as bruised and battered emotionally is that the trick played on them both risked appearing callous. While their shared love of writing, argument, wit and, in this production, books, made it obvious that this Beatrice and Benedick belonged together, nevertheless, the plan to play games with such emotionally vulnerable people seemed dangerous, especially in relation to a Beatrice played as despairing, with her nearest and dearest failing to register her distress, despite her obvious boozing.

Creative pausing also featured during the final admission of love between Beatrice and Benedick in 4.1, particularly during the 'Kill Claudio' (288) sequence. After the hurly-burly of Claudio's denunciation, and its immediate aftermath, this sequence was paced very slowly. A major pause was taken after Benedick's 'I do love nothing in the world so well as you' (267) before he added 'Is not that strange?' (268). The pause after Beatrice's 'Kill Claudio' (288) was immense. Benedick responded 'No, [instead of 'Ha'] not for the wide world' (289). The pause between 'Enough' and 'I am engaged, I will challenge him' (328) was also marked. This created a thoughtful, slow-moving but still compelling sequence, in part, because for Beale, this is the climax of Benedick's story, a moment of profound heroism. However, the heroism Beale detected was critically dependent on Benedick being middle-aged.

In an interview, available on YouTube, Beale explores his reading in detail.[14] For him, when Benedick takes the 'extraordinary decision to support a wronged woman against an army of men', he changes sides, abandoning the hard drinking, macho world. After Don Pedro and his military entourage depart in 4.1, Benedick is left onstage, an outsider, with a family whose lives have been wrecked. Benedick is convinced that his friend Claudio is *as* wronged as Hero and, although he doesn't have any evidence, he guesses Don John is to blame. When Beatrice demands he 'kill Claudio' that is outrageous; however, Benedick agrees to challenge a man twenty years younger than himself, much fitter and probably a better swordsman. Benedick looks death in the face and decides 'well if Beatrice wants me to do that I will risk my life.' For Beale then, Benedick is the bravest man he has ever played.

Hytner agreed with Beale that Benedick is willing to do 'something suicidally brave for Beatrice' in committing to fight a duel he is bound to lose.[15] Any duel has to involve risk, but an experienced soldier pitted against a lamb who is yet to become a lion (1.1.15) is actually reasonable odds in Benedick's favour, unless he is hampered by, for example, being embodied by the 47-year-old, not very athletic looking, Beale. A younger Benedick, or a more athletic, mature Benedick would appear less 'suicidally brave'. This thoughtful, nuanced and psychologically realistic reading of Benedick's dilemma ennobled him but risked making Beatrice appear more unreasonable and destructive. This was exacerbated as Beale's Benedick had also developed a much closer relationship with the audience earlier in the play, and often talking directly, self-deprecatingly but engagingly, to them. Laurie Maguire notes that: 'He even holds up for our inspection the paper on which his ineptly rhymed sonnet is written – the paper he refuses to let the onstage audience see in Act Five, he is willing to share with us.'[16] Benedick's wryly confessional connection with the audience contrasted with Beatrice's comparative lack of direct engagement with them; Wanamaker played speeches such as 'What fire is in mine ears?' (3.1.107) as introspective musings, rather than directing her questions to the audience.[17]

The maturity of Beatrice and Benedick in Hytner's *Much Ado* led Georgina Brown to express 'some doubts about the sex factor',[18] while Nicholas de Jongh commented: 'John Gielgud and Peggy Ashcroft famously led the way in the Fifties, revealing how these roles could be moulded to suit middle-aged performers or an unheterosexual actor of Gielgud's make-up.'[19] Beatrice did seize the initiative and kiss Benedick at 'Peace I will stop your mouth' (5.4.97);[20] however, during the dance at the end of the play, Beatrice and Benedick peeled off from the rest of the dancers and – perhaps slightly out of breath? – settled down to talk. Their enjoyment of witty, engaged conversation, rather than the physicality of dancing, was presented in what was, in effect, a tableau vivant. This intelligent, bookish, witty, conversation-loving, aspiring-to-authorship, mature pair of second-time-round lovers may have offered an empathetic image to many in the National Theatre audience, given the traditional subscriber demographic.

The psychological realism that created this Beatrice and Benedick was also, crucially, supported by the realistic, coherent and plausible Messina created on the Olivier stage; as Michael Billington put it 'Hytner gives us a real world occupied by recognisable people'.[21] This commitment to stage realism was signalled from the outset by a rolling start as Leonato's household assembled one by one for breakfast and sat down at the table to eat real food. The sense of a living community was generated and the large cast size – twenty-five – enabled Hytner to create an impression of authentic hustle and bustle around the main plot lines; servants went about their business, cleaned glasses, swept, played music and could easily eavesdrop on the upper classes. The strong sense of a real extended household, accustomed to working and living together was epitomized in the care taken over the role of Antonio's son.[22] Picking up on Leonato's line 'How now, brother, where is my cousin your son? Hath he provided this music?' (1.2.1–2) Hytner brought the character on stage, casting Matthew Woodyatt in the role. Subsequently Leonato's 'O I cry you mercy, friend' (1.2.22–3) was changed, with 'friend' replaced by 'nephew', and the prompt copy indicates that as the attendants crossed the stage in 1.1 they were 'led by Antonio's son' even though no one in the audience would have picked up on this tiny detail.

Rehearsal reports also indicate the care taken over the production's realism; for example, Beatrice was reading a book during breakfast; Wanamaker 'requested that her book could be something like Tennyson, Wordsworth or Browning – or possibly a Greek (Ovid, etc.).'[23] For the arrival of Don Pedro's victorious army there was a request for: 'Flowers instead of petals to scatter. Rather than women strewing petals which would then get left on stage, the Army will carry flower stems when they enter, as if they have been given them by Sicilian Villagers as they march through the town on their triumphant return.'[24] However, given the Beatrice-and-Benedick-had-a-previous-relationship approach, it is not surprising that what reviewer Jane Edwardes remembered of this moment was Benedick arriving 'with a bunch of flowers, which he fails to deliver' to Beatrice.[25]

Leonato – the second-largest role in the play, in terms of lines – was also played, by Oliver Ford Davies, as a complex, fully rounded and unusually sympathetic character. Davies is well known for playing senior, statesmen-like roles,[26] but at 68 years of age in 2007, he was only ten years older than Wanamaker. However, costuming and characterization made Leonato appear significantly older than his niece. Ageing Leonato helped to clarify his familial role, and foregrounded his position as patriarch, as governor of Messina and, apart from Don Pedro, as the highest-ranking character in the play. Leonato appeared very old compared with Hero – Susannah Fielding was 22 but looked younger – and possibly more like a grandfather than father. Davies's Leonato, however, had an intensely close relationship with his only daughter. While the generation gap between Hero and Beatrice endowed Beatrice with a maternal aspect – and Beatrice was certainly old enough to be Hero's mother – the Leonato/Hero relationship gained a Lear/Cordelia inflection.

Davies had played King Lear in 2002 and some reviewers detected a Lear-like quality injected into Leonato's journey during 4.1, the church scene, usually the moment when Leonato loses audience sympathy.[27] His treatment of Hero, and in particular his expressed hope that, if what Claudio and Don Pedro say is true (123 ff.), she should die, is harsh. Davies made Leonato more sympathetic than usual, however, by playing him as anguished by what was done to Hero, furious, but then also quickly won round to questioning the accusations made against her. Leonato certainly, as it were, rejected his Cordelia, Hero, in public and then raged upon the heath that was created in the church; however, unlike Lear, this Leonato became reconciled to his daughter extremely quickly. He was emotionally destroyed by the attack on Hero and the issue of his personal honour was only one aspect of the greater outrage of the public shaming of his beloved daughter. Davies's willingness to allow Leonato to display distress alongside his anger helped rehabilitate this character for a modern British audience and perhaps the hardest line Leonato has to say – 'Hence from her, let her die' (154) – was spoken through sobs; this Leonato was so emotionally devastated he had become incapable of rational thought.

Davies's Leonato moved on from rage so quickly that 'Being that I flow in grief / The smallest twine may lead me' (4.1.249–50) became a keynote.[28] The moment the Friar mentioned 'the errors that these princes hold' (4.1.163), Leonato listened intently. When Leonato protested against the Friar's line of argument, he sounded as if he was asking to be proved wrong. By the time of Benedick's 'The practice of it lives in John the bastard' (188), a line which was emphasized, Leonato was completely converted. While his threat to tear Hero to pieces had been downplayed, by contrast, 'if they wrong her honour' (191) was at full throttle with Leonato now thirsting for revenge. Hero and Leonato embraced here, fully reconciled, both determined to right Hero's wrong. They exited together, with Leonato supporting his beloved daughter, a gesture that anticipated Leonato's declaration of faith 'My soul doth tell me Hero is belied' (5.1.42).

Davies argues that Shakespeare struggles to make 4.1. plausible, citing several unrealistic features:

> Beatrice, who knows Borachio must be lying when he confessed he had had sex with Hero 'a thousand times in secret' (4.1.94), has to be silenced by Leonato. Benedick, who could have denounced Don John much earlier in the scene, is uncharacteristically made to say 'I am so attired in wonder / I know not what to say' (144–5). Hero merely says, 'I talked with no man at that hour, my lord' (86), before she faints.[29]

Meanwhile, for Leonato, the damning testimony is when Don
Pedro states:

> I am sorry you must hear. Upon mine honour,
> Myself, my brother and this grieved count
> Did see her, hear her, at that hour last night,
> Talk with a ruffian at her chamber window,
> Who hath indeed, most like a liberal villain,
> Confessed the vile encounters they have had
> A thousand times in secret.

(4.1.88–94)

Leonato assumes he is hearing Borachio's testimony by means
of Don Pedro's report here. Davies comments 'This is hard,
incontrovertible evidence'.[30] Consequently, 'Leonato's initial
anger and despair is extreme' but 'understandable'. Because
she has been publicly shamed, Hero is unmarriageable; she
faces a future in a convent or living secluded in her family
home. For Davies, 'Leonato will be "killed", either by his own
hand, or dead within the year through shame, because his
emotional investment in his daughter is so intense.'[31] However,
Leonato's suffering galvanizes him, transforming him from the
rather obsequious host of the opening; by the beginning of 5.1.
Leonato has become an avenger figure, hell-bent on clearing
his daughter's name. Davies argues 'Leonato is given a
remarkable journey [. . .] It is the most complete exposition of
a father taking charge throughout the play of his daughter's
future happiness until Shakespeare came to write *The
Tempest*'.[32] Davies also references Shakespeare's own life
history at the time *Much Ado* was written; for Davies, Hero is
probably 'no more than 15' – the age of Susanna Shakespeare
in 1598 – with Claudio 'no more than 16 or 17'.[33]

Hytner's Claudio, Daniel Hawksford, was 27 and looked it,
and was characterized as prone to explosive outbursts of
temper. By the time that Claudio attempted to throttle Hero in
church, the audience had already seen him attempt to throttle
Don John, when he first raised doubts about Hero. Earlier,

Claudio also became extremely agitated over Don Pedro's offer to woo Hero on his behalf, and Claudio's repeated, but unsuccessful, attempts to interrupt or demur, when Don Pedro proposed the scheme, implied both insecurity and the understanding that 'a count cannot contradict a prince'.[34] Claudio's subsequent violent jealousy situated Hero as stuck between an Othello or Leontes-like fiancé and a Lear-like father.

Susannah Fielding's young-looking and inexperienced Hero seemed to go into shock in 4.1, being too stunned to be able to speak out and deny the claims made against her until after her accusers had gone. The scene was staged to emphasize the violence that was being done to her and how disorienting that was. When Hero arrived in the chapel, Claudio gently removed her veil and took her hands; when he answered 'No' to Friar Francis's 'You come hither, my lord, to marry this lady?' (4.1.6), Hero looked to her father in confusion and was clearly relieved when Leonato explained 'To be married *to* her' (7, emphasis added). In the subsequent exchange, Hero kept her eyes fixed on Claudio, unable to comprehend her fiancé's accusations, while Claudio kept hold of her hands, before then violently shoving her back into Leonato's arms.

Within this context of domestic violence in public, Hero's silence became a withdrawal, an act of self-preservation. As both Leonato and Claudio oscillated between tenderness and then violence towards her, they made it almost impossible for Hero to judge how best to react: in Claudio's final speech before leaving, he initially appeared to approach Hero tenderly; the tenderness quickly turned into disgust and violence; finally Beatrice had to shield Hero from physical attack. A similar trajectory occurred when, after recovering from her swoon, Hero was able to hug Leonato, before then being violently pushed aside as Leonato exclaimed 'O she is fallen / Into a pit of ink' (4.1.139–40). Hytner's decision to make this scene male-dominated also contributed to a sense of real physical threat. The only women present were Hero and Beatrice as the other female characters were 'all at home getting the reception ready'.[35] The rehearsal reports state that the aim was to 'isolate Hero more (Beatrice being the only other woman there)' and some of the male members of the Watch were drafted in as supernumeraries to increase this effect. As the soldiers were located upstage, this male, military presence essentially guarded the door of the chapel, trapping Hero in with her accusers. By interpolating a cry of 'no' in response to Don Pedro's accusation that she had met Borachio 'A thousand times in secret' (4.1.94), Fielding's Hero did make a protest, but she was silenced, intimidated by the overwhelming, macho aggression she was encountering.

The church scene was one of several moments when Fielding gave Hero depth by playing her silences and creating significant subtext. From the beginning of the play Fielding played between the lines to signal that Hero was extremely attracted to Claudio; so in 2.1 she sat slightly apart from the group, ignoring Beatrice's witticisms, waiting impatiently for the maskers – especially Claudio – to arrive. Hero also took the lead when her betrothal was confirmed; while Claudio was summoning up the courage to kiss her in public, Hero – as Beatrice suggests (2.1.285–6) – pressed ahead and kissed him. The most significant increase in Hero's agency, however, appeared in 5.3. As Claudio, barefoot and in sackcloth, prostrated himself upon her 'grave', Hero, accompanied by Leonato, stood upstage, watching him. Eventually Leonato looked questioningly at Hero; she nodded, indicating that she chose to go ahead with the second-time-round marriage ceremony. Fielding commented: 'seeing the change in Claudio, weeping, singing and hanging the epitaph helped me imagine forgiving him'.[36] When, having experienced the extremes of Claudio's volatility, Hero still decided that Claudio was the husband she wanted, it was, at least, from a position of knowledge and she was aware she was choosing to marry a human volcano.

Hytner's *Much Ado* excelled in the careful excavation and presentation of realistic characters and situations, to such an extent that the production often headed in the direction of

Shakespeare-as-Chekhov.[37] This *Much Ado* had a large country house setting, with characters on the brink of disaster, despair, possibly suicide. Sound effects suggested the real, living and working community of Messina was just offstage; dogs barked, cicadas chirruped, bells tolled. There was nothing of the postmodern, post-dramatic or the Brechtian. In addition, a drift towards the literary, and the novel, was suggested in a programme essay, written by novelist Philip Hensher,[38] who sees *Much Ado* 'from the beginning to end, as a novel without knowing it; a novel before such a thing existed'. Hensher states, 'The plot of mock-hostilities between a man and a woman yielding to love seems to me essentially one of the novel rather than the drama' and he aligns the play with novels such as *Pride and Prejudice*. Hensher does not, however, acknowledge the radical instability of theatre; the appearance, age and demeanour of Elizabeth Bennet will not change with successive readings but each new production of *Much Ado*, each new cast, brings a different set of meanings to the play; Hytner's *Much Ado* would have generated very different meanings if Beatrice had been cast as the same age as Hero.

As Hytner's *Much Ado* morphed into a cross between a Chekhovian country house play and *The Portrait of a Lady*, it is worth noting that several key players in the production were particularly well placed to offer detailed and nuanced 'three-dimensional literary criticism' of the play. Oliver Ford Davies gained a DPhil in history, from Oxford, before choosing an acting career over academia and a lectureship at Edinburgh University; both Hytner and Beale read English Literature at Cambridge and would have been trained in quarrying literary and historical text.[39] However, in the original performances of *Much Ado*, with players learning just their parts plus cue lines, without access to the rest of the play, there would have been little in the way of detailed exploration of text, character motivation or creation of what was later called subtext. In addition, the non-illusory casting practices of Shakespeare's single-sex company would mean that the gap between the actor and his role could be pronounced, and often foregrounded, in a way that would be incongruous within a production committed to wholesale realism. Consequently it is not surprising that there were several moments in Hytner's production when the realism did not work, when Shakespeare's grounding in an anti-illusionistic playhouse was in tension with the production's realist aesthetic. One of the most noticeable instances of such tension related to *Much Ado*'s use of substitution and interchangeability.

The successful substitution of one woman for another is crucial to the Hero plot of *Much Ado*: on the eve of their wedding Claudio mistakes Margaret for Hero, and in the final scene Hero is substituted for Leonato's fictitious niece. This act of substitution in *Much Ado* has its roots in the bed-trick, a convention widely used in plays from the period in which 'a sexual encounter occurs in which at least one partner is unaware of the other partner's true identity'.[40] However, in a performance context dominated by realism, this dramatic convention was troubling; the interchangeability of clearly different bodies put a strain on realist conventions.

In the name of theatrical clarity, the roles of Hero and Margaret are generally played by actors of a similar age and build, a convention to which Hytner's realist staging adhered. However, Hytner's *Much Ado* went to great effort to individualize each character and this problematized the straightforward exchange of one woman for the other. For example, while Hero and Margaret wore dresses of a similar style and shade, they were characterized quite differently, with Fielding's Hero played as prim and well-spoken and Niky Wardley playing a slightly older and more down-to-earth Margaret, who spoke with a Yorkshire accent. Although the difference in the characters' accents made it harder to accept Claudio and Don Pedro's mistake – Don Pedro says he saw and heard Hero with Borachio – Margaret was excluded from 4.1 to avoid the problem of Margaret's response to the denunciation of Hero; her absence provided a reason why Margaret didn't speak out and explain the misunderstanding. The production later went further in creating sympathy for

Margaret, as during the scene change between 5.1 and 5.2 she was seen standing alone and in tears. Rehearsal notes include a request for a suitcase for Margaret 'as if she is packing up and leaving in Scene 5.2', which suggests that she was at that stage envisaged as either feeling guilty or being punished.[41]

In addition to the four named female roles of Hero, Beatrice, Margaret and Ursula of Shakespeare's text, Hytner cast four extra female performers. The programme identifies three of these as 'Ladies of the House' and the fourth as a new character named 'Meg'. Replacing the Boy of Shakespeare's text, Meg was a housemaid for Leonato and, as well as being given the Boy's lines in 2.3 and the Messenger's lines in 3.5, she was allowed a significant amount of stage time; she frequently appeared in the background of scenes, and during scene changes, contributing to the realistic depiction of Leonato's working household. The rehearsal notes chart a remarkable character development for such a minor role: starting out as 'Wench' instead of 'Boy', the character soon acquired her name, as well as additional lines, and a specific position in the hierarchy of Leonato's household.[42]

In a production context in which even the most minor characters had a backstory, the decision to name this character 'Meg' must take on significance. As a diminutive of Margaret, 'Meg' had to be linked, if only associatively, with Hero's waiting woman. Indeed, as Meg was identified by name *before* Margaret was, the first 'Margaret' to be addressed after 2.2, when Borachio and Don John plan their deception involving 'Margaret', was this new character of Meg. Later on, Hero also refers to Margaret as 'Meg' (3.4.7), and this created a lexically porous relationship between the two characters.

In their embodiment, however, Meg and Margaret were very distinct. Contemporary casting conventions dictate that Hero and Margaret should adhere to the petite dimensions expected of the ingénue and both Fielding and Wardley conformed to these expectations. Meg, on the other hand, was played by a plus-sized young actor, Jessica Gunning, whose physical presence marked her out as different from the other women of the household.⁴³ Yet, despite embodying an alternative to the conventions of desirable femininity in terms of size, Meg was physically substituted for a romantic lead, Beatrice, in 3.2. In order to eavesdrop on Hero and Ursula, Wanamaker borrowed Meg's straw hat, mop and bucket. Disguised as Meg, and having sent Meg away, Beatrice concentrated on listening, edged closer to Hero and Ursula, and became careless in her mopping. After knocking the bucket into the pool, and with Ursula and Hero glaring at her, Beatrice-as-Meg had to lean over into the pool. As she toppled in, Beatrice, hilariously, put all her energies into trying to keep Meg's wide-brimmed hat in place, so that her face could not be seen, and her disguise as Meg preserved.

The rehearsal reports indicate that this substitution was for comic effect alone, and the requirements of realism were discussed and taken on board: 'So that it is believable that Hero and Ursula could mistake Beatrice for a servant, it was thought that Beatrice could be wearing an Apron and carrying a Tea Towel with her sleeves rolled up and her hands covered in flour as if she has been baking.'⁴⁴ A more radical reading of this comic substitution would be that by indicating the complexity of the act of embodiment, the production was able to question both the dramatic convention of the bed-trick and the casting conventions that have developed since women's performance became legalized in the seventeenth century. The pantomimic confusion of Hero and Ursula when they looked for Beatrice upstage, only to realize that the older, slimmer Beatrice had substituted for younger, plus-sized Meg, was played for laughs, but this sequence also questioned the notion of the interchangeability of female bodies which is the bedrock of the narrative of Hero's defamation.

Another tension created by Hytner's commitment to realism related very specifically to Beatrice's age. In 2007, Wanamaker was a celebrity, with many details of her life, including her actual age, very much in the public domain; indeed, for some, Wanamaker's celebrity status would have disrupted, and haunted, the realism of this *Much Ado*. Wanamaker regularly

featured on British television as Susan Harper, the mother in
the popular BBC sitcom *My Family* (2000–2011).[45] For those
who followed *My Family*, Wanamaker's mature, maternal
Susan could have ghosted her Beatrice;[46] Susan and Beatrice
share an acerbic wit, and the repartee between Susan and her
husband Ben (Robert Lindsay) may have underscored the
merry war between Beatrice and Benedick. Wanamaker was
also, however, known for playing Madam Hooch, the flying
instructor at Hogwarts School of Witchcraft and Wizardry, in
Harry Potter and the Philosopher's Stone (2001).[47] Michael
Quinn argues that celebrity casting adds an extra layer of
meaning to a performance, as the characteristics of the actor,
the dramatic character, and the stage figure interact with the
celebrity's public persona in a way that 'keeps them from
disappearing entirely into the acting figure or the drama.'[48]
For some of the audience, particularly younger members,
Wanamaker's Madam Hooch, and games mistress stereotypes,
may also have been part of the mix in responses to her Beatrice.

In the context of contemporary London theatre, however,
depicting Beatrice as mature, as a 'woman of a certain age' also
had a political significance. On average, women are
outnumbered by two to one on England's stages, and this
inequality is even more pronounced in performances of
Shakespeare.[49] Of those roles that are available to women,
many are cast primarily by age, with older women almost
invisible in classical performance. For example, data from
2013 and 2014 indicates that in productions mounted by
the RSC and Shakespeare's Globe in these years, performance
opportunities decreased with age for both genders, but
markedly so for women: female performers made up just
16 per cent of the actors aged over 45 performing at these
prestigious classical venues.[50] While the Act for Change
project's 'Women of a Certain Age' campaign has highlighted
the dearth of roles available for older female performers across
a variety of media, including film and television,[51] these bleak
statistics for older female performers are, in part, caused by
Shakespeare's ongoing importance in the repertoire.[52] In the

canon of Shakespeare's most revived plays, such as *A Midsummer Night's Dream*, *Merchant of Venice*, *Taming of the Shrew*, *Twelfth Night*, *Othello* and *Henry V*, young women predominate, whereas some of Shakespeare's most remarkable older women appear in plays that are rarely revived, such as *Coriolanus*, *The Merry Wives of Windsor* and *King John*.

In the years since Hytner's production a number of high-profile productions of *Much Ado* have imagined Beatrice as a woman of a certain age.[53] What is remarkable about this trend for middle-aged, twenty-first century Beatrices is the role played by celebrity status. When a jobbing actor plays Beatrice she tends to be in her late twenties or early thirties, whereas when a celebrity plays the role she tends to be older and her celebrity then stamps an age on the character in a unique way.[54] Casting directories require actors to categorize themselves based on their apparent age, but in a performance context dominated by celebrity, the *actual* age of the performers – as detailed in newspaper interviews and *Wikipedia* entries – will contribute to the theatrical semiotic. The tension between contemporary ageism and celebrity in casting Beatrice suggests that, in the hierarchy of casting requirements, celebrity can trump ageism, but that for jobbing actors ageism remains an issue even in a role, like Beatrice, where there is a track record of mature actresses playing the role with success.

Celebrity casting, however, resulted in a critical mauling for Mark Rylance's 2013 Old Vic production of *Much Ado*, starring Vanessa Redgrave (76) and James Earl Jones (84). The uniformly negative reviews almost all mentioned the age of Beatrice and Benedick, associating this with low energy levels, lack of projection and uncertainty over lines, and some reviewers even detailed the combined age of the leading actors as 158.[55] While this fixation on age may, in part, be due to ageism, it was facilitated by a production aesthetic in which the consequences of the casting were not worked through. Rylance's relocation of the play to 1940s rural Britain, with Don Pedro's army depicted as American GIs, represented a realist approach to the play, with Jones and his fellow soldiers played as African American airmen. However, while the colour-conscious casting contributed to a realist aesthetic, the age element did not; for example, Jones looked too old for active service. As Simon Edge remarked, 'You can't help wondering why Earl Jones's Benedick is a boon companion to the youthful Claudio';[56] Edge added 'The age-blindness also means we don't get the normal clues – nieces look like aunts, cousins like grandfathers';[57] Michael Billington's one-star review in *The Guardian* also described the production as 'age-blind';[58] however, the actors' maturity was important in the production's reception, and Rylance asserted that, by casting 'elderly' actors as Beatrice and Benedick, 'the young couple [Hero and Claudio] have much more room'.[59] This does not suggest an 'age-blind' approach and, if the age of Redgrave and Jones's Beatrice and Benedick was intended to signify, their maturity was not coherently or consistently thought through in terms of the world evoked onstage. By contrast, many reviews of Hytner's production remarked on the powerful signification of an older Beatrice and Benedick, with Charles Spencer stating that 'the age of the actors actually adds to the pleasure and point of the piece'.[60]

Overall, Hytner's production turned *Much Ado* into a realistic exploration of recovering relationships. While Beatrice and Benedick picked up the pieces from their previous relationship, Hero and Claudio might also, potentially, be in recovery mode, given the agency imported for Hero in 5.3. There was also, possibly, another, subtextual, recovering relationship, between Margaret and Balthasar. In 2.1. Margaret appeared to reject the drunken, amorous Balthasar as a suitor, pushing him away from her,[61] but the couple were reunited in the final scene, and danced together for the finale. Theatre production is always a form of adaptation, and often appropriation, but Hytner's Chekhovian *Much Ado* indicates the extent to which casting is also part of the adaptation and appropriation continuum; casting a Beatrice and Benedick 'of a certain age' shifted meanings, refashioned and remade the play in performance, and facilitated the generation of a very specific subtext, one which was grounded in the notion of Beatrice and Benedick being second-time-round lovers.

While *Much Ado* worked well with Hytner's chosen approach, the leisurely tempo and pausing that went with playing Beatrice and Benedick as middle-aged slowed down the pacing; the compensation on offer was the detailed, three-dimensional criticism produced. Beale has explained that, in performance, he tries to: 'lead the audience through a detailed argument about a character, while embracing a role's contradictions and leaving himself open to the inspiration of the moment'.[62] Hytner's *Much Ado*, in Beale's words, also led 'the audience through a detailed argument' about the characters, the situations and the age of the protagonists of *Much Ado*. His nuanced and realist *Much Ado* allowed Beale to discover heroism in a middle-aged Benedick facing certain death in the duel with Claudio, while Wanamaker's performance made a persuasive case for playing Beatrice as a woman of a certain age.

Postscript

After this chapter was completed, both Zoë Wanamaker and Nicholas Hytner have recently published discussions of the 2007 *Much Ado*. See *Balancing Acts* by Nicholas Hytner (London: Jonathan Cape, 2017) and 'Zoë Wanamaker on Beatrice', in *Shakespeare on Stage 2* by Julian Curry (London: Nick Hern Books, 2017), 279–302.

6

New Directions

Much Ado or Love's Labour's Won? – Does It Matter Which?

Lois Potter

In its 2014–2015 season, the Royal Shakespeare Company performed *Much Ado About Nothing* as a sequel to *Love's Labour's Lost*, retitling it *Love's Labour's Won*. When this pairing was announced, one journalist wondered 'whether it's commercially wise to attach the *Love's Labour's Won* name to a script that would have more sway with potential patrons under its actual title.'[1] In fact, the double bill, directed by Christopher Luscombe, was such a success that the RSC brought it back in the 2016–2017 season. It also marketed the DVD of the production as *Love's Labour's Won*, with *Much Ado* as the subtitle.[2] There were many reasons for the success of the two plays. Both, especially *Love's Labour's Lost*, were heavily cut and trimmed of anything that might not be easily understood. Both had a delightful musical score by Nigel Hess. They were family-friendly Christmas shows (a Christmas tree played a prominent part in *Much Ado*). *Love's Labour's Lost*, in particular, had been softened into a more likeable play. The Pageant of the Nine Worthies – in the text, an attempted entertainment that is sabotaged by the rudeness of its spectators – became a charming musical event, with the spectators encouraging rather than insulting the performers. Perhaps a still greater attraction was the *look* of the production. The beautiful set, with scene changes that were a pleasure in themselves, represented Charlecote Manor in the second decade of the twentieth century. Most of the audience would have recognized the familiar world of *Downton Abbey*, the most popular television programme of recent years.

It was in the context of the long hot summer of 1914 that the audience was invited to see the silly game-playing and courtship of *Love's Labour's Lost*. The sudden news of the death of the King of France became, emotionally, the equivalent of the assassination of Franz Ferdinand and the declaration of war. Though the play ends with the departure of the women, the production reversed the emphasis: after saying farewell, the men exited and re-entered in uniform, clearly bound for France. The play, then, followed the trajectory of Series 1 of *Downton Abbey*. In Series 2 the tone darkened; part of the stately home was turned into a hospital; and few of the young men were the same when they returned from the Front. It was this world that was evoked at the beginning of *Much Ado*, which opened, supposedly, four years later. The hall of the stately home was now occupied by hospital beds, and Beatrice and Hero wore nurse uniforms. It seemed that Beatrice, rather than Berowne, had been obliged to 'jest a twelvemonth in a hospital' (*LLL* 5.2.859).[3] The beds were empty, however, and perhaps some of her edginess might have resulted from the loss of a sense of purpose. After the men's return from the war, however, the beds and the uniforms disappeared. The production attempted to keep the war in mind through Don John's arrival on crutches and the fact that Dogberry's speech disorders seemed the result of gas or shell shock (and thus, as Peter J. Smith, for example, noted, not funny at all).[4] But, as

Carol Chillington Rutter pointed out in *Shakespeare Survey*, there was no real sense of the effects of the war on the characters on the home front – hardly surprising, since there is nothing in the text of the play to support it.[5]

Ironically, at almost exactly the same time as the RSC, Scott Kaiser was producing his own *Love's Labour's Won*, performed at Seattle University in 2014 and (in repertoire with *Love's Labour's Lost*) at the Illinois Shakespeare Festival in 2015. This new play, according to the detailed plot description on the website, reunites the lovers in 1918 Versailles, just as the armistice is about to be signed. All the characters from the earlier play reappear, but in the context of the issues raised by the 1914–1918 war: prisoners, arms sales, spying.[6] These are just the issues that some reviewers missed in the RSC *Much Ado*, though it is hard to see how the text would have allowed them to be incorporated.

It should be noted that the idea of renaming *Much Ado* came not from the director but from Gregory Doran, artistic director of the RSC. Luscombe duly laid emphasis on lines that might link the plays, but the connections between them were largely visual and benefited from awareness of the *Downton Abbey* parallels, such as the 'upstairs/downstairs dynamic' with the servants Ursula, Margaret and Borachio, whom Gretchen E. Minton compared to the footman Thomas in the television series.[7] Though Jami Rogers wrote in *Shakespeare Bulletin* that the productions 'were impossible to view in isolation',[8] this is in fact how many spectators saw them (often attending only the more popular *Much Ado*) and the early reviews had to focus on one at a time, though usually with some comment on the renaming. Peter J. Smith felt that they were a 'forced marriage', while Michael Billington felt that parallels 'abound' and that the pairing 'made total sense'.[9] Now that the productions are available on DVD, there will undoubtedly be more detailed analyses of the two-part structure, and my chapter is not going to compete with the intelligent reviews that have already appeared. (With what I suspect was a typical academic reaction, I enjoyed the

productions a great deal – in part because the audience was
enjoying them so much – but also regretted their evident
distrust of much of the plays' language.) Rather, I shall take my
cue from Peter Kirwan's comment: 'the implication that the
two plays are *narrative* sequels is bunk, but the *thematic*
connection implied by the titles need not be.'[10] Let's see where
that idea will take us.

What was *Love's Labour's Won*?

Love's Labour's Won, listed among Shakespeare's comedies
by Francis Meres in 1598, is the most tantalizing, and most
coveted, lost work of the Renaissance. In numerous detective
stories involving Shakespeare's life and/or afterlife, it has
become the successor to that favourite nineteenth-century plot
device: the priceless Indian jewel that brings death to everyone
who owns it. At one time, it was considered possible that
Meres was simply mistaken, or disingenuous, about its
existence. Then, in 1953, the antiquarian bookseller Solomon
Pottesman discovered an early seventeenth-century bookseller's
list (dated 19 August 1603) including both *Love's Labour's
Lost* and *Love's Labour's Won*. He showed it to T.W. Baldwin,
who researched its provenance and published his conclusions
in 1957.[11] There has been some disagreement over the
interpretation of the list, but it does show that *Love's Labour's
Won* got into print, and thus that a copy might yet surface in
some unexpected place.[12]

Though it has been possible to conjecture about the other
'lost' play, the Shakespeare–Fletcher *Cardenio*, whose title
hero shares the name of a character in *Don Quixote*, nothing
is known about *Love's Labour's Won* apart from the fact that
Meres listed it as a comedy. As Roslyn Knutson's 'Lost Plays'
website points out, plays whose titles make them look like
sequels (she instances *A Knack to Know a Knave* and *A Knack
to Know an Honest Man*) do not always turn out to have
anything to do with their predecessor.[13] Even plays that present

themselves as sequels do not necessarily observe consistency in characters' names and personalities. Fletcher's *The Woman's Prize* is a good example: the only names carried over from *The Taming of the Shrew* with their original identities are those of Petruchio and his now-dead wife Katherine, while the characters called Bianca and Tranio bear no relation to those in the earlier play. Sequels to popular plays were common, especially in the 1590s, and Shakespeare had written a number of them. Most of the sequels were easily recognizable because they were called Part Two (or, in one case, Part Three), though *The Merry Wives of Windsor* offers a completely new title, perhaps because it is not so much a sequel to the Henry IV plays as a Falstaff play that takes place in a parallel universe.[14] So *Love's Labour's Won* may have been a completely different work, now lost. A glimpse of a scene supposedly from this play was performed, memorably, in an episode of *Doctor Who* (2007), and an internet search of fan and fantasy websites will quickly reveal many other attempted recreations, usually with some sinister explanation for the play's disappearance.

On the other hand, *Love's Labour's Won* may – and this has been a popular view for over a century – be an alternative title for some other Shakespeare comedy. The plays most often proposed as possible candidates are two comedies that may pre-date Meres's list but are not included on it: *The Taming of the Shrew* (though the Folio text may be a later revision) or *Much Ado About Nothing*, first published in 1600, which may have had its first performances just after Meres wrote his survey of contemporary writers. Evidence that Shakespeare plays were sometimes revised for later revival has led to speculation about three other plays that in their present form are usually considered later than 1598: *As You Like It*, *All's Well That Ends Well* and *Troilus and Cressida*. Since Meres mentioned *A Midsummer Night's Dream* (first published 1600), it is unlikely to be identical with *Love's Labour's Won*, but the two plays have obvious intertextual connections. Depending on their respective dates, Berowne's 'Jack hath not Jill' (*LLL* 5.2.863) may hark back to *A Midsummer Night's*

Dream and Puck's assurance that 'Jack shall have Jill' (3.2.461),[15] or, on the other hand, Puck's line, and the four pairings-off in *Dream*, may be a comment on the 'unsatisfactory' ending of the earlier play. F.N. Lees and David Ormerod have pointed out that *As You Like It* offers an even closer relation to *Love's Labour's Lost*, since it is also set in France, depicts the wrestler Orlando as a sort of Hercules, and ends with four weddings.[16] *All's Well That Ends Well* is, like *Love's Labour's Lost*, a proverbial title, and Henry Woudhuysen has pointed out other links: the settings (near the Spanish border); the characters called Dumaine; characters whose names (Moth, Parolles) mean 'word' or 'words'; a sick king.[17] *Troilus and Cressida* seems a much less likely possibility; presumably it has been proposed because of its deferred ending, since Pandarus announces that he will be making his will 'here' (in the theatre?) in a month's time.

The Taming of the Shrew is a more serious candidate, even though its original version may be earlier than *Love's Labour's Lost*. It has been argued that, since the bookseller's list includes *The Taming of a Shrew*, Shakespeare's *Shrew* play cannot have been *Love's Labour's Won*. The indefinite article, however, is significant, since a play of that name was printed in 1594. Given the rules of the Stationers' Company that forbade publication of anything that might damage the sales of a work still on the market,[18] it is possible that the existence of *A Shrew* would have forced the Lord Chamberlain's Men to perform and publish the play under a different title. John Fletcher's sequel to *The Shrew* is titled *The Woman's Prize*, while *The Tamer Tamed* is only its subtitle. Martin Wiggins notes that there is no evidence of the title used in the first performances (he dates these between 1607 and 1611, with a preference for 1610); at its revival in 1633 it was called *The Tamer Tamed*.[19] There is some evidence of revision in *The Shrew*, possibly for a revival, a fact that further complicates any attempt to link it to *Love's Labour's Won*. But it seems clear that, by the time the 1623 Folio was in preparation, it was no longer thought necessary to take account of the existence of *A Shrew*.

Indeed, *The Shrew* and *Much Ado* might be seen as alternative sequels to *Love's Labour's Lost*, in that both of them develop one theme of that play, the sex war / wit combat, and treat it in dramaturgically similar ways. As Alexander Leggatt notes, each play depicts two pairs of wooers, a conventional and an unconventional one, 'with correspondingly different types of characterization'.[20] This structure is initially anticipated in *Love's Labour's Lost*, with Berowne distinguished from the other three courtiers by his irreverent attitude, but once he has fallen in love he is only the most articulate of a basically similar group of wooers, who, like the women, act in unison. Beatrice's declaration that she will return Benedick's love by 'Taming my wild heart to thy loving hand' (3.1.112) may not only allude to *The Shrew* but draw a deliberate contrast with it: as Sheldon Zitner writes, 'it is Beatrice herself who will do the taming'.[21] Zitner also suggests, interestingly, that Benedick's 'Sweet Beatrice, wouldst thou come when I called thee?' (5.2.41) might remind the audience that Kate's entrance, after Petruccio had sent for her in the final scene of *The Shrew*, had been the 'public proof' of her 'taming'; Beatrice is a much less tamed heroine.[22]

The phrase 'Love's labour's lost' was proverbial, but it has been thought that allusions to the labours of Hercules in both *The Shrew* and *Much Ado* might be another link with it. In *The Taming of the Shrew* Gremio says of Petruccio's intention to woo and wed Katherina, 'leave that labour to great Hercules, / And let it be more than Alcides' twelve' (*TS* 1.2.256–7).[23] Don Pedro describes his plan to make Beatrice and Benedick fall in love as 'one of Hercules' labours' (*MA* 2.1.336–7). Hercules is mentioned in many Shakespeare plays, usually as a physically powerful hero who overcame a series of ordeals. His helplessness as a lover was, however, equally important. Henry Woudhuysen, arguing persuasively for the influence of Sir Philip Sidney on *Love's Labour's Lost*, has drawn attention to a passage in *A Defence of Poetry* which not only mentions character types appropriate for comedy (including a schoolmaster and braggart who might have inspired Holofernes and Armado) but also cites the story of Hercules spinning wool out of his love for Omphale as an example of a subject that is delightful as well as ridiculous.[24] The Hercules–Omphale story reappears in Benedick's contention that Beatrice would have outgone her classical prototype in enslaving and humiliating the hero. But if one looks for a justification of the *Love's Labour's Won* title, *All's Well That Ends Well* makes the most sense, although it seems chronologically impossible. Helena is set two tasks by her wayward husband, and she performs them both successfully.

These suggested parallels assume, of course, that audiences at one play will notice references to the title, or the plot, of another one – which in most cases they have probably not seen for some time. As a theory about Elizabethan audiences and the original titles given by Shakespeare or his company, this seems to me highly unlikely. Such connections would become visible in paired revivals (such as happened, as early as 1633, with *The Shrew* and *The Tamer Tamed*) and also for the kind of reading audience that was made possible by the Folio. Repertory companies usually emphasize the connections between the Shakespeare plays in their season; it is one way, of course, to draw audiences to the lesser-known works.

Love's Labour's Lost was not performed in its original version between the closing of the theatres in 1642 and the nineteenth century, whereas *Much Ado* was highly popular. I doubt that the unpopularity of the earlier play was due to its inconclusive ending. Restoration audiences had seen other plays (George Etherege's *The Man of Mode*, for instance) which postpone the marriage of the central characters. But some later audiences seem to have wanted what we call closure. In her theatrical history of the play, Miriam Gilbert comments that the first significant revival, by Madame Vestris at Covent Garden in 1839, was so elaborate in its final pageantry that the audience may have been unaware that the couples had parted at the end.[25] The twentieth century, on the other hand, has generally liked the fact that the play ends in a minor key. In fact, some productions of *Much Ado* have made its ending almost as inconclusive as that of its predecessor, avoiding any easy sense of closure. Combining the two plays allows the audience to have both the dying fall and the happy ending. To suggest, as Luscombe did, that the space between them was filled by the experience of war helps to explain the difference between their two worlds.

The (merry?) war

The resemblances between *Love's Labour's Lost* and *Much Ado* do not in the end add up to much more than a pair of witty lovers and a comic constable. There are no real equivalents in the later play for the Princess of France, Costard, Armado, Moth, Holofernes and Sir Nathaniel. *Love's Labour's Lost*, moreover, has no villains, even comic ones. The closest thing to malevolence is the women's destruction of the masque of Russians, followed by the men's destruction of the Pageant of the Nine Worthies. One play is set in Navarre, one in Sicily. The characters in *Love's Labour's Lost* are mostly French, those in *Much Ado* mostly Italian. Even their two Spanish characters are different: Armado, like the Prince of Aragon in *The Merchant of Venice*, is often played with a comic Spanish accent. Theatrical tradition used to give foreign accents to comic characters even when they were related to non-comic characters speaking standard English, but most modern productions do not go this far. Comic Spaniards are in the tradition of Italian comedy, where ridicule of the country's occupiers had a political edge. The Don Pedro of *Much Ado* is a very different figure.

Don Pedro of Aragon, in Bandello's source narrative, is based on the historical figure who became King of Sicily in 1282 after the 'Sicilian Vespers', a bloody national uprising against the occupying French. This fact is clearly irrelevant to the play. As far as I know, no production has ever set the play in the thirteenth century; there is no sense of Don Pedro's foreignness, and no suggestion that other characters, including Benedick and Claudio, might likewise be Spaniards rather than

Italians. The name of Don John the Bastard might recall the best known historical figure of that name, the heroic victor of the Battle of Lepanto, but he is obviously not the same person. In some productions of *Much Ado* he has been played comically. Like the use of the names of Navarre, Berowne, Dumaine and Longaville in *Love's Labour's Lost* (themselves associated with a bloody civil war), the play thus has a teasing relationship with history. Perhaps the only conclusion to be drawn is the arbitrariness of names as a guide to identity, something that had recently been a problem with the name of Oldcastle in *1 Henry IV*.

The historical context is equally uncertain. *Much Ado About Nothing* begins with the news that Don Pedro and his men are returning from what is initially described as 'this action' (1.1.5–6), 'a victory' (8), and then, by Beatrice, as 'the wars' (29), a term that is taken up by the Messenger (45–6). Period-specific productions always need, of course, to have some idea as to which war these characters are talking about. Directors now are probably less likely than they once were to make Don Pedro's army into comic dressed-up soldiers who have clearly never been in any real danger. One of the most successful American productions (Central Park, New York, 1972, dir. A.J. Antoon) evoked the Spanish-American War of the late nineteenth century. John Barton, who had given *Othello* a Victorian military setting in 1971, turned Messina into a garrison in Victorian India in 1976. As Pamela Mason notes, the production effectively blamed the military culture, more than Don John, for its treatment of Hero, and was thus able to forgive him at the end (he was even paired off with Ursula).[26] The most extreme emphasis on the background of war was Di Trevis's RSC production of 1989, in which a helicopter airlifted a wounded soldier to the stage, and 'Don Pedro and his soldiers entered in battle dress, exposing the leisured complacence of the civilians.'[27] The helicopter would have suggested the Vietnam war to most spectators.

Kenneth Branagh's film of *Much Ado* (1993) followed a *Henry V* (1989) that was considered realistic in its treatment of war. So, in rehearsals, he had the cast improvise answers to questions about the war in the background: 'How long had the soldiers been away? What kind of war had it been? How violent? Which of our men had been killers? How often had they visited Leonato prior to this? How well did they all know each other? How old were they? How long did these soldiers expect to live?' He felt that Don Pedro, Don John and Claudio were all 'soldiers for whom time spent away from war is precious' and that this explained the rapidity of Claudio's decision to marry Hero and Don Pedro's agreeing to help him.[28] It is unlikely, however, that most viewers of the film would be conscious of this backstory. His film version of *Love's Labour's Lost* (2000) set the play in 1939 and, like Luscombe's production, changed the emphasis of the ending so that its focus was less on the grief of the Princess and the departure of the women than on the departure of the four young men for the impending war. In 2006 an American musical freely based on *Much Ado* offered a glimpse of the other end of the story: it was called *The Boys Are Coming Home* and translated the action to the USA after the Second World War, with the renamed Bea 'reminiscent of the famous icon Rosie the Riveter'.[29]

But the 1914–1918 war has, at least in Britain, the most poignant associations. Because of its high death rate among young officers, the assumption at the end would be that it was unlikely that all four young men would return alive from the front. Robin Phillips, at Stratford, Ontario (1978), set *Love's Labour's Lost* in 1914 and at the very end the audience heard what Ralph Berry described as 'a distant rumbling. . . . The principals paused, looking at each other, puzzled. Was it thunder? Or gunfire?' Quoting this description, Miriam Gilbert noted the resemblance to Bernard Shaw's *Heartbreak House* with its depiction of a leisured class on the verge of its own annihilation.[30] It seems to have been Ian Judge, in his RSC production of 1993, who initiated the idea of making the men depart for the war at the end. Pamela Mason, though she found the production generally unmoving, felt that 'an evocation of the Great War briefly brought a chilling edge to the closing sequence.'[31] In fact, Carol Chillington Rutter's comment on the end of the 2014

Love's Labour's Lost was that 'we'd seen it all before' (and she noted that Luscombe had played Moth in Judge's production).[32]

In the context of these evocations of a real war, the plays' metaphorical language acquires a different resonance. The wooing of the four women in *Love's Labour's Lost* is figuratively seen as a war: 'Saint Cupid, then! And, soldiers, to the field!' (*LLL* 4.3.340). In *Much Ado*, Beatrice and Benedick fight a 'skirmish of wit' (*MA* 1.1.59) whenever they meet; Margaret and Benedick refer, in a bawdy metaphor, to swords and bucklers; metaphor becomes literal and threatening when Benedick answers Claudio's 'Wilt thou use thy wit?' with 'It is in my scabbard. Shall I draw it?' (*MA* 5.1.124–5). That 'merry war' (*MA* 1.1.58) is an oxymoron means that interpretations of *Much Ado* can choose which word to emphasize.

Much Ado as metatheatre

It is not unusual for modern theatre companies to conflate a number of Shakespearean characters within the same play. Usually these are minor figures: several servants and officials may be given to a single actor in order to save money and to provide a more interesting role. Conflation of characters across two plays is most likely to happen in productions of a sequence of history plays, and for the same reason. When *The Taming of the Shrew* and *The Tamer Tamed* are performed together, the names of some characters in the Fletcher play are changed to create a more obvious continuation of the Shakespeare comedy. The RSC did not – could not – follow this practice with *Much Ado*. It is impossible to imagine Dogberry rechristened Dull, or Beatrice and Benedick renamed: the fact that 'Benedick' has one more syllable than 'Berowne' would ruin lines like 'And, Benedick, love on, I will requite thee' (*MA* 3.1.111). Renaming the characters in *Love's Labour's Lost* would be still more disastrous, given the amount of rhyme and wordplay associated with them.

Some of the RSC's cross-casting was thematic, while some was clearly theatrical. That is, it was not the actor of Dull (Chris

McCalphy) who played Dogberry, but the actor of Costard (Nick Haverson), in each case filling the role that would have been taken by the leading low comedian of the Elizabethan stage. The actor of the ridiculous Spaniard Don Armado (John Hodgkinson) was also the Spaniard Don Pedro. Holofernes (David Horovitch) was Leonato while Holofernes' constant companion Sir Nathaniel (Thomas Wheatley) was Leonato's brother Antonio. For no obvious reason, Longaville (William Belchambers) was Conrade and the King of Navarre (Sam Alexander) reappeared as the villainous Don John. There were fewer roles for the women in *Much Ado*. Leah Whitaker, who had played the Princess, disappeared from the second play, which needed only *one* powerful woman. Two of her ladies (Frances McNamee and Flora Spencer-Longhurst) became Ursula and Hero respectively. Perhaps the casting of Emma Manton, the Jaquenetta, as Margaret was meant to suggest a parallel between two women who might benefit from upward mobility through sex appeal. Only one other casting choice made a difference to the production. Gretchen E. Minton found the mildness of Claudio's behaviour in the church scene, even when he was accusing Hero, improbable in someone who had just been through the violence of war.[33] The audience, however, would have remembered the performance of the same actor (Tunji Kasim) as Dumaine in *Love's Labour's Lost*: he is traditionally 'the youngest and most naïve of the men'[34] and the teddy bear that he carried in the climactic poem-reading scene was probably the best-remembered feature of that production. The fact that he was so innocent and lovable lessened the tension in what is usually *Much Ado*'s most emotionally violent scene, but also made it easier to accept his ultimate reunion with Hero.

Apart from this casting, it was only the pairing of Michelle Terry and Edward Bennett – first as Rosaline and Berowne, then as Beatrice and Benedick – that was meaningful for the narrative aspect of the two plays. In the parallel universe that the RSC production assumed, neither relationship involves love at first sight. Readers and spectators of *Much Ado* have never been willing to believe that Beatrice and Benedick fall in love purely as the result of a practical joke on the part of Don Pedro and his fellow-conspirators, and the text offers several hints that this mutual attraction has been there all along, waiting only for a catalyst. Their backstory might include a prior life as Berowne and Rosaline.

Of course, this prior life is Shakespeare's, not theirs, but something from one play may carry over into the other. When the Princess and her ladies are talking of the French lords they are about to meet, each lady mentions one in particular, and the Princess easily recognizes that all three of them are in love. It is characteristic of the play that these descriptions focus almost exclusively on the *wit* of the men. It is Longaville, according to Maria, who has 'a sharp wit matched with too blunt a will, / Whose edge has power to cut' (*LLL* 2.1.49–50). By contrast, Rosaline's description of Berowne indicates that his wit (which doesn't exceed 'the limit of becoming mirth': 2.1.67) brings nothing but delight to those who experience it:

> His eye begets occasion for his wit,
> For every object that the one doth catch
> The other turns to a mirth-moving jest,
> Which his fair tongue, conceit's expositor,
> Delivers in such apt and gracious words
> That aged ears play truant at his tales
> And younger hearings are quite ravished,
> So sweet and voluble is his discourse.

> (*LLL* 2.1.69–76)

Yet for the rest of the play she seems determined to be as unpleasant as possible toward him. Their first exchange, initiated by Berowne, is:

BEROWNE [*to Rosaline*]
    Did I not dance with you in Brabant once?
ROSALINE
    Did I not dance with you in Brabant once?

BEROWNE
  I know you did.
ROSALINE   How needless was it then
  To ask the question!

(LLL 2.1.114–17)³⁵

There is a possible parallel with the opening encounter between Benedick and Beatrice, who, unlike Rosaline, initiates it. When Beatrice tells him that no one is listening to him, Benedick's retort – 'What, my dear Lady Disdain! Are you yet living?' (*MA* 1.1.112–13) – seems meant to imply that he has not thought about her since his departure. In that context, perhaps Berowne's question to Rosaline, in its suggestion that he doesn't remember her as well as she remembers him, is sufficiently hurtful to motivate the change from her initial warmth to the hostility that she shows in the rest of the play. This reaction is probably not playable; it belongs to the curious intertextual area opened up by the pairing of the two plays. Similarly, the constant references to perjury, which the men in *Love's Labour's Lost* commit first (knowingly) toward their oath to study and then (unknowingly, through deception) toward the women they love, may carry over into *Much Ado*, where Beatrice angrily tells Benedick, 'He is now as valiant as Hercules that only tells a lie and swears it' (4.1.319–20). She might be referring either to Claudio or to Benedick himself, if their past relationship includes something that she considers a betrayal. Beatrice's anger is directed, above all, at Claudio's duplicity in delaying his accusations against Hero until he could disgrace her publicly at the wedding. Characteristically, however, even this accusation is itself phrased wittily: 'What, bear her in hand until they come to take hands' (4.1.302–3). As Claire McEachern notes with regard to another line, 'Beatrice's rage seems only to hone her quibbling power' (314n).

When Rosaline addresses Berowne in the final scene of *Love's Labour's Lost*, all sense of his charm and wit has gone; she makes him sound more like Maria's earlier description of Longaville:

Oft have I heard of you, my lord Berowne,
Before I saw you, and the world's large tongue
Proclaims you for a man replete with mocks,
Full of comparisons and wounding flouts,
Which you on all estates will execute
That lie within the mercy of your wit.

(*LLL* 5.2.829–34)

The apparent interchangeability of Berowne and Longaville, like the confusion over the names of Katherine and Rosaline in speech prefixes elsewhere in the play, may simply indicate that Shakespeare was initially undecided about the names of his characters.[36] It also suggests, however, that he may have been equally undecided about his attitude to their wit combats. In the sex war of *Love's Labour's Lost* both the men and the women become increasingly irresponsible in their 'mocks' and thus virtually indistinguishable. Though much criticism, beginning with the influential essay by Anne Barton,[37] has insisted that the women in this play are much kinder than the men, this is really true only in their reactions to the actors who perform the Pageant of the Nine Worthies. The Princess and her ladies may sometimes claim that their behaviour is meant to be reformative, but their competitive instinct is lethal: the Princess decides to spoil the men's attempted entertainment, declaring that 'The effect of my intent is to cross theirs' (5.2.138), while Rosaline's 'That same Berowne I'll torture e'er I go' (5.2.60) shows, as Alexander Leggatt writes, 'something sadistic' in her attitude.[38] And yet, although her final address to Berowne seems unfair in the circumstances, her reply to his protests is arguably the most effective statement in the play:

A jest's prosperity lies in the ear
Of him that hears it, never in the tongue
Of him that makes it.

(*LLL* 5.2.849–51)

It is a statement that carries weight. Beyond the characters' immediate situation, it touches on the behaviour of the actors themselves, in a play that already has been conspicuously self-reflexive. Rosaline's changing attitude to Berowne, from apparent admiration to hostility to a desire to reform him, seems less that of the character than of the playwright. And it is this ambivalent and essentially moralizing attitude to wit and jesting that becomes the main subject of *Much Ado About Nothing*.

Unlike Berowne and Rosaline, Benedick and Beatrice are not only distinguished from the other characters but subjected – equally – to harsh criticism of the very wit that makes them entertaining. As in *Love's Labour's Lost*, however, the desire to be part of the world of wit affects most of the characters. Even Dogberry, faced with a serious and unequivocal denial from Conrade ('Marry, sir, we say we are none'), calls him 'a marvellous witty fellow' (4.2.26–7). One reason why *Much Ado* is so gloriously actable is that this collective obsession makes it difficult for speaker, listener or audience to know when anyone is being serious; thus, there is immense scope for director and actors to make the numerous 'tonal choices' that Claire McEachern, in her edition, admirably describes.[39] Almost everything is open to interpretation, down to the quality of Balthasar's singing (and thus the sincerity both of his apologies for it and of Benedick's negative comments).[40] Modern directors, who cannot always count on having a fine singer available, can only be grateful for the openness of the text.

The sheer difficulty of assessing tone is made clear at once in the dialogue between Beatrice and the Messenger, who becomes so bewildered that Leonato finally has to try to explain her behaviour ('You must not, sir, mistake my niece': 1.1.57). The Messenger's 'I will hold friends with you, lady' (1.1.86) suggests a truce, providing the first proof that what has just been described as a merry war is by no means confined to Beatrice and Benedick. Perhaps the most obvious example of confusion over what is and is not funny occurs when Claudio attempts to sound Benedick on the subject of Hero:

CLAUDIO
> Is she not a modest young lady?

BENEDICK
> Do you question me as an honest man should do, for
> my simple true judgement? Or would you have me
> speak after my custom, as being a professed tyrant to
> their sex?

CLAUDIO
> No, I pray thee; speak in sober judgement.

(1.1.157–162)

Despite this request, which could hardly be more explicit,
Benedick proceeds to enjoy himself in a series of quibbles,
finishing with some double talk ('were she other than she is,
she were unhandsome; and being no other but as she is, I do not
like her') that leads Claudio to complain, 'Thou thinkest I am
in sport. I pray thee tell me truly how thou lik'st her' (166–9).

Beatrice gets herself into a worse situation when her decision
to play on the double meaning of Don Pedro's offering to 'get
you' a husband (2.1.295) leads her to sound as if she were
proposing to him: 'I would rather have one of your father's
getting' (296–7). She makes matters worse with 'Hath your
grace ne'er a brother like you?' (297) – that is, *not* like Don
John. Whether Don Pedro's 'Will you have me, lady?' (300) is
a serious proposal or a joking one, it is potentially an
embarrassing situation, as she recognizes when, after making
another joke, she apologizes for it. The best example of an
attempt to read meaning into another person's language is of
course Benedick's riff on Beatrice's 'Against my will I am sent
to bid you come into dinner' (2.3.238–9). His determination to
find 'a double meaning in that' (2.3.249) is perhaps the funniest
moment in the play – but, as Pamela Mason astutely comments,
'Benedick is indeed reading a subtext in Beatrice's words which
she is repressing.'[41] After all, there usually *is* some sort of
double meaning in her words.

In the wedding scene, on the other hand, seriousness is
mistaken for a joke. When he is asked, 'You come to marry this

woman?' Claudio's 'No' (4.1.5) would halt the wedding at once, if her father did not immediately assume that the young man is quibbling about the language of the ceremony. It is theatrically effective: the audience is kept in suspense as to when his outburst will occur, and meanwhile Leonato and Claudio bandy words and Benedick throws in an interjection about interjections 'of laughing' (4.1.19–20), either because he thinks they are joking or in an effort to get the ceremony back on track. Against this background of joking, Claudio's rejection of Hero is all the more of a shock, and this in turn allows the scene between Beatrice and Benedick to be the masterpiece that it is. McEachern describes the movement of the play as 'difficulty held at bay for a rather long period, followed by a protracted flurry of resolution',[42] and it is clear from the theatrical history of this scene that some actors felt that the resolution was achieved too quickly. In eighteenth- and nineteenth-century productions it became traditional to interpolate extra lines and parting looks to draw out the church scene and, as John F. Cox puts it, to make 'the developing relationship between Beatrice and Benedick seem less provisional than in the quarto text'.[43] In fact, no one who analyses the scene on paper seems completely comfortable with its tone, although it rarely fails in performance. It is often seen as disastrous if there is audience laughter on Benedick's 'Is not that strange?' (4.1.268) or on Beatrice's 'Kill Claudio' (288). Yet the actors should still be able to exploit the reaction without losing the scene's complex effect. The audience itself is now in the position of the play's characters, not knowing whether to take the situation seriously.

Comic cross-purposes are no longer comic in 5.1, when Don Pedro and Claudio continue their increasingly inappropriate joking until Benedick has challenged Claudio. 'He is in earnest,' says Don Pedro, hardly able to believe it (5.1.189). It is possible that, having mistaken the serious for the comic, these two men get it wrong again in the final scene, taking Beatrice and Benedick to be serious when they are really engaged in a private joke ('Then you do not love me?' 'No truly, but in friendly recompense': 5.4.82–3), and trying laboriously to bring them back together. But perhaps the couple *are* serious: some productions have made them trap themselves in their own wit to an extent that 'dismayed both of them'.[44]

The RSC production of the *Love's Labour's* plays put the emphasis on an ongoing relationship which developed because of its (imported) historical context and despite the fact that it was embodied in the actors rather than the characters. Nor is it the characters who experience the movement from the somewhat confused attitude toward wit in *Love's Labour's Lost* to the complex interplay of the serious and comic in *Much Ado*. If this happened, it happened, of course, to the author, probably over only two or three years of his working life. If one were to use these plays as a way of understanding Shakespeare's development as an author, one might tell a very different story about what happened in the space between them. This story would be based largely on the playwright's experience as an actor. The bad reception given to the amateur performers in *Love's Labour's Lost* and *A Midsummer Night's Dream* depicts the kind of failure that would not have been at all funny in a real acting career. The ability to judge and control audience response, and particularly to 'get laughs', is crucial to an actor's livelihood. As an actor who was also an author, Shakespeare had had to deal with someone who found his comic treatment of Sir John Oldcastle offensive, renaming the character and solemnly telling his audience that 'Oldcastle died a martyr and this is not the man' (*2 Henry IV*, Epilogue, 29–30). He wrote some of his funniest comedies immediately after an event that may have come between the two plays I have been discussing: the death of his son Hamnet. Thus, he would have every reason to understand how it is possible to make jokes without being 'merry', how joking can become mechanical, and how both joking and the refusal to joke can be used to wrong-foot others. Rosaline's awareness of the importance of the audience to 'a jest's prosperity' becomes part of the process by which Beatrice and Benedick begin (it is only a beginning) to understand the effect that they have on one another. In a good production of *Much Ado About Nothing*, uncertainty about response inside and outside the play world creates an unusual degree of audience rapport with the actors, who are only as funny as they are allowed to be. If it takes the concept of a world war to make a modern audience recognize the ambivalence of the play's attitude to comedy, then there may be some justification for the two-part division of *Labour*.

7

New Directions

Much Ado About Nothing and Social Media

Christy Desmet

Shakespeare is no stranger to new media. He appears on Facebook; he is the subject of websites and blogs; and his aphorisms are repeated, 140 characters at a time, on Twitter. The story of *Much Ado* on social media, as for Shakespeare generally, begins with YouTube, founded in 2005 and still going strong as a repository for archiving and disseminating Shakespearean content on the internet. Amateur content with Shakespearean themes appeared on the site almost from the beginning. By 2008, teenaged videographers were representing, remixing and parodying Shakespeare's plays in ten-minute productions that varied greatly in quality, but radiated enthusiasm and a sense of community. School projects started to pop up on the site with increasing regularity, as teachers and students took advantage of YouTube's affordances. In the current YouTube scene, commercial videos have become more numerous, advertising films and theatre productions from the Royal Shakespeare Company down to regional and college theatres. At the same time, however, the spread of Shakespearean content across different social media platforms and the emergence of new, hybrid artistic genres – such as the video blog and web series – takes Shakespeare beyond the confines of YouTube into a broader intermedial network. Within this more dispersed environment, the most innovative appropriations of *Much Ado About Nothing* can now be found.

Much Ado About YouTube

As a crowd-sourced 'accidental archive', YouTube changes constantly, so chronicling its landscape proves to be an ongoing process. The YouTube interface itself exercises a crucial role, 'shap[ing] what we notice'.[1] Other factors, such as language, country in which the search is being conducted, and the user's IP address, play a role.[2] On 2 June 2016, for instance, a search on the following word strings brought up the results in Table 7.1.

TABLE 7.1 *YouTube results 2 June 2016*

Search term	Results
'Hamlet'	1,020,000
'Romeo and Juliet'	890,000
'Much Ado About Nothing'	836,000
'Macbeth'	655,000
'A Midsummer Night's Dream'	329,000
'Othello'	265,000
'Twelfth Night'	110,000

TABLE 7.2 *YouTube results 12 February 2017*

Search term	Results
'As You Like It'	212,000,000
'Romeo and Juliet'	4,860,000
'Hamlet'	1,110,000
'Macbeth'	703,000
'A Midsummer Night's Dream'	620,000
'Twelfth Night'	414,000
'Othello'	288,000
'Much Ado About Nothing'	218,000

These numbers are not surprising, in that tragedies and those Shakespeare plays that dominate the secondary school curriculum get produced more often than others online as well as in the theatre. Repeating the search on 'Much Ado About Nothing' on 12 February 2017 produced the findings in Table 7.2.

In this experiment, some of the conditions affecting YouTube's search mechanism were controlled; for instance, I searched in the USA from the same IP address each time. But other factors, such as YouTube's algorithm – the formula by which the application weights items in a search – and the serendipitous infusion of musical groups and album titles that may have produced an outsized number of hits for *As You Like It*, are not controllable.[3] The very fact that I had been researching and writing about YouTube Shakespeare over the past six months, increasing substantially my own activity on the site during that time, undoubtedly had an effect on my personal search results, accounting perhaps for the proportionately larger number of hits for all play titles at the later date.

Searching specifically for 'Much Ado About Nothing' on 12 February 2017 produced from YouTube the following 'hits' on the first page of results displayed: the official trailer (1) and short clips (4) from the venerable 1993 Kenneth Branagh *Much Ado*; the official trailer (1) and clips from the 2012 Joss Whedon film (2); complete two-hour recordings of live school productions (2); 'teaser' clips from the David Tennant and Catherine Tate production at Wyndham's Theatre advertising the full film for sale from Digital Theatre (15); The Geeky Blonde's seventeen-minute production, the only true 'fan video' from the youth sector on this page; and at the bottom, the popular teen video blog from Australia, 'Nothing Much to Do' (1). Finally, there were three 'educational' videos summarizing the plot of *Much Ado About Nothing*. One, 'Video Summary – Much Ado About Nothing', undoubtedly comes from actual students, their accents suggesting a US location.[4] The other two are much more professional, in terms of both production values and sponsorship. The 1 minute, 21 second version of *Much Ado* by '60second Recap' plays off the tongue-in-cheek ethos of amateur productions, but is actually part of the packaging for College Coach, the entrepreneurial business of a young graduate from Bryn Mawr College (USA) that offers to match students to the college appropriate for them. The video's gently moralizing conclusion, 'Deception can be evil or harmless depending on the circumstances. So think before you judge', perhaps signals its participation in the school ethos of bowdlerized Shakespeare.[5]

The Royal Shakespeare Company gets into the act with their 'Animated Synopsis of Love's Labour's Won', which at 20,433 views seems to be performing relatively well within the crowded marketplace of YouTube.[6] Like the commercial videos, the RSC effort relies on clear summary and euphemism (e.g. 'Don John attempts to ruin Claudio and Hero's marriage, making Claudio think that Hero has been unfaithful') to make the play's sexual content suitable for family audiences. Published by RSC Education, the video nevertheless does not contain much metadata nor connect itself to other RSC productions, and so the video's broader purpose remains obscure, perhaps purposefully so. Some comments seem, at least, to come from students who appreciate having the play's plot clarified, although other commenters are focused on the video's technical merits. The 'related videos' section, listed on the right-hand side of YouTube's web interface, reveals more educationally oriented examples. Overly Sarcastic Productions, which includes *Much Ado* in its roster of Shakespeare summaries, identifies Don John as a 'villain so cardboard, he can be played by Keanu Reeves'.[7] There is also a *Much Ado* from the venerable amateur series, 'Finger Puppet Shakespeare'.[8] From this snapshot and based on my study of the fate of other plays on YouTube, the *Much Ado* landscape is generally consistent with that of other plays in 2016–2017, if a bit more sparsely populated than that of the more popular plays.

The best of the amateur offerings, by far, is the Geeky Blonde's reduced version of *Much Ado About Nothing*. I found this hidden gem not through YouTube's search function, but through critical paratext – specifically, Stephen O'Neill's discussion of this young videographer.[9] Trimming the play for YouTube's small screen and abbreviated time span and following the pattern established in her other videos, within the fictional frame the Geeky Blonde is directed to *Much Ado* by her sock puppet Shakespeare ('sockspeare'), then performs a telescoped, but quite coherent, version of the play, with herself acting each and every part. The performance, as O'Neill argues, is well acted and polished but very much tongue-in-cheek and full of cultural irony. For instance, the Geeky Blonde notes that one of Leonato's lines of greeting to Don Pedro – 'when you depart from me, sorrow abides and happiness takes his leave' (1.1.96–7) – is reproduced on, of all things, her 'Shakespeare love quote' mug, from which she drinks coffee that has been brewed for her by the sock puppet. Beatrice answers Benedick's greeting 'my dear Lady Disdain' (1.1.112), with a plain English retort: 'Oh hello Benedick, I see you've become the third syllable of your name more than ever'. (Benedick jokes are a staple in social media *Much Ado*s.) The exchange ends by turning back to the Shakespeare text, as Beatrice exclaims, 'You always end with a jade's trick' (138) and the Geeky Blonde makes a coy scholarly reference to the archaic sexual meaning of that phrase. Following Beatrice's extended disquisition on how much Benedick 'sucks', Hero responds, 'O Beatrice, I'm sure you'll find a non-sucky husband someday', and the witty Beatrice recoils with teenaged humour: 'No, boys have cooties. I'm smarter than all of them'. As Don John reveals Hero's supposed perfidy to Claudio and Don Pedro, the Geeky Blonde says drily, 'These are some standup guys'. When Don John escapes, the Blonde comments, 'Poor villain management'. In this manner, the production alternates between a tour de force one-woman show and sardonic adolescent commentary.

Convergence culture: Joss Whedon's *Much Ado*

In *Shakespeare and YouTube: New Media Forms of the Bard*, Stephen O'Neill acknowledges that new media platforms do not necessarily compete with or replace one another; thus, YouTube, by distributing blockbuster films in whole or part, 'may even sustain or disperse' those films.[10] Recently, YouTube Shakespeare has begun to show further signs of what Henry Jenkins calls 'convergence culture', the 'circulation of media content – across different media systems, competing media economies, and national borders'.[11] As David Bell elaborates, 'convergence' refers to 'when bits of media' become 'indistinguishable'; the same video, for example, may be published on YouTube or embedded in a news article. 'Convergence happens', furthermore, 'when media hybridize and recombine, as when movies are distributed over the Internet to download, or podcasts of radio shows can be listened to on an MP3 player or via a PC'. The proliferation of social media and web platforms has sparked not just movement of content from one platform to another, but more active 'convergence and multi-platform intertextuality'.[12] Intertextuality, a term derived from narratology and literary appropriation, refers to tropes that are shared across media; a set of conventions, for instance, that initially characterizes amateur YouTube videos, finds its way, through an aesthetic back-formation, into mass-distribution commercial films – in this case, the Joss Whedon *Much Ado About Nothing* (2012), which reflects the ethos, narrative and filmic conventions, and aesthetic flair of earlier YouTube productions. The Whedon film itself becomes a mediating touchstone for further hybrid forms of amateur social media, in this case two teen video blogs, or vlogs, and one web series based on *Much Ado About Nothing*, all of which date from 2014.

Amateur Shakespeare production on YouTube between 2005 and 2016 has featured families or groups of young friends whose interactions obviously are tinged with off-camera personalities and relations. The videos, which perforce rely heavily on ready-made settings, developed a set of standard locations in which Shakespeare's plots could unfold. Not surprisingly, the interiors of ordinary, middle-class homes often were featured: Othello's accusations against Desdemona were staged on living-room couches, nefarious plots unfolded in family kitchens, characters exited dramatically by stomping up or down staircases and slamming doors, and fatal duels took place in parks and gardens. For *Hamlet*, in particular, bodies of water became de rigueur; and while some videographers sought out local rivers and streams to stage the now-standard, although extra-diegetic, scene of Ophelia's drowning, others found a handy setting in the suburban swimming pool. Many of these tropes resurface in the Whedon *Much Ado*.

The film, famously, was filmed over twelve days on a slim budget at Whedon's Santa Monica home, featuring a cast of friends and actors from his various films and television series. Amy Acker, who played Fred on *Angel*, is Beatrice; Alex Denisof, of *Angel* and *Buffy*, is Benedick; Hero is Jillian Morgese from *The Avengers*; Nathan Fillion, from *Firefly* and *Serenity*, plays

Dogberry – and so forth. Douglas Lanier suggests the possibility of intertextual play among these productions: for instance, 'Might the romantic reconciliation between Beatrice in Benedick in *Much Ado* be seen as a redemption of the tragically broken relationship between Fred and Wesley on the series *Angel*, particularly because both sets of lovers are played by the same actors?'[13] More important for the purposes of this chapter, however, is the spirit of amateur performance mixed with celebrity lore that pervades the film's origins and ethos. The YouTube channel Backstage offers a series of short video interviews with the cast of *Much Ado*, covering such topics as when each actor met Joss Whedon (some traditional auditions, but most of them embellished by a chance meeting in a restaurant or other locale); how much Shakespeare each actor had done previously (a few had professional credentials, but others nothing beyond high school drama); and reminiscences about the legendary Shakespeare readings and brunches at Whedon's home that some had attended.[14] The Shakespeare reading, long a staple of amateur and quasi-amateur Shakespeare performance, brings Shakespeare into the home and emphasizes the closeness of friends in and out of role. Lanier find evidence of this ethos within Whedon's interpretation of the play, where according to him, the 'circle of friends' acts as a 'substitution for or extension of traditional family'.[15]

The Whedon *Much Ado* also takes advantage of found settings and unity of place. The entire action takes place within Whedon's grounds and house, which was designed with house parties in mind by his architect wife Kai Cole. Whedon himself has said that 'the house informs what the movie is. It has a combination of sunny spaciousness and dark labyrinthine intrigue'.[16] Within this paradoxical space of West Coast light and Shakespearean dark doings, the kitchen is the centre, where most social encounters, surrounded by the ubiquitous vessels of alcohol that mediate social relations, take place.[17] Here occur the marriage negotiations between Don Pedro and a somewhat inattentive Leonato, who has dozed off, while Benedick cleans up bottles left in the garden after the party and

Ursula and Borachio engage in heavy flirting. Beatrice and Don Pedro exchange pleasantries, until a tipsy Beatrice wobbles up the stairs to bed, reinforcing the suburban two-storey floor plan as separating communal from private spaces. Here also takes place the gulling of Beatrice, who in a slapstick routine, first falls downstairs in a gesture reminiscent of amateur YouTube videos, then hides behind and under various cabinets and pieces of furniture to escape notice as she overhears the plot.

The living room and adjoining grounds of Whedon's estate are the location for the party in which Don Pedro woos Hero on Claudio's behalf. The villains' manipulation of Claudio begins in the emblematic swimming pool of amateur videos. Claudio rises from the water's depths wearing a snorkelling mask and balancing carefully a cocktail, while other characters pop up behind him to whisper conspiratorially about Hero's shortcomings, which would make her an unfit wife for Don Pedro, and thus to imply that Hero has already betrayed Claudio's love. The gulling of Benedick occurs with Don Pedro, Leonato and Claudio performing their parts in the living room while Benedick, on the lawn beyond the French doors, dashes from bush to bush to overhear what they say.

The outdoors is an ambivalent place in this symbolic economy, subjected as it is to extreme variations of light and dark; stairs leading from garden to house are also liminal, a boundary between benefactors and malefactors. Benedick the committed bachelor jogs and exercises up the steps to and from the amphitheatre, but Conrade and Don John also conspire near those same stairs, where they are nevertheless overheard by the Watch. Hero's shaming and eventual marriage both take place outdoors, in the amphitheatre that Cole designed for Whedon's Shakespeare readings. The boundary between inside and outside is not only morally flexible but also porous, especially during the masked party; furthermore, as Lanier notes, the presence of acrobatic dancers as entertainment outdoors brings the possibility of scopophilia (emblematic of in-house intrigue) into the great outdoors.[18]

The upstairs bedrooms in *Much Ado*, a private place in US suburban homes, are disturbingly public and subject to violation. The film opens with an extradiegetic scene in which Benedick sneaks out of Beatrice's room after they have spent a night together. Beatrice, for her part, pretends to be asleep to avoid an awkward farewell; a later flashback, explicating Beatrice's remark to Don Pedro that she had once loaned her heart to Benedick, shows passion mixed with copious amounts of alcohol.[19] Don John receives information from Borachio about Claudio's impending marriage in another bedroom, where he is involved in a sexual tryst with Conrade (a woman, in this version). Borachio invades a very private moment, although Conrade allows John to continue caressing her under the covers and the viewer, positioned above and looking through a skylight, is doubly implicated in the voyeurism, spying on both the spies and the lovers.

A more complex violation is the intrusion of men into what must have been the childhood bedroom of Beatrice and Hero, to which Benedick and Claudio have been assigned for the house party. The room, with twin beds and a feminine decor, still contains a dollhouse and a host of stuffed animals. As they drop off their luggage, the young men joke among themselves about women and wrestle playfully on the beds. The worst violation of all, the false report of Hero's meeting with a man at her chamber window, occurs in the bedroom of a mature woman, ostensibly that of Hero. We glimpse a dressing table and a bed strewn with discarded clothes as Margaret primps and prepares for her meeting. But Borachio brings the garment, which eventually will serve as Hero's ill-fated wedding dress, from outside, dominating the feminine space with his masculine sexual preferences. And while the film is explicit that more than talking takes place between the two (we are privy to a shot of their lower bodies, with Margaret's skirt hiked up high on her thighs), Borachio lures Margaret outside as much as she invites him into the bedchamber. The feminine space is violated not only directly by the appearance of a man, but simply by being opened up to the dangers of dark night that stream through the bedchamber window.

Lanier has noted the mix of filmic techniques in *Much Ado About Nothing*, a combination of the 'three camera setup' used in live television and roving, handheld digital cameras that are standard in the world of amateur YouTube.[20] Whedon, of course, is a seasoned producer of television shows, but he is also familiar with social media production. *Dr. Horrible's Sing-Along Blog*, a 43-minute production in three acts, is a vlog married to full-scale musical: a kind of *Rocky Horror Show* designed from the start for the tiny screen and social media viewing habits. The story, in which a hapless would-be villain, Dr. Horrible, falls in love with a girl at the laundromat, only to lose her to his nemesis Captain Hammer, ends with the villain's triumph, but the heroine's death, and a rousing final chorus. The production of the vlog, made under a tight budget, was intended from the beginning for free release on open venues and was attentive to its emerging fan sites.[21] The Whedon *Much Ado* has a number of features in common with *Dr. Horrible*: in particular, a reliance on handheld cameras, the use of ready-made sets, a preoccupation with the mediatization of ordinary life, and a spirit of camaraderie and insouciant wit among players in the cast.

'Hello, people of the internet!': *Nothing Much to Do, SHAKES* and *A Bit Much*

Media convergence, Jenkins stresses, depends on active user participation.[22] The latest form of Shakespeare available on YouTube is the youth-oriented video blog, or vlog. This genre tends towards convergence culture in that it is spread over multiple media platforms. The vlog is also typical of Jenkins's participatory culture in that the creators launch a production without being sure of its audience and also respond to its fans throughout production. *Nothing Much to Do* is the most popular Shakespearean example to date in this genre.[23]

The brainchild of four New Zealand teens who call themselves the Candle Wasters (a phrase taken from Shakespeare's play, 5.1.18), *Nothing Much to Do* (2014) was recorded and broadcast on social media over the space of about a year in Auckland, New Zealand. The creators of this vlog take the tropes from amateur social media production that Whedon had imported into art film and bring them back home to their native environment.[24] In this way, the markers of YouTube Shakespeare migrate into commercial film and return to inform a new artistic genre within social media. The inaugural video opens with 'Beatrice' addressing the camera – 'Hello, people of the internet!' – seeking an audience that the actors seemed unsure existed but that the series would soon find. (Although audience attention waned somewhat as the 79-episode epic rolled on, the first video garnered 90,000 views on YouTube alone.)

The first episode of *Nothing Much to Do*, punning on the uneventful nature of teen life, begins with the premise that Beatrice, whose parents have moved to Australia for reasons of employment, has relocated to Auckland to live with the family of her favourite cousin, Hero. They and their friends at Messina High School become the vlog's dramatis personae. For various reasons, the parents of Hero have also left the country for an extended period of time, leaving the kids in charge of the house. Once this premise is established, *Nothing Much to Do* cleaves pretty closely to the Shakespearean plot line, translated into a teen idiom in the style of such Shakespeare films as *Ten Things I Hate About You* and *She's the Man*. John and 'Robby Borachio' plot against Hero, the collective of friends conspire to bring Beatrice and Benedick together, and – in a contemporary touch – the series ends with a reformed, romantic Benedick bringing together Pedro, an 'all around nice guy', and Balthasar, who has been the group's principal musician, playing everything from keyboard to ukulele. Dogberry and Verges have an expanded role, pontificating on the nature of detective work, and finally, at the end of the series, finding and returning to its owner a cat that has been missing for seven months. Hero's shaming comes on the occasion of her sixteenth birthday party. Unlike the Whedon film, which delivers the Shakespearean text trimmed but never altered, *Nothing Much to Do* gets its punch from plain English translations of Shakespeare: Claudio fumes, 'You put on this cute little face, but underneath, you're just a slut'. As in Whedon's film, where an official photographer is present at public events, including Hero's shaming, this scene also is on record and ends with Pedro shouting, 'Shut that camera off!' Hero's 'death', refigured as a hospital stay, ends when the friends come together to send a get-well video message and Hero herself appears at the park where they are gathered; she greets Claudio with a low-key, exhausted and not very sentimental exclamation of 'shit'.

Like Whedon's film and the amateur productions of other Shakespeare plays that populate YouTube, *Nothing Much to Do* relies on found settings – in this case, the symbolic opposition between Messina High and Hero and Beatrice's home. As in the Whedon film, Hero's bedroom assumes a central place in the series' symbolic universe. Beatrice and Hero regularly blog from two chairs facing the camera, with the bed and Hero's wall decorations visible in the background. In the second Q&A with their internet audience hosted by the cousins, when asked what would be her ideal bedroom, Hero responds, 'pretty much what I have now, except more fairy lights'. There is even a special episode, 'Sci-fi Room Tour | Nothing Much To Do', that begins with Beatrice reading in bed and lecturing on *Frankenstein*, then moves into a panoramic survey of the objects in Hero's room, ranging from a nested Russian doll, a miniature classic car and old windup watches on the desk to a survey of her books, posters of Benedict Cumberbatch on the wall (even though he is supposed to be Beatrice's celebrity crush) – and, of course, the aforementioned fairy lights. While Whedon's film tempts the viewer to allegorize props – for instance, the dollhouse in the child's bedroom as emblem for gender relations in Messina – the objects of Hero's bedroom in *Nothing Much to Do* are copious but resist literary interpretation. The only item that could be considered remotely related to the plot is a poster identifying different birds, visible often when Beatrice and Hero blog, to Benedick's rant about 'birds' in one of his early blogs (Episode 9, 'Birds'). In this episode, Benedick waxes rhapsodic about a schoolmate who drives to the top of the mountain on which the school sits and accidentally kills birds that smash into his car. Other episodes refer to and mock this effort at *cinéma réalité*.

Surrounding and complementing the central bedroom are a few other rooms with quasi-symbolic significance. The gulling of Benedick takes place in the kitchen, with the dupe eavesdropping from the garage, and – again, as in Whedon – taking a pratfall that makes his presence obvious and a subject for comedy. Various cooking videos are also produced in the kitchen, a space of bonding and conviviality. There is also a sleepover, or rather the aftermath of a sleepover, when the girls gather in the living room in their pyjamas. This innocent encounter jars against the living room's repurposing as the party space in which Claudio slut-shames Hero. Finally, there is the bathroom, from whose empty tub Benedick, fully clothed, regularly blogs and later cuddles with Beatrice. Apparently, Benedick has no room of his own.

Outside the house, there is an eerie sense that no one besides the participants in this drama exists and that the social landscape in which the drama takes place is quite restricted. We never see the inside of Messina High School, just the grounds. Even the spacious park in which Hero's return and the general reconciliation take place is empty of the accidental 'actors' one might expect to find in a public place. Ironically, the principals in this series are isolated from both the outside world and one another. The saga of Messina High School concludes by moralizing the nearly year-long event in which people have communicated through blogs but failed at interpersonal relations: 'Face to face communication is always best'.

Nothing Much to Do was not only successful, but artistically satisfying. The series generated a strong fan base and included both creditable original music and witty references to the affordances and limitations of its medium. The use of the house as found setting resonates strongly with the Whedon film, and a similar spirit of camaraderie pervades the whole venture. On the level of narrative, just as Whedon hinted at a prior sexual entanglement between Beatrice and Benedick, *Nothing Much to Do* chronicles the early teen friendship between Beatrice and Benedick and its erosion into mutual animosity created through misunderstanding. Finally, the series exploits fully the resources of cross-media platforms.

Another amateur vlog series, this time by American teens, was *SHAKES* (2014), renamed 'The Town's the Thing' when the creators decided to do a second season. The series, which consists of fourteen videos, takes place in the ostensibly Southern small town of Shakes, even though none of the actors has a recognizably Southern accent. This cast also maintained a presence on Tumblr, Facebook and Twitter, exploiting the affordances of convergence culture. As with *Nothing Much to Do*, I came to this production, created by Kathryn Ormsbee and Destiny Soria, indirectly, this time through Luke McKernan's curated blog BardBox, which emphasizes again the growing importance of scholarly paratexts to navigating the terrain of popular and amateur Shakespeare.[25]

SHAKES is a mashup of three plays: *Romeo and Juliet*, *Hamlet* and *Much Ado About Nothing*. The drama opens with Hamlet, Ophelia, Romeo, Juliet and Beatrice at an outdoor performance of Shakespeare's *Romeo and Juliet*. As they watch the impassioned moment in which Juliet attempts to drain the last drops of poison from Romeo's vial, the young people exchange negative comments about how boring or unrealistic the drama is. Impervious to the charms of Shakespeare's tragedy, they will nevertheless soon find themselves living his plots. The episode quickly moves into comedy as Benedick, newly returned to town to take up his position as a reporter for the *Globe*, a traditional newspaper, interrupts from behind the seats and Beatrice, startled, accidentally slaps him in the face. Their mutual acrimony nevertheless takes up where it had left off when they graduated from high school. In this version, the three girls live together as roommates, as do the boys. Within the fiction, Hamlet is studying law, while the accommodating Ophelia works in her father's pharmacy but also writes an advice column for the *Herald*, Beatrice's online media news outlet. Romeo and Juliet have no visible means of support: Romeo plays bad music covers on the ukulele and seems to be in college, while Juliet is a mild kleptomaniac. Hamlet suspects that Ophelia's father, a pharmacist and now the town mayor who combines the roles of Polonius and Claudius, killed his father.

For the first half of the series, the 'merry war' (1.1.58) between Ben and Bea takes centre stage. He has a degree from Columbia Journalism School, while she started the *Herald* as a blog straight out of high school and so lacks his credentials. They bicker about the relative merits of their news outlets. Then Benedick publishes an exposé of Beatrice's two arrests for disorderly conduct under the influence of alcohol, which occurred during his absence at college. What Ben does not know, and what the other two women tell him, is that Beatrice had been given a 'free ride' or full scholarship to Columbia Journalism School, but stayed home to care for her mother, who was disabled by a stroke, until her death. The arrests reflect the fact that she 'was going through a lot' at the time. Benedick is chastened, but the damage is done.

At Juliet's birthday party, the moment in the *Much Ado* plot where the slut-shaming of Hero should take place, we get instead a truncated version of *Hamlet*'s closet scene, thus completing the mashup. Instead of Claudio denouncing Hero, we hear Hamlet tell Ophelia that she is too eager to please, and thinks that every problem can be solved by chamomile tea. In the ensuing melee, Hamlet and Juliet break into Ophelia's house (by flinging a 'Gnomio' garden gnome through the door), and Hamlet discovers in the father's desk his own father's heart pills.

When the rest of the gang appears, Ophelia confirms that the pills are sugar pills, so apparently the fake heart medicine is at fault for Hamlet Sr's fatal heart attack. The climactic episode begins with Ophelia submerged, fully dressed, in the bath until unexpectedly, she rises suddenly from the water in a gesture reminiscent of Glenn Close in *Fatal Attraction*. Ophelia, rather than sinking beneath the waters, has decided to testify against her father and then leave town; Romeo and Juliet break up, and Beatrice and Benedick come together with renewed love. Hamlet, on the run, holes up in a dark place and soliloquizes about just how tired he is, uttering 'to sleep . . . to dream . . . living or dying: what's the difference if you are already in hell?' The screen fades to black, implying that Hamlet takes the pills he removed from Ophelia's house and commits suicide. Or does he, if the pills are fake? In a final 'Word From the Creators', the two women writer-producers offer a public service message about suicide that refers viewers to the National Suicide Hotline.

The set for *SHAKES* is centred, once again, around the opposition between a suburban house and the surrounding town. The gulling of Benedick and Beatrice takes place in the house; he eavesdrops on the girls gossiping about him in the kitchen, then reveals himself with a noisy pratfall that recalls Benedick's slapstick efforts in the Whedon film. Beatrice is tricked by a faked advice letter while the girls are gathered in Ophelia's bedroom. Benedick's dawning recognition and vow to love Beatrice occurs on the local playground, with Ben meditating on the bottom of the slide and then in a swing.

The series uses almost no Shakespearean language, with Hamlet's 'To Be or Not to Be' soliloquy, transposed to the scene of his suicide, being the notable exception; but even here, few of Shakespeare's words are actually used. Nor, after the initial insertion of an actual Shakespeare performance, does the series refer with particular self-consciousness to its Shakespearean subtext.

There are two clever intertextual moments in the early episodes. In the first, Juliet reads *Macbeth* upside down in bed, just as Beatrice, of *Nothing Much to Do*, reads and rhapsodizes about *Frankenstein*. (The *Macbeth* is the Yale 'Annotated Shakespeare' edition, but obviously the scholarly text is over Juliet's head.) In the second, the receptionist at Ben's place of work is reading Norrie Epstein's *Friendly Shakespeare*. The series plays on the characters' alienation from 'classical' Shakespeare, but once the *Hamlet* plot takes over, this strain of reference to Shakespeare is abandoned. *SHAKES*, in fact, combines a sentimental take on the resilience of young people with a knowing scepticism about Shakespeare's relevance to life.

A Bit Much (2014) is a mini 'web series' (comprising ten episodes) written by Colleen Scriven that is 'inspired by' *Much Ado*.[26] The scene is Camp Messina in upstate New York. Ben (Benedick) and Bridget (Beatrice) have known each other since they were seven, when both started coming to the camp. Now Ben is the head boys' counsellor and Bridget the head girls' counsellor. As the blog *The Shakespeare Standard* reports, writer/director Colleen Scriven came up with the idea for her web series from a combination of sources: a 2014 Theater for a New Audience production in New York and old *Flash Gordon* serials that she watched in a film-history class. 'I was wondering why that particular format had died out, and then realized it hadn't at all; it had just been reformatted for the web', Scriven said. 'I started thinking about the process of cutting up a big story into those mini episodes'.[27] Thus, the web series combines an interest in Shakespeare appropriation with an interest in media history. In *A Bit Much*, Scriven also drew on her experiences with the bard in high school:

> My drama club and teacher were particularly passionate about staging his shows with unique twists, so before I graduated I was lucky to play Puck in a 'summer of love' inspired production of *A Midsummer Night's Dream* and Feste in *Twelfth Night* in a speak-easy setting. I think these little modernizations helped show how timeless the characters and language were, which later helped me write *A Bit Much*.[28]

In the same video blog, actors Liv Benger (Bridget) and David Dimitruk (Ben) also stress the ease of translating Shakespeare into a contemporary setting: *A Bit Much* takes place in New York instead of Sicily; the lords and ladies before are now campers and counsellors, and the characters are given updated names. In the creators' eyes, this Shakespeare spinoff not only continues the tradition of television serials in a new medium, but is also tied to live drama and both high art and school culture.

The series opens with Leo, Bridget's father, welcoming this summer's counsellors to the camp, even though 'I know you'd rather be watching *Dawson's Creek*, chattin' on the AOL'. One counsellor asks 'How old *is* he?' playing on the now familiar trope of new media ironically mocking the old. There is additional byplay about television shows, as Haley (Hero), Bridget's cousin who is staying with her while her own parents fight their way through a divorce, measures life in relation to the *Gilmore Girls* and *Grey's Anatomy*. As in the other social media productions of *Much Ado About Nothing*, Bridget and Ben have a lifelong friendship that went sour, this time by a disastrous sexual encounter in the recent past.

A Bit Much offers a somewhat older and more worldly group of teens. Haley, the youngest and least knowledgeable about sex, is only seventeen and vomits when she drinks too much. Corey (or Claudio), an awkward nerd, nevertheless is eager to lose his virginity with Haley. Relationships among the characters are generally more tangled. Bridget, who shelters her feelings behind a mask of sarcastic humour, has slept with both Pedro and Ben, who are now college students, and Pedro makes a play for Haley as well as Bridget. The unravelling of *Much Ado*'s narrative in a summer camp resembles a daytime soap opera more than Shakespeare, but some fine comic acting makes the campy plot riveting. Best of all is the casting of Boris (Borachio) as a social outlier and the marvellously evil villain, John, as none other than Pedro's pesky younger brother. John hates being at camp, but he loves creating mischief for the older kids, and lures Corey to overhear, rather than actually see, Boris

and Margaret stage the faked encounter between Haley and
Pedro. But all is well that ends well, as in Shakespeare's play.
The young people are reconciled and decide to pair off into
stable, more committed relationships beyond the conventional
summer fling. As in *Nothing Much to Do*, traditional virtues
are restored and celebrated. Finally, when little John's perfidy is
revealed, Pedro enters dramatically to announce, 'In the car.
Now. I called Mom'. 'You called *Mom*?' demands the little
villain, who is quickly mollified when he figures out that being
in trouble with Mom means not having to return to camp.

In terms of both its ironic spirit and cinematography, *A Bit
Much* is the most sophisticated of the new media *Much Ado*
spinoffs. Scriven graduated magna cum laude from Brooklyn
College (USA) and has an impressive set of credentials in film,
drama, web productions and stand-up comedy. Other actors in
the production are also accomplished college and professional
actors. The production values and script, likewise, are of higher
quality than is usual in amateur Shakespeare on the web.
Finally, *A Bit Much* demonstrates the greatest awareness of
new media as an experimental art form. Some cast members,
for instance, have also participated in another effort, 'What if
Shakespeare's characters had Snapchat'.[29] Several brief snippets,
recorded on a smartphone, record *Hamlet*'s closet scene and
Mercutio outside a bar ranting about women. In a fascinating
reversion to YouTube's glory days of amateur production, these
Shakespearean bits show artistic merit mingled with witty
relocations of the plays to contemporary suburban America. In
a final gesture of convergence culture, the line between not only
improvised drama and mediated video but also amateur and
professional culture has been breached.

Conclusion: family resemblances

Earlier amateur Shakespeare on YouTube created new genres
and conventions by intense memetic activity – appropriation,
imitation, replication and remix of previous amateur videos. In

this way, within short order there emerged Lego Shakespeares, Barbie *Hamlet*s and rewritings of Branagh's *Hamlet* as Ophelia's story.[30] The striking thing about this later cluster of productions – the commercial Whedon film of *Much Ado* and the three amateur vlogs, *Nothing Much to Do*, *SHAKES* and *A Bit Much* – is their ability to cohere as an incipient social media Shakespeare genre despite being fewer and more far-flung than when artistic creation was concentrated in YouTube. Although all three appeared in 2014, two years after the Whedon *Much Ado*, direct citations of Whedon or one another remain elusive. The first episode of *Nothing Much to Do*, which has the boys wrestling on Hero and Beatrice's twin beds, might point toward the parallel scene in the child's bedroom at the beginning of Whedon's *Much Ado*. There is also an incipient intertextual tie between *Nothing Much to Do* and *SHAKES*, as in the latter Romeo writes music and plays the ukulele, although much less proficiently than Balthasar from *Nothing Much to Do*. Perhaps the ironic parallel is meant to be noticed, perhaps it is a moment of direct imitation – but perhaps not.

Nor do these dispersed Shakespearean efforts exploit YouTube's capacity for commenting on one another directly to create what Patricia Lange has called 'videos of affinity' – that is, videos and videographers who talk directly to one another and 'try to establish communicative connections to people, often members of a social network'[31] – much less an 'interactive amateur video-making collective' of the kind responsible for such viral imitations as 'Harlem Shakes'.[32] Under these circumstances, the narrative of Shakespeare adaptation (which involves two-way, intentional reference and imitation) or Shakespeare appropriation (which pilfers and also donates material from one artefact to another) threatens the carefully policed border between Shakespeare and 'not Shakespeare', making appropriation a matter of contingency – perhaps even of mere chance – rather than artistic imitation or conversation. In 2009, Thomas Elsaesser characterized the YouTube user as a 'Web 2.0 flaneur', wandering through the YouTube landscape experiencing alternately 'epiphanies' and troughs of 'entropy', a dialectic of success and failure as users surf the web in search of new material.[33] In 2016, the best of social media *Much Ado About Nothing* suggests that this dynamic is, if anything, more exacerbated than ever. Encountering media hybrids of Shakespeare piecemeal and on multiple platforms, Elsaesser's insouciant flaneur is increasingly a stranger adrift in a strange land.

But the news is by no means all bad. The emergence of the newest versions of *Much Ado* on social media points to not only new developments within social media production and consumption, but also new artistic configurations. The video blog and web series examples of *Much Ado About Nothing* discussed here are witty, skilful dramas produced by very talented artists. However the Whedon film and these slightly later spinoffs relate (or not) to one another, they have enriched the Shakespearean scene. Even more fascinating is the very way in which social media Shakespeare is changing. Once, YouTube was the province of enthusiastic amateur videographers from the youth sector. Now, professional theatre companies and commercial enterprises on YouTube mimic their ethos and methods. At the same time, the increased professionalization of amateur Shakespeare production in social media has elevated the amateur video into high art. This is convergence culture.

8

Resources

'How Apt It Is to Learn' – Studying and Teaching *Much Ado About Nothing*

Brett Greatley-Hirsch and Sarah Neville

In this chapter, we survey recent print editions of the play and pertinent online resources, and propose critical approaches to studying and strategies for teaching the play from thematic, critical-theoretical, textual and performance perspectives. A selected annotated bibliography of relevant criticism immediately follows the discussion of each critical approach.

A survey of recent print editions

Much Ado About Nothing first appeared in print as a quarto edition of 1600 (or 'Q'), printed by Valentine Simmes for the

stationers Andrew Wise and William Asply. This edition serves
as the basis for all subsequent texts of the play. A copy of Q
annotated with references to performance was used as copy
when the play was later printed in the First Folio of 1623 (or
'F1'), introducing some 140 (mostly minor) changes to the
text, including the insertion of act divisions and a number of
stage directions. With only these minor variations to take into
account, modern editions of *Much Ado* are largely more
focused on the play's historical contexts, critical reception and
performance history than its textual issues.

Collected works editions

The Arden Shakespeare Complete Works. Gen. eds Richard
    Proudfoot, Ann Thompson and David Scott Kastan, rev. edn.
    London: Arden Shakespeare, 2011.
The Complete Works of Shakespeare. Ed. David Bevington, 7th edn.
    New York: Pearson Longman, 2014.
The RSC Shakespeare: Complete Works. Gen. eds Jonathan Bate
    and Eric Rasmussen. New York: Modern Library, 2007.
The New Oxford Shakespeare: The Complete Works. Gen. eds Gary
    Taylor, John Jowett, Terri Bourus and Gabriel Egan. Oxford:
    Oxford University Press, 2016.
The Norton Shakespeare. Gen. ed. Stephen Greenblatt, 3rd edn.
    New York: W.W. Norton, 2015.

Much Ado has appeared in every edition of Shakespeare's
collected works since the First Folio was printed in 1623. With
space at a premium, modern printed editions of Shakespeare's
collected works typically offer limited play-specific introductory
materials and commentary. Annotations, if and when they are
provided, are generally confined to glosses of unfamiliar terms
and concise explications of relevant cultural, historical and
topical references. If textual notes are included at all, they are
strictly kept to a minimum, or otherwise relegated to separate
reference volumes (as in the case of the New Oxford
Shakespeare) or to subscription-based, digital-only content (as
in the case of the Norton Shakespeare). Some collected works

editions, like *The Arden Shakespeare Complete Works*, simply provide a text without any annotation or commentary to assist the reader. The economical approach to annotation and commentary adopted by many collected works editions makes them ideal reference volumes, whereas single-text editions, able to provide more generous critical and editorial material and assistance to the reader, may represent a better option for teaching and learning.

Single-text editions

Bate, Jonathan, and Eric Rasmussen, eds. *Much Ado About Nothing*, RSC Shakespeare. London: Macmillan, 2009.

Cox, John F., ed. *Much Ado About Nothing*, Shakespeare in Production. Cambridge: Cambridge University Press, 1997.

Mares, F.H., ed. *Much Ado About Nothing*, New Cambridge Shakespeare, rev. edn. Cambridge: Cambridge University Press, 2003.

McEachern, Claire, ed. *Much Ado About Nothing*, Arden Shakespeare (Third Series), rev. edn. London: Arden Shakespeare, 2015.

Mowat, Barbara A., and Paul Werstine, eds. *Much Ado About Nothing*, Folger Shakespeare Library. New York: Folger Shakespeare Library, 1995.

Zitner, Sheldon P., ed. *Much Ado About Nothing*, Oxford Shakespeare. Oxford: Oxford University Press, 1993.

All of the major print series offer single-text editions of *Much Ado* suitable for personal study and classroom use, though each has its particular editorial quirks and critical priorities. Some, like the Folger Shakespeare Library edition of *Much Ado*, edited by Barbara A. Mowat and Paul Werstine, incorporate features designed to meet the specific needs of a student readership, such as useful scene-by-scene plot summaries and generous facing-page explanatory notes (illustrated with relevant contemporary images sourced from the Folger Shakespeare Library's collection of early modern printed books), as well as an introduction addressing the play's language and an annotated list of recommended further reading. The Folger edition of *Much Ado* also includes an interpretative essay by Gail Kern Paster on masculine anxieties about marriage and sexual betrayal, which serves as an excellent model of a historically informed close reading of the play for students new to thinking and writing critically about Shakespeare.

Intended for a more advanced readership, the other single-text print editions of *Much Ado* listed above offer introductory materials and commentary of comparatively greater breadth and depth. While the introductions cover much of the same critical ground, attending to fundamental contexts including gender, sex and social rank, as well as detailed discussion of *Much Ado*'s sources, language and structure, these single-text print editions differ in their treatment and coverage of the play in performance.

In keeping with his remarks about the need for editors to keep footnotes short and few, Sheldon P. Zitner's commentary for the Oxford Shakespeare edition of the play is thrifty but serviceable. By contrast, his introduction is ample and wide-ranging, including discussion of *Much Ado* in relation to Shakespeare's other romantic comedies (1–5), its date and sources (5–14), title, place and setting (14–18), as well as critical readings of the play's characters grouped by dramatic function and social position: 'Lovers' (19–38), 'Brothers' (38–42) and 'Gentlewomen, Conspirators, and Others' (42–8). Zitner's introduction is also notably sensitive to issues of dramaturgy, with insightful discussion of the play's 'Plot Construction' (48–50), 'Act, Scene, and Pace' (50–2), 'Contrasts and Links Between Scenes' (52–6) and 'Local Effects' (56–8). Annotations throughout the text further demonstrate Zitner's keen eye for performance possibilities. His discussion of the play's stage history is impressively detailed, paying particular attention to nineteenth-century productions ('Stage History', 58–70). However, as it was published in 1993, Zitner's performance history is now dated; covering only stage productions up to 1991, Zitner's discussion necessarily excludes the many important stage productions and screen adaptations of *Much Ado* which have since appeared.

If Zitner's edition for the Oxford Shakespeare was remarkably sparing in its commentary, F.H. Mares's edition for the New Cambridge Shakespeare is equally notable for its attempt to avoid promoting any particular critical reading of *Much Ado*. Mares's discussion of 'The Criticism of the Play' (29–41) is something of a misnomer, since it engages with little scholarship, ruminates on the theoretical limits of interpretation and is arguably more concerned with restricting – rather than opening up – readings of the play: 'I do not dispute the infinite variety of possible readings', Mares writes, 'but in my view that infinite variety is constrained within certain bounds' (30). His treatment of the play's 'Stage History' (10–29) is more generous and especially detailed in its coverage of twentieth-century stage productions. When first published in 1988, Mares's edition surveyed major stage productions of *Much Ado* up to the early 1980s; it was subsequently reprinted in 2003 with an additional essay on 'Recent Stage, Film and Critical Interpretations' by Angela Stock (48–59), which briefly addressed British stage productions up to 2000 as well as Kenneth Branagh's 1993 film adaptation. In the course of her short stage history, Stock offers a perceptive observation about Beatrice's age on stage: 'Like the decision to play her as a self-assertive character, frumpy spinster, defensive feminist or domineering Amazon, her supposed age is a good indication of a production's idea of romance and its views of gender relations' (54). While concisely written – it spans only four pages – and necessarily selective, Stock's survey of post-1980s criticism on *Much Ado* is a much-needed supplement to Mares's original.

Of the single-text editions surveyed here, Claire McEachern's revised edition of *Much Ado* for the Arden Shakespeare (Third Series) offers generous annotations and perhaps the most lengthy critical introduction, almost a third of which is taken up with 'Building a Play: Sources and Contexts' (4–52), a detailed examination of Shakespeare's transformation of the play's prose narrative sources. This is followed by consideration of *Much Ado*'s 'Structure and Style' (52–82), a notably brief discussion of the play's critical reception (124–31), and a section on textual analysis (131–51). McEachern's discussion of 'Staging *Much Ado*' (82–124) eschews the conventional chronological survey of productions and focuses instead on how productions have addressed certain 'questions of staging' – such as choices of tone and setting (social, geographical, temporal) – and 'their implications for the play's effect' (84). For the revised edition, McEachern appends a new 'Additions and Reconsiderations' section to the introduction (153–81). While McEachern offers some discussion of recent scholarship, the 'Additions and Reconsiderations' section is almost entirely devoted to analysis of stage and screen productions appearing in the interim since the first edition was published in 2006, and might have been more usefully integrated into the relevant introductory sections.

In keeping with the theatrical auspices of the series, Jonathan Bate and Eric Rasmussen's RSC Shakespeare edition of *Much Ado* privileges matters of performance in its introduction and commentary. Annotations (prepared by Eleanor Lowe and Héloïse Sénéchal) are glosses of unfamiliar terms with the occasional concise contextual note. Like the Folger, the RSC edition offers scene-by-scene analysis by Esme Miskimmin (102–13). In addition to Bate's general introduction (1–12), the edition includes an overview of the play's performance history by Jan Sewell (115–26) and discussion of Royal Shakespeare Company productions by Penelope Freedman (126–41), as well as interviews with actors and directors by Bate and Kevin Wright (142–63). Critics derided the decision by the RSC editors to use F1 as a base (or 'copy') text for the *Complete Works* edition as an uncritical fetishization of the Folio. Since the single-text edition reproduces the *Complete Works* text, the objection remains – this is the only modern edition of *Much Ado* taking F1 as its copy-text, and the textual notes (100–1) record the numerous readings from Q favoured over those of F1.

Readers interested in matters of performance to the exclusion of critical reception and historical context might consider using an edition in the Shakespeare in Production series, launched by Cambridge University Press in 1996, in which the New Cambridge Shakespeare text of the plays are annotated with interpretations from (predominantly major British and North American) stage and screen productions. In the introduction to his edition of *Much Ado* for the series (1–85), John F. Cox tracks the play's stage history up to Michael Boyd's 1996 RSC production, analysing theatrical trends and points of departure (such as Victorian constructions of Beatrice, 35–43, and various twentieth-century settings, 74–5) and attending to film and television adaptations (81–4). Cox's annotations offer valuable insights into the ways that directorial decisions and the treatment of specific speeches, passages and even individual words have resulted in radically different interpretations of the play.

A glance at online resources

Digital editions

Drama Online, Bloomsbury/Faber & Faber: http://www. dramaonlinelibrary.com/.
Folger Digital Texts, Folger Shakespeare Library: http://www. folgerdigitaltexts.org/.
Internet Shakespeare Editions: http://internetshakespeare.uvic.ca/.
The Norton Shakespeare Digital Edition, W.W. Norton: https:// digital.wwnorton.com/shakespeare3.
Oxford Scholarly Editions Online, Oxford University Press: http://www.oxfordscholarlyeditions.com/.

At time of writing, there are no completed 'born-digital' editions of *Much Ado* – that is, editions with no prior existence in print. Gretchen Minton and Cliff Werier are preparing the first born-digital scholarly edition of *Much Ado* for Internet Shakespeare Editions, which, when complete, will offer an annotated modern-spelling text of the play with collations of textual variants and historical editions, critical and textual introductions, and a performance history, supplemented with additional contextual materials and multimedia content. At time of writing, the edition provides accurate semi-diplomatic transcriptions and facsimile images of the Q and F1 texts, as well as facsimile images of the play as printed in the Second, Third and Fourth Folios, and in the 1709 and 1733 collected works editions by Nicholas Rowe and Lewis Theobald respectively. All content published by the Internet Shakespeare Editions is subject to rigorous peer review and is completely 'open access' – that is, made freely available online.

Some of the print editions of *Much Ado* mentioned in the previous section are also available online – or soon will be. *Folger Digital Texts* makes the texts of the Folger Shakespeare Library editions freely available online. While *Folger Digital Texts* accurately replicate the formatting, lineation and pagination, they do not reproduce any of the critical apparatus or commentary present in the print volumes.

Drama Online, a platform developed by Bloomsbury in partnership with Faber & Faber and available by institutional subscription, incorporates digitized versions of the Arden Shakespeare series, including McEachern's edition of *Much Ado*. The *Drama Online* interface provides added analytical functionality, allowing users to generate 'part-books' for each character, and to compare words and speeches between acts and characters.

Digitized versions of *The New Oxford Shakespeare* materials (including Anna Pruitt's modern- and original-spelling editions of *Much Ado*), as well as individual volumes from the Oxford Shakespeare series (including Zitner's edition of *Much Ado*), are accessible through the *Oxford Scholarly Editions Online* platform published by Oxford University Press. Ordinarily, *Oxford Scholarly Editions Online* is available only by institutional subscription; however, personal subscriptions are now included with the purchase of *The New Oxford Shakespeare* print volumes.

The Norton Shakespeare Digital Edition reproduces the same text of *Much Ado* prepared by Trudi Darby as the print version, with the addition of the nine 'textual comments' and four 'performance comments' that are referred to – but not reproduced – in the print edition. Curiously, while *Much Ado* survives in two early versions (Q and F1), the play is represented in both print and digital editions of *The Norton Shakespeare* solely by a text based on Q – despite the 'single-text editing' rationale described by the general textual editors justifying separate editions of both early versions. Access to *The Norton Shakespeare Digital Edition* is by registration of an individual code, whether supplied with purchase of the print edition or purchased separately.

Although it is still currently in development, the *Cambridge World Shakespeare Online* will bring digitized versions of the New Cambridge Shakespeare series – including Mares's edition of *Much Ado* – together with the *Cambridge Guide to the Worlds of Shakespeare*, articles from *Shakespeare Survey*, and other works of reference and criticism published by Cambridge University Press.

Prompt-books

The Shakespeare Collection, Gale: http://gale.cengage.co.uk/
    shakespeare.
*Shakespeare in Performance: Prompt Books from the Folger
    Shakespeare Library*, Adam Matthew Digital: http://www.
    shakespeareinperformance.amdigital.co.uk/.

'Prompt-books' of *Much Ado* – that is, copies of the play annotated for specific performance, noting entrances and exits, emended lines and changes to the text, and other stage business – offer unique insights into the ways that actors, directors and other theatre practitioners have approached the play. Given their value as historical records of performance, especially in the absence of other archival material, many prompt-books have been digitized. *The Shakespeare Collection*, a database published by Gale and available by institutional subscription, offers digitized microfilm of significant Shakespeare prompt-books, six of which are prompt-books and rehearsal scripts of *Much Ado* from productions between 1804 and 1949. The database also includes digitized microfilm of Gordon Crosse's unpublished theatrical diaries, which record his responses to over 500 performances he attended in the United Kingdom between 1890 and 1953; of these, there are twenty entries for *Much Ado* dated from 1895 to 1952. Published by Adam Matthew Digital and similarly available by institutional subscription, *Shakespeare in Performance* is a digital archive of the Folger Shakespeare Library's collection of more than 1,000 prompt-books dating from the seventeenth to the twentieth century, representing productions from the UK, the USA and further abroad. It contains thirty-eight prompt-books of *Much Ado* between 1788 and 1926.

Archival materials

Digital Image Collection, Folger Shakespeare Library: http://luna.
    folger.edu/.
Discover Shakespeare, Shakespeare Birthplace Trust: http://
    collections.shakespeare.org.uk/.
Shakespeare in Performance Database, Internet Shakespeare
    Editions: http://internetshakespeare.uvic.ca/.

The Folger Shakespeare Library's *Digital Image Collection* provides access to an impressive and growing digitized collection of artworks, archival and promotional materials, costumes, set and costume designs, and production photographs, dating from the seventeenth century to the present day. Hundreds of these digitized materials relate to *Much Ado*, including twenty-five nineteenth-century watercolour illustrations from Charles Kean's scrapbook (Folger ART Vol. d49). The *Digital Image Collection* is freely accessible, and use of its materials, unless under non-Folger copyright, is subject to a Creative Commons Attribution–ShareAlike (CC-BY-SA) licence.

In addition to its own impressive museum and library, the Shakespeare Birthplace Trust maintains the Royal Shakespeare Company's archives and collections, which include more than 4,000 artworks depicting stage productions and artistic interpretations of Shakespeare's work since the seventeenth century, as well as costumes, props and designs from the 1800s to the present day. Objects are catalogued in the Trust's *Discover Shakespeare* database, and digital facsimiles and images are often available. The database also contains information for over 4,000 RSC productions since 1879, including more than eighty productions of *Much Ado*, many with digitized photographs. *Discover Shakespeare* is free to use, but use of digitized materials varies – some digital objects are subject to a Creative Commons Attribution–NonCommercial–NoDerivs (CC-BY-NC-ND) licence, while others are subject to copyright or require licensing from the Royal Shakespeare Company.

Theatre companies from around the world contribute digitized archival materials to the Internet Shakespeare Editions' *Shakespeare in Performance* database. Hundreds of these artefacts relate to *Much Ado*, including still photographs of productions, theatre programmes, prompt-books, posters and press clippings. While the Internet Shakespeare Editions is open access, permissible uses vary from artefact to artefact because individual theatre companies determine the copyright status for the material they contribute to the *Shakespeare in Performance* database.

Digital audio and video

BBC *Shakespeare Archive Resources*, BBC: http://shakespeare.ch.
   bbc.co.uk/.
Digital Theatre Plus: http://www.digitaltheatreplus.com/.
Drama Online, Bloomsbury/Faber & Faber: http://www.
   dramaonlinelibrary.com/.
MIT Global Shakespeares Video & Performance Archive, MIT:
   http://globalshakespeares.mit.edu/.

To commemorate the 400th anniversary of Shakespeare's
death, the British Broadcasting Corporation (BBC) launched
the *BBC Shakespeare Archive Resource*, making hundreds
of digitized images, video recordings of productions, and
television and radio programmes from the 1950s to 1989
freely available to schools, colleges and universities across
the United Kingdom. (British users unattached to institutions
of formal education and users outside of the UK are unable
to access this content.) Resources for *Much Ado* include
video recordings of Franco Zeffirelli's 1965 National Theatre
production and Stuart Burge's 1984 BBC Television
Shakespeare production, an audio recording of John Powell's
1969 BBC Radio 3 production, and numerous photographs.

A number of repertory theatre companies have begun to
make digital video recordings of their Shakespeare productions
available to rent or purchase on demand. For example, the
2011 production of *Much Ado* directed by Jeremy Herrin for
Shakespeare's Globe London may be rented or downloaded
to own through the Globe's *Globe Player* service, or streamed
by subscription to *Drama Online*. *Digital Theatre Plus*,
available by institutional subscription, offers streaming video
recordings of theatre productions and interviews, including the
2011 Wyndham Theatre production of *Much Ado* (starring
Catherine Tate and David Tennant), Joseph Papp's 1972 CBS
TV production of the New York Shakespeare Festival's
Broadway staging (starring Kathleen Widdoes and Sam
Waterston), and Donald McWhinnie's 1978 BBC Television
production. Users can also rent or buy an increasing number of
film adaptations and televised stage productions from general
vendors of digital video, such as Amazon Video, including
the 1993 Kenneth Branagh and 2012 Joss Whedon film
adaptations.

The *MIT Global Shakespeares Video & Performance
Archive* is a growing collection of streaming video-recorded
stage and screen productions of Shakespeare sourced from
around the world. Recordings are freely accessible online, and
are supplemented with critical essays, actor and crew interviews,

scripts, and subtitles for foreign-language productions. Among others, the *Archive* includes video recordings of a 2003 Portuguese-language production of *Much Ado* from Brazil, and a 1986 production in Mandarin adapting the play for *huangmei* (Chinese opera). Productions like these demonstrate the range of global, cultural responses to Shakespeare outside the Anglophone theatrical tradition.

Critical approaches and lenses for classroom study

Textual history and sources

Much Ado first appeared in print as a quarto edition of 1600 published by stationers Andrew Wise and William Asply. The play had been mentioned in the Stationers' Company register on 4 August 1600, where it appeared in a list of four plays belonging to the Lord Chamberlain's Men that were 'to be stayed', possibly an attempt to forestall or prevent their publication by unauthorized agents. However, only a few weeks later, on 23 August 1600, Wise and Asply entered for their copy the rights to both *Much Ado* and *2 Henry IV*. The title page of their edition (or 'Q'), which was printed by Valentine Simmes, advertised both the play's theatrical origins and its authorship: 'Much adoe about | Nothing. | *As it hath been sundrie times publikely* | acted by the right honourable, the Lord | Chamberlain his seruants. | *Written by William Shakespeare*'. A copy of Q annotated with references to performance was later used as copy for the First Folio of 1623 (or 'F1'). More detailed textual introductions can be found in the editions surveyed above.

Several of the play's textual cruxes offer opportunities for class discussion. Details such as Q's silent 'ghost' characters of Innogen, Leonato's wife (mentioned in the entry directions to 1.1 and 2.1), the 'kinsman' (2.1.0) and the Town Clerk (4.2.0) hint at Shakespeare's writing process and offer possibilities for performance. Do these characters really exist? If so, what do they signify? Michael D. Friedman ('"Hush'd"') suggests that Innogen's silent presence is part of the play's focus on marital and musical harmony. Likewise, stage directions and variant speech prefixes that use the names of actors and musicians demonstrate the ways that roles were written with specific talents in mind (Kathman). One crux in particular allows for an exploration and rebuttal of editorial emendation: Leonato's 'Peace! I will stop your mouth' (5.4.97), which is sometimes transferred to Benedick (Maurer).

Stories of unjustly spurned women are common in romance literature, but Ariosto's *Orlando Furioso* (translated into English by John Harington in 1591) and Matteo Bandello's *La Prima Parte de la Novelle* (translated into French by François de Belleforest in 1569) are generally agreed to be direct sources for Hero's plot in *Much Ado*. Critics have nonetheless focused on the ways that Shakespeare adapts or amplifies elements within his sources (McEachern, 'Fathering'; Moisan; Salingar). Additional studies have focused on the influence of Baldassare Castiglione's *The Book of the Courtier* on the character of Benedick (Collington, '"Stuffed"'), ballad culture (Collington, '"Pennyworth"'), and the association of jest books with Beatrice (Munro).

Collington, Philip D. 'A "Pennyworth" of Marital Advice: Bachelors and Ballad Culture in *Much Ado About Nothing*'. In *Shakespeare's Comedies of Love*, edited by Karen Bamford and Richard Knowles, 30–54. Toronto: University of Toronto Press, 2008. Argues that 'Shakespeare's witty courtship culture is both a product of, and participant in, England's ballad culture.'

Collington, Philip D. '"Stuffed With All Honourable Virtues": *Much Ado About Nothing* and *The Book of the Courtier*'. *Studies in Philology* 103, no. 3 (2006): 281–312. Examines influences of Castiglione's *Courtier* on the characterization of Benedick and on thematic events in the play such as sprezzatura and service.

Friedman, Michael D. 'The Editorial Recuperation of Claudio'. *Comparative Drama* 25, no. 4 (1991): 369–86. Explores how editorial emendations construct the character of Claudio and affect stage treatments of him.

Friedman, Michael D. '"Hush'd on Purpose to Grace Harmony": Wives and Silence in *Much Ado About Nothing*'. *Theatre Journal* 42, no. 3 (1990): 350–63. Concludes that the play's musical harmony signifies a marital concord predicated on female silence.

Kathman, David. 'Actors' Names as Textual Evidence'. *Theatre Notebook* 63, no. 2 (2009): 70–9. Outlines evidence for the historical musician John Wilson, whose name appears in F1 and who likely played Balthasar in a post-1611 revival of the play.

Maurer, Margaret. 'Leonato and Beatrice in Act 5, Scene 5, Line 97 of *Much Ado About Nothing*'. In *Reading What's There: Essays on Shakespeare in Honor of Stephen Booth*, edited by Michael J. Collins, 89–98. Newark: University of Delaware Press, 2014. Argues for maintaining the Quarto and Folio readings, which assign the line to Leonato, instead of the editorial tradition which transfers it to Benedick.

McEachern, Claire. 'Fathering Herself: A Source Study of Shakespeare's Feminism'. *Shakespeare Quarterly* 39, no. 3 (1988): 269–90. Argues that Bandello's tale and Shakespeare's play show 'marked differences' in the patriarchal relationship between Hero and Leonato; in *Much Ado*, their bond is marked as much by personal investment as by public perception.

Moisan, Thomas. 'Deforming Sources: Literary Antecedents and Their Traces in *Much Ado About Nothing*'. *Shakespeare Studies* 31 (2003): 165–83 Asserts that the play's use of Bandello and Ariosto as sources is characterized by 'furtiveness' and 'ambivalence', both of which are also mirrored in the play's approach to character and politics.

Munro, Ian. 'Shakespeare's Jestbook: Wit, Print, Performance'. *ELH* 71, no.1 (2004): 89–113. Examines Benedick's accusation that Beatrice derives her humour from a popular book of jests to conclude that female wit is suspiciously rote rather than genuine, setting 'feminine print and masculine performance' in direct opposition.

Salingar, Leo. 'Borachio's Indiscretion: Some Noting about *Much Ado*'. In *The Italian World of English Renaissance Drama*, edited by Michele Marrapodi, 225–38. London: Associated University Presses, 1998. Finds Shakespeare critically adapting Bandello to produce a 'bittersweet comedy' from a 'triumph of magnanimity over falsehood'.

Genre and language

Much Ado about Nothing was written during Shakespeare's mid-career prose period, and the play is roughly 70 per cent prose to 30 per cent verse. This high percentage of prose offers students a clear visual signal as they consider the form and content of characters' speeches. Such interpretations have also found purchase in criticism: Jonas A. Barish and William W. Morgan demonstrate the ways that shifts between prose and verse can delineate nuances in theme, plot and character, while Nicholas Potter applies this study of form particularly to the play's examination of courtly and romantic love. Students may wish to be attentive to the percentage of the play that is spoken by each character or pairs of characters (figures that are available in collected works editions such as *The New Oxford Shakespeare* and *The RSC Shakespeare: Complete Works*). For example, Beatrice and Benedick speak nearly 30 per cent of the lines of the play to Claudio and Hero's 15 per cent, and despite the havoc he wreaks in Messina, villain Don John speaks less than 5 per cent of the play's lines.

Another recurring theme in criticism of the play's language examines the ways in which the play's surface wittiness can mask more sinister interpretations. Language is a medium for expressing social hierarchies and power, and critics have long been attentive to the play's discursive subtext (Straznicky; Slights; McKeown; Turner). In his introduction to *The Norton Shakespeare* edition of the play, Stephen Greenblatt notes that 'the more one attends to the language of *Much Ado About Nothing*, the more its whiplash merriment seems saturated with violence' (1398), and Russ McDonald likewise points out that the play 'explores the human damage that language can do'.[1] In particular, the malicious and false report of unchastity levelled against Hero is especially damaging, and critics have sought to place the slander of *Much Ado* in its Elizabethan contexts. In 1992, S.P. Cerasano published an article on gender-based slander in the context of Elizabethan law, a theme that has been picked up in greater detail by Nancy E. Wright (focusing on legal determination of intention) and Cyndia Susan Clegg (contrasting approaches to slander in secular and ecclesiastical law). Slander is levelled most damnably against Hero, but false report is used to humorous effect towards Beatrice, Benedick and Dogberry. In exploring the humour in Dogberry's 'ass' sequence alongside Hero's defamation, Steve Cassal offers a contrast in slanders that makes the discursive issues at play readily comprehensible to undergraduate students. The multivalency of puns within the play has also garnered special focus, as they point towards the inherent ambivalence of signifier and signified, thereby offering an opportunity for characters to display linguistic prowess (McCollom; Cummings).

Barish, Jonas A. 'Pattern and Purpose in the Prose of *Much Ado About Nothing*'. *Rice University Studies* 60, no. 2 (1974): 19–30. Explores the effects of rhetorical prose, particularly as they pertain to manners and fashion.

Cassal, Steve. 'Shakespeare's *Much Ado About Nothing*'. *Explicator* 64, no. 3 (2006): 139–41. Contrasts the tragically slanderous language used to defame Hero with the humorous slander used against Dogberry to demonstrate the synchronicity of plot and subplot.

Cerasano, S.P. '"Half a dozen dangerous words"'. In *Gloriana's Face: Women, Public and Private in the English Renaissance*, edited by S.P. Cerasano and Marion Wynne-Davies, 167–183. Detroit, MI: Wayne State University Press, 1992. Notes Hero's use of the phrase 'honest slander' to mark Beatrice's faults, and considers slander alongside Elizabethan law.

Clegg, Cyndia Susan. 'Truth, Lies, and the Law of Slander in *Much Ado About Nothing*'. In *The Law in Shakespeare*, edited by Constance Jordan and Karen Cunningham, 167–88. Basingstoke and New York: Palgrave Macmillan, 2007. Considers slander in the context of sixteenth-century English law, suggesting that the play 'embodies an essentially conservative world view that reaffirms both chivalric honor and the older, more traditional ecclesiastical jurisdiction [as opposed to the secular courts] as the appropriate venue for mitigating slander's damage'.

Cummings, Peter. 'Verbal Energy in Shakespeare's *Much Ado About Nothing*'. *Shakespeare Yearbook* 8 (1997): 448–58. Outlines the 'linguistic sophistication of Shakespeare's title-word dissections, puns, and wordplays'.

Everett, Barbara. '*Much Ado About Nothing*: The Unsociable Comedy'. In *English Comedy*, edited by Michael Cordner, Peter Holland and John Kerrigan, 68–84. Cambridge: Cambridge University Press, 2007. This seminal and often-reprinted essay argues that the play is one of Shakespeare's most psychologically complex comedies, deftly masking its seriousness behind humour.

Kreps, Barbara. 'Two-Sided Legal Narratives: Slander, Evidence, Proof, and Turnarounds in *Much Ado About Nothing*'. In *Taking Exception to the Law: Materializing Injustice in Early Modern English Literature*, edited by Donald Beecher, Travis DeCook, Andrew Wallace and Grant Williams, 162–78. Toronto: University of Toronto Press, 2015. Considers the play's use of 'judging facts' to create a binary between truth and error.

McCollom, William G. 'The Role of Wit in *Much Ado About Nothing*'. *Shakespeare Quarterly* 19, no.2 (1968): 165–74. Suggests that 'wit is organic' in *Much Ado*, focusing on four forms of linguistic play: puns, 'allusive understatement', 'flights of fancy' and parody.

McKeown, Roderick Hugh. '"I Will Stop Your Mouth": The Regulation of Jesting in *Much Ado About Nothing*'. *Shakespeare* 12, no. 1 (2016): 33–54. Puts feminine wit in a broader social context, finding that Hero's aggressive language goes 'largely unremarked' by critics.

Morgan, William W. 'Verse and Prose in *Much Ado About Nothing*: An Analytic Note'. *English* 20, no. 108 (1971): 89–92. A short article, particularly appropriate for students, exploring the juxtaposition of the play's prose and verse.

Potter, Nicholas. 'Romance and Realism in *Much Ado About Nothing*'. In *Critical Essays on Much Ado About Nothing*, edited by Linda Cookson and Bryan Loughrey, 54–62. Harlow: Longman, 1989. Considers the play's depiction of courtly and romantic love language, particularly as indicated by the contrasting forms of verse and prose.

Slights, Camille Wells. *Shakespeare's Comic Commonwealths*.
Toronto: University of Toronto Press, 1993, 171–89. Analyses the
play's 'metadiscourse' to suggest that the play is 'centrally
concerned [. . .] with the power of language and with language as
an articulation of power'.

Straznicky, Marta. 'Shakespeare and the Government of Comedy:
Much Ado About Nothing'. *Shakespeare Studies* 22 (1994):
141–71. An exploration of the linguistic power dynamics at work
within the play, which ultimately call into question the play's
happy resolution.

Turner, John. 'Claudio and the Code of Honour'. In *Critical Essays
on Much Ado About Nothing*, edited by Linda Cookson and
Bryan Loughrey, 21–30. Harlow: Longman, 1989. Finds that
social class is central to understanding both the character of
Claudio and the play's ambivalent genre.

Wright, Nancy E. 'Legal Interpretation of Defamation in
Shakespeare's *Much Ado About Nothing*'. *Ben Jonson Journal* 13,
no. 1 (2006): 93–108. Considers Don John's defamation of Hero
in the context of Renaissance law, focusing on the question of
malicious intent.

Sex and gender

The pun on 'nothing' in the play's title encourages audiences to
view the play as a witty war between the sexes: if men have a
'thing' between their legs, women have 'no thing'. The second
pun on 'nothing' in *Much Ado About Nothing* plays on
Elizabethan pronunciation: 'nothing' was often pronounced
'noting', and the title hints that the root of its dramatic conflicts
stems from conflicting perspectives and misinterpretation.
Many critics have explored the ways that Messina's male and
female characters espouse differing views on marriage and
gender norms. Harry Berger Jr's 1982 influential article on the
play's 'sexual and family politics' offers a useful starting point
for considering the play's normalized gender roles and attitudes
towards virtues such as constancy, as well as characters'
(chiefly Hero's and Beatrice's) responses to them. Carol Cook's
comprehensive exploration of the play's gendered discourse

finds that *Much Ado About Nothing* 'masks, as well as exposes, the mechanisms of masculine power', rendering its comic ending less a comprehensive resolution than a suspicious 'artful dodge'. In 'The Ambivalent Blush', Andrew Fleck offers a case study that demonstrates the effects of men's 'reading' of women and their bodies; this theme is dissected further in Stephanie Chamberlain's examination of Claudio's use of metaphor in calling the disgraced Hero a 'rotten orange' – a fruit that rots from the inside out, and thus may yet appear outwardly unspoiled.

The play's plot assumes audiences have a basic understanding of early modern English courtship and marriage customs, which can be supplied by essays by Ian Frederick Moulton and Germaine Greer. (The latter's focus on the role of lovers' 'go-betweens' is especially useful in considering marriage as a couple's contract with society at large.) Alison Findlay places Hero and Claudio's marriage ceremonies within the larger context of Shakespeare's oeuvre to find that they are particular celebrations of feminine virtue and nostalgia.

Other critics have focused their attentions more specifically on the play's careful construction of masculinity (Lane), drawing particular attention to the way that misogyny is designed to create a closed community of men (Davis). Susan Harlan's freely available online essay considers masculinity as a by-product of the play's militaristic backstory, which informs the way that male characters consult each other about romance. Ann Pellegrini notes that heterosexual marriage also promotes a 'closing of ranks' that can push villain Don John into the position of 'queer anti-hero'.

Berger, Harry, Jr. 'Against the Sink-a-Pace: Sexual and Family Politics in *Much Ado About Nothing*'. *Shakespeare Quarterly* 33, no. 3 (1982): 302–13. This often-reprinted article explores the gender conventions expected of Messina's male and female residents, as well as their subversion.

Chamberlain, Stephanie. 'Rotten Oranges and Other Spoiled Commodities: The Economics of Shame in *Much Ado About Nothing*', *Journal of the Wooden O Symposium* 9 (2010): 1–10.

Investigates the economic metaphors underlying Shakespeare's 'gendered commodity exchanges' within marriage.

Cook, Carol. '"The Sign and Semblance of Her Honor": Reading Gender Difference in *Much Ado About Nothing*'. *PMLA* 101, no. 2 (1986): 186–202. An exploration of the multivalency of gender signification in the play, where men are interpreters and women are objects to be 'read'.

Davis, Lloyd. 'Rethinking Misogyny: Shakespeare, Gender, and the Critical Tradition'. *Shakespearean International Yearbook* 6 (2006): 185–211. Considers misogyny as a displacement of homoerotic desire in a variety of comedies, including *The Taming of the Shrew*, *The Winter's Tale* and *Much Ado*.

Findlay, Alison. 'A Day to Remember: Wedding Ceremony and Cultural Change'. *Shakespeare* 8, no. 4 (2012): 413–23. Surveys weddings in Shakespeare's plays, including *Much Ado*, and argues they are sites of nostalgia.

Fleck, Andrew. 'The Ambivalent Blush: Figural and Structural Metonymy, Modesty, and *Much Ado About Nothing*'. *ANQ* 19, no. 1 (2006): 16–23. Explores Claudio's justification for his denunciation of Hero by considering the interpretative significance of her blush.

Greer, Germaine. 'Shakespeare and the Marriage Contract'. In *Shakespeare and the Law*, edited by Paul Raffield and Gary Watt, 51–63. Oxford: Hart, 2008. Draws attention to the role of 'go-betweens' in establishing early modern marriage contracts, demonstrating the public (not just private) nature of the institution.

Harlan, Susan. '"Returned from the wars": Comedy and Masculine Post-War Character in Shakespeare's *Much Ado About Nothing*'. *Upstart: A Journal of English Renaissance Studies*, 24 June 2013. https://upstart.sites.clemson.edu/Essays/returned-from-the-wars/returned-from-the-wars.xhtml. This freely available online essay considers militaristic constructions of masculinity to explore male characters' approaches to heterosexual romance.

Howard, Jean E. 'Renaissance Antitheatricality and the Politics of Gender and Rank in *Much Ado About Nothing*', In *Shakespeare Reproduced: The Text in History and Ideology*, edited by Jean E. Howard and Marion F. O'Connor, 163–87. New York: Methuen, 1987. This essay, later incorporated into Howard's *The Stage and Social Struggle in Early Modern England* (London: Routledge,

1994), considers the play's treatment of social class and gender alongside Elizabethan ideological tracts.

Lane, Robert. '"Foremost in Report": Social Identity and Masculinity in *Much Ado About Nothing*'. *Upstart Crow* 16 (1996): 31–47. Considers how social dynamics and interactions construct attitudes to masculinity and male identity.

Moulton, Ian Frederick. 'Courtship, Sex, and Marriage'. In *The Ashgate Research Companion to Popular Culture in Early Modern England*, edited by Andrew Hadfield, Matthew Dimmock and Abigail Shinn, 133–48. Farnham: Ashgate, 2014. Offers a broader context for *Much Ado b*y exploring ideas about early modern marriage and courtship.

Pellegrini, Ann. 'Closing Ranks, Keeping Company: Marriage Plots and the Will to be Single in *Much Ado About Nothing*'. In *Shakesqueer: A Queer Companion to the Complete Works of Shakespeare*, edited by Madhavi Menon, 245–53. Durham, NC: Duke University Press, 2011. Finds Don John to be a 'queer anti-hero' who calls attention to the way heterosexual marriage promotes insularity, or a 'closing of ranks'.

Peterson, Kaara L. 'Shakespearean Revivifications: Early Modern Undead'. *Shakespeare Studies* 32 (2004): 240–66. Compares Hero and Juliet's false deaths and resurrections to explore the purification process needed to rehabilitate hysterical women.

Music

In her edition, Claire McEachern describes *Much Ado* as a play 'replete with the melodious conventions of aristocratic courtship: masked balls, serenades before chamber windows, lute warbling and sonnet writing' (80). While few early musical settings for such 'serenades' and 'lute warbling' survive, scholars have located contemporary sources for two of the songs in *Much Ado*: a non-theatrical setting of 'Sigh no more' (sung by Balthasar at 2.3.60–75) for three voices by Thomas Ford dating from the 1620s, and 'The God of Love' (sung briefly by Benedick at 5.2.26–9), a ballad composed by William Elderton during the 1560s and frequently parodied and imitated. Scholars have scrutinized the 'melodious conventions' of song and dance in *Much Ado*, drawing attention to their relationship to rhetoric and language (Nelson; Womack), their role in furthering the play's central themes of misinterpretation and duplicity (Moseley), and as platforms for subversive commentary (Sheppard). Mark Womack's short analysis of 'Sigh no more' demonstrates the kinds of critical insights that may be gleaned from a close reading of the songs that students – and, though they are unlikely to admit it, scholars – frequently gloss over in their reading. Whereas Michael D. Friedman sees parallels between musical and marital harmony, Philippa Sheppard interprets the songs in *Much Ado* as opportunities for social critique. However, such opportunities are not always successfully exploited: Sheppard argues that the 'jolly treatment' of 'Sigh no more' in Kenneth Branagh's film adaptation of *Much Ado* 'obscures the lyrics' bitter taste'.

Students might usefully compare the ways that different productions of *Much Ado* use song and dance: what mood do the musical settings convey, and do these choices contradict or reinforce the lyrics? Given the range of cultural, social and symbolic associations, many of them gendered, what effect does the choice of a particular musical instrument to accompany a song have on its meaning? Students might also consider the implications of using different musical genres in performance, or of varying the (feigned or actual) abilities of the performers: does it matter if Benedick cannot sing in tune?

Friedman, Michael D. '"Hush'd on Purpose to Grace Harmony":
    Wives and Silence in *Much Ado About Nothing*'. *Theatre Journal*
    42, no. 3 (1990): 350–63. Draws parallels between musical
    harmony and marital concord, arguing that Beatrice's loss of
    power in taking a husband also represents a loss of language as
    she exchanges verbal mastery for dutiful silence.
Moseley, Charles. '"Men Were Deceivers Ever"'. In *Critical Essays
    on Much Ado About Nothing*, edited by Linda Cookson and
    Bryan Loughrey, 45–53. Harlow: Longman, 1989. Links song
    and dance in *Much Ado* to the central themes of verbal and
    visual misunderstanding and duplicity.
Nelson, Brent. 'Faith and Sheep's Guts in *Much Ado About
    Nothing*'. *Shakespeare* 12, no. 2 (2016): 161–74. Traces explicit

and implied references to music in the play, arguing that music
provides a thematic framework of social/musical harmony and
discord.

Sheppard, Philippa. '"Sigh No More Ladies" – The Song in *Much
Ado about Nothing*: Shakespeare and Branagh Deliver Aural
Pleasure'. *Literature/Film Quarterly* 33, no. 2 (2005): 92–100.
Argues that the treatment of 'Sigh no more' in Kenneth Branagh's
1993 film adaptation obscures the song's (potential) function as
cynical commentary on the inconstancy of men.

Womack, Mark. 'Balthasar's Song in *Much Ado About Nothing*'. In
Shakespeare Up Close: Reading Early Modern Texts, edited by
Russ McDonald, Nicholas D. Nace and Travis D. Williams,
57–63. London: Arden Shakespeare, 2012. Provides a close
reading of 'Sigh no more', arguing that 'scrupulous attention to
the language', even of a short song, 'is the only way to
understand how Shakespeare transforms a mere vehicle for
transmitting conceptual freight into an amusement park ride for
the minds and ears of his audience'.

Performance history and dramaturgy

Several book-length performance histories of *Much Ado
About Nothing* are available. John F. Cox's 1998 volume in
the Shakespeare in Performance series (mentioned above,
in the single-text editions section) offers accounts of notable
performances alongside a text of the play, enabling quick and
easy searching for approaches to particular moments. Alison
Findlay's more recent Shakespeare Handbook on *Much Ado*
provides an investigation of the play's 'theatrical potential',
offering students and teachers of the play insight into watershed
productions and critical trends. Findlay has written extensively
on women in theatre, and her volume is particularly attuned to
the way the play's conflicting themes of love and war, or
attraction and repulsion, are expressed in particularly gendered
ways. Penny Gay's 'A Kind of Merry War' provides an accessible
and shorter history of post-Second World War productions.

Performance-oriented critics have been drawn especially
to the effect of Beatrice's request that Benedick 'Kill Claudio'

(4.1.288). Beatrice is deadly serious, but the line often draws laughter from audiences, much to the dismay of directors. Articles by John F. Cox and Philip Weller defend this audience impulse, and Sarah Antinora posits that such humour is needed to remedy the disquiet caused by Hero's defamation. Critics have also been interested in the phenomenological aspects of a play that relies so heavily on depictions of eavesdropping and watching others. Ros King uses *Much Ado* as a case study to consider how audiences engage with plays *as play*, a crucial element of human learning. Nova Myhill pays attention to the way *Much Ado* requires audiences to query their own privileged roles as eavesdroppers and observers, demonstrating how ideas about 'truth' are constructed by untested assumptions about the objectivity of witnesses.

Antinora, Sarah. 'Please Let This Be Much Ado about Nothing: 'Kill Claudio' and the Laughter of Release'. *Ceræ: An Australasian Journal of Medieval and Early Modern Studies* 1 (2014): 1–21. This freely available article considers audience reactions to Beatrice's request of Benedick alongside Freud to posit that laughter here is a valuable and 'communal emotional response'.

Cox, John F. 'The Stage Representation of the "Kill Claudio" Sequence in *Much Ado About Nothing*'. *Shakespeare Survey* 32 (1979): 27–36. A performance history of Beatrice's request that Benedick 'Kill Claudio' from the eighteenth through to the mid-twentieth century.

Findlay, Alison. *Much Ado About Nothing: A Guide to the Text and the Play in Performance*. London: Palgrave Macmillan, 2011. The *Much Ado* volume of the Shakespeare Handbooks series offers a comprehensive historical overview of notable performances of the play, as well as a summary of its critical history, and is particularly attentive to the play's approach to questions of gender and fashion.

Gay, Penny. '*Much Ado About Nothing*: A Kind of Merry War'. In *As She Likes It: Shakespeare's Unruly Women*, 143–77. London: Routledge, 1994. Offers a performance history of the play from the 1950s through to the early 1990s.

King, Ros. 'Plays, Playing, and Make-Believe: Thinking and Feeling in Shakespearean Drama'. In *Embodied Cognition and*

Shakespeare's Theatre: The Early Modern Body-Mind, edited by
Laurie Johnson, John Sutton and Evelyn Tribble, 27–45. New
York and Abingdon: Routledge, 2014. Considers the role of
audiences within the play and considers 'the extent to which
mindfulness and the expression of feeling among performers and
audience can be tested in the dynamic play of the playhouse'.

Myhill, Nova. 'Spectatorship in/of *Much Ado About Nothing*'. *Studies
in English Literature, 1500–1900* 39, no. 2 (1999): 291–311.
Investigates how the play's focus on witnessing and 'noting'
unsettles an audience's traditional position of privileged observer.

Weller, Philip. '"Kill Claudio": A Laugh Almost Killed by the
Critics'. *Journal of Dramatic Theory and Criticism* 11, no. 1
(1996): 101–10. Explores directors' attempts to suppress the
humour in Beatrice's request.

Adaptations

Though the play is less frequently adapted than some other
comedies, film adaptations of *Much Ado About Nothing* have
nonetheless found popular favour. Students may benefit from
reading the play alongside viewings of the films to consider
the ways that in making *Much Ado About Nothing* 'more
accessible', film adaptations are required to make cuts that
limit or forestall certain interpretations at the expense of
others. Kenneth Branagh's bright 1993 star-studded film
features himself and his then-wife Emma Thompson in the
roles of Beatrice and Benedick, alongside Denzel Washington
(Don Pedro), Keanu Reeves (Don John), Robert Sean Leonard
(Claudio), Kate Beckinsale (Hero) and Michael Keaton
(Dogberry). The cheerfulness of Branagh's production is the
result of careful cutting: William Brugger demonstrates that
Branagh removed most of the play's references to cuckoldry.
Likewise, Jacek Fabiszak finds that Branagh's choice to situate
the play in a 'fairy-tale' version of Messina amplifies the
strangeness of its setting for modern audiences unaware of
Renaissance England's default assumptions about *Much Ado*'s
'exotic' Italian locale.

Much as Baz Luhrmann's 'punk' *Romeo + Juliet* brought Shakespeare's tragedy to the attention of teenage viewers, Joss Whedon's contemporary 2012 adaptation of *Much Ado About Nothing* offered a fresh take on the comedy for fans of his feminist approaches to comics and speculative fiction. Douglas Lanier notes that Whedon's *Much Ado* is difficult to contextualize: as it was shot in black-and-white, the film evokes the 'screwball comedies' of the 1930s and 1940s, yet its theme of on-again, off-again love in a time of turmoil suggests it is also of a piece with other texts in the 'Whedonverse'. Occasional and accessible articles in the online publication *Slayage: The Journal of Whedon Studies* have consequently followed, exploring the film's 'normalization of surveillance culture' (Smith) and how the early modern gender and racial norms of the text are set at odds with the film's contemporary Californian setting, causing the audience to experience cognitive dissonance (Wilcox).

Finally, as an example of 'Shakespeare in the world', students may be delighted to know that *Much Ado About Nothing* is the first Shakespearean comedy to be translated into the fictional language of Klingon. In keeping with the ethos of the *Star Trek* universe, the text of Wil'yam Shex'pir's *paghmo' tIn mIS* (literally translated, *The Confusion is Great Because of Nothing*) 'has been painstakingly restored to its original Klingon language' by linguist Nick Nicholas. For those unfamiliar with Shakespeare's role in the *Star Trek* imaginary (and Klingon more generally), Karolina Kazimierczak offers a useful primer.

Brugger, William. 'Sins of Omission: Textual Deletions in Branagh's *Much Ado About Nothing*'. *Journal of the Wooden O Symposium* 3 (2003): 1–11. Examines Branagh's editing choices in creating the screenplay, which is roughly half as long as the play.

Fabiszak, Jacek. 'Kenneth Branagh's Multicultural and Multi-Ethnic Filmed Shakespeare(s)'. *Multicultural Shakespeare: Translation, Appropriation, and Performance* 12, no. 27 (2015): 75–86. Considers the effects of Branagh's interracial casting decisions as

well as the distancing or romanticizing effects of settings for his
film versions of *Much Ado About Nothing* and *Hamlet*.

Kazimierczak, Karolina. 'Adapting Shakespeare for *Star Trek* and
Star Trek for Shakespeare: The Klingon *Hamlet* and the Spaces of
Translation'. *Studies in Popular Culture* 32, no. 2 (2010): 35–47.
Explores connections between Shakespeare and the *Star Trek*
universe to provide a context for the choice to translate *Hamlet*
and *Much Ado About Nothing* into Klingon.

Lanier, Douglas M. '"Good Lord, for Alliance": Joss Whedon's
Much Ado About Nothing'. *Représentations: La revue
électronique du CEMRA* 1 (2014): 117–42. This online, freely
available essay explores Whedon's decision to focus his modern-
day adaptation on the play's friendships, rather than make much
of the familial (particularly paternal) relationships.

Oppenheimer, Jean. 'An Indie Twist on Shakespeare'. *American
Cinematographer* 94, no. 7 (2013): 56–63. Considers the
cinematography of Joss Whedon's *Much Ado About Nothing*.

Smith, Philip. '"I Look'd Upon Her With a Soldier's Eye": The
Normalization of Surveillance Culture in Whedon's *Much Ado*'.
Slayage: The Journal of Whedon Studies 14, no. 1 [43] (2016).
http://www.whedonstudies.tv/uploads/2/6/2/8/26288593/smith_
slayage_14.1.pdf. Demonstrates that Whedon's film 'intimat[es] a
hawkish neo-colonial political stance' and 'normalizes modern
discourse on privacy and national security.'

Wilcox, Rhonda V. 'Joss Whedon's Translation of Shakespeare's
Much Ado About Nothing: Historical Double Consciousness,
Reflections, and Frames'. *Slayage* 11:2–12:1 (2014). http://www.
whedonstudies.tv/uploads/2/6/2/8/26288593/wilcox_
slayage_11.2–12.1.pdf. Considers the cognitive dissonance
caused to audiences encountering the gender or racial norms of
Shakespeare's day in a contemporary setting.

NOTES

Introduction

1   Samuel Johnson, *Selections from Johnson on Shakespeare*, ed. Bertrand H. Bronson with Jean M. O'Meara (New Haven, CT and London: Yale University Press, 1986), 14.

2   W.H. Auden, *Lectures on Shakespeare*, ed. Arthur Kirsch (London: Faber, 2000), 119.

3   On the connection between literature and the night-time city, see Matthew Beaumont, *Night Walking: A Nocturnal History of London* (London: Verso, 2015).

4   Ewan Fernie, *Shakespeare for Freedom: Why the Plays Matter* (Cambridge: Cambridge University Press, 2017), 92.

5   Lynda E. Boose, 'Scolding Brides and Bridling Scolds: Taming the Woman's Unruly Member', *Shakespeare Quarterly* 42, no. 2 (1991), 179–213.

6   Mihoko Suzuki, 'Gender, Class, and the Ideology of Comic Form: *Much Ado About Nothing* and *Twelfth Night*', in *A Feminist Companion to Shakespeare*, ed. Dympna Callaghan (Oxford and Malden, MA: Blackwell Publishers, 2000), 125.

7   Alison Findlay, *Illegitimate Power: Bastards in Renaissance Drama* (Manchester: Manchester University Press, 1994).

8   *Hero and Leander*, in *Christopher Marlowe, Complete Plays and Poems*, ed. E.D. Pendry and J.C. Maxwell (London, Melbourne and Toronto: J.M. Dent, 1976), l. 175. The poem was entered in the Stationers' Register on 28 September 1598.

9   R.E.R. Madelaine, 'Oranges and Lemans: Much Ado About Nothing, IV.i.31', *Shakespeare Quarterly* 33, no. 4 (1982), 491.

10 Claire McEachern, ed., 'Introduction', *Much Ado About Nothing* (London: Arden Shakespeare, 2015), 20.

11 Peter J. Smith, *Social Shakespeare: Aspects of Renaissance Dramaturgy and Contemporary Society* (Basingstoke: Macmillan, 1995), 33.

12 Roderick Hugh McKeown, ' "I Will Stop Your Mouth": The Regulation of Jesting in *Much Ado About Nothing*', *Shakespeare* 12, no. 1 (2016): 35–54, 51.

13 Peter J. Smith, 'Review of *Much Ado About Nothing*', *Cahiers Élisabéthains* 88 (2015): 184–6, 185.

14 Geoffrey Bullough, ed., *Narrative and Dramatic Sources of Shakespeare* (New York: Routledge, 1963), vol. II, 72.

15 Angela Stock, 'Recent Stage, Film and Critical Interpretations', in *Much Ado About Nothing*, ed. F.H. Mares (2nd ed., Cambridge: Cambridge University Press, 2003), 56.

16 Compare Edmund Spenser, Amoretti 67: 'Strange thing me seemd to see a beast so wyld, / So goodly wonne with her owne will beguyld'. *Edmund Spenser's Poetry*, ed. Hugh Maclean and Anne Lake Prescott (New York: W.W. Norton, 1993).

17 Stanley Cavell, *Pursuits of Happiness: The Hollywood Comedy of Remarriage* (Cambridge MA: Harvard Film Studies, 1984).

18 Jane Austen, *Pride and Prejudice*, ed. James Kingsley (Oxford: Oxford University Press, 1990), 29.

19 Quoted in Chapter 4 of this volume, by Duncan Salkeld: London Metropolitan Archives, *Repertories of the Court of Aldermen*, Rep 21, 31ᵛ (19 February 1584).

Chapter 1

1 David Wiles, *Shakespeare's Clown: Actor and Text in the Elizabethan Playhouse* (Cambridge: Cambridge University Press, 2005), 137.

2 The reputation for playing Dogberry as corpulent continued in Miller's *The Universal Passion* (1737) where the character was renamed Porco.

3 Margaret Cavendish, *CCXI Sociable Letters Written by the Thrice Noble, Illustrious, and Excellent Princess, the Lady*

Marchioness of Newcastle (London: William Wilson 1664),
Letter CXXIII (244–5).

4   *Bell's Edition of Shakespeare's Plays As They Are Now
    Performed at the Theatres Royal in London, Regulated From the
    Prompt Books of Each House, With Notes Critical and
    Illustrative by the Authors of the Dramatic Censor*, Volume II
    (London, 1774), 268, 285, 274.

5   William Hazlitt, *Characters of Shakespeare's Plays* (London,
    1817), 303.

6   Darl Larsen, *Monty Python, Shakespeare and Renaissance
    Drama* (Jefferson, NC: McFarland Publishers, 2003), 63.

7   Hermann Ulrici, *Shakespeare's Dramatic Art* (1839), trans.
    L. Dora Schmitz cited in Horace Howard Furness, ed., *A New
    Variorum Edition of Shakespeare, Much Ado About Nothing*
    (New York: Dover Publications, 1964), 373.

8   E.W. Sievers, *William Shakespeare* (Gotha, 1886) cited in
    Furness, *New Variorum*, 377.

9   John A. Allen, 'Dogberry', *Shakespeare Quarterly* 24, no. 1
    (1973): 46.

10 Ibid., 38, 39.

11 Charles Gildon, 'Remarks on the Plays of Shakespeare' in *The
    Works of William Shakespear*, Volume 1 (London, 1709), xvii.

12 Charlotte Lennox, *Shakespear Illustrated: Or the Novels and
    Histories, on Which the Plays of Shakespear Are Founded,
    Collected and Translated From the Original Authors. With
    Critical Remarks. The Third and Last Volume. By the Author of
    The Female Quixote* (London, 1754), III, 267, 263, 270.

13 James Miller, *The Universal Passion* (London, 1737), 72. All
    subsequent references are to page numbers in this edition.

14 Elizabeth Griffith, *The Morality of Shakespeare's Drama
    Illustrated* (London, 1775), 159, 155, 159, 161.

15 Charles Gildon, 'Remarks on the Plays of Shakespeare' in *The
    Works of Mr William Shakespear*, Volume 7 (London, 1710),
    304–7.

16 *Bell's Edition*, Volume II, 278

17 Ibid., 286, 279.

18 William Warburton, *The Works of Shakespear* (1747), cited in
    Furness, *New Variorum*, 210.

19 Griffith, *Morality*, 159.

20 *Bell's Edition*, II, 292.

21 A.C. Swinburne, *A Study of Shakespeare* (1884), cited in
    Furness, *New Variorum*, 354.

22 F.J. Furnivall, 'Introduction' to *The Leopold Shakespeare*
    (London: Cassell and Company, 1877), liv–lvi.

23 F. Kreyssig, *Vorlesungen uber Shakespeare* (1862), 217, cited in
    Furness, *New Variorum*, 375–6.

24 Mrs Inchbald, *British Theatre* (1822), cited in Furness, *New
    Variorum*, 348.

25 Henrietta Palmer, *The Stratford Gallery; or the Shakespeare
    Sisterhood, Comprising Forty-Five Ideal Portraits* (New York:
    Appleton and Co. 1859), cited in *Women Reading Shakespeare
    1660–1900: An Anthology of Criticism*, ed. Ann Thompson and
    Sasha Roberts (Manchester: Manchester University Press, 1997),
    112.

26 Grace Latham, 'Julia, Silvia, Hero and Viola', New Shakespeare
    Society, *Monthly Abstract of Proceedings* (London: February
    1891), cited in Thompson and Roberts, *Women Reading
    Shakespeare*, 171.

27 Janice Hays, 'Those "soft and delicate desires": *Much Ado* and
    the Distrust of Women', in *The Woman's Part: Feminist Criticism
    of Shakespeare*, ed. Carolyn Ruth Swift Lenz, Gayle Greene and
    Carol Thomas Neely (Urbana: University of Illinois Press, 1980),
    79–99, 79.

28 Carole McEwin, 'Counsels of Gall and Grace: Intimate
    Conversations Between Women in Shakespeare's Plays', in Lenz
    et al., *The Woman's Part: Feminist Criticism of Shakespeare*,
    117–32.

29 Elizabeth Schafer, *Ms-Directing Shakespeare: Women Direct
    Shakespeare* (Basingstoke: Palgrave Macmillan, 2000), 83–5.

30 Michael D. Friedman, '"For Man Is a Giddy Thing and This Is
    My Conclusion": Faith and Fashion in *Much Ado about
    Nothing*', *Text and Performance Quarterly* 13, no. 3 (1993):
    267–82.

31 Carol Thomas Neely, *Broken Nuptials in Shakespeare's Plays* (New Haven, CT: Yale University Press, 1985).

32 Harry Berger Jr, 'Against the Sink-a-Pace: Sexual and Family Politics in *Much Ado About Nothing*', *Shakespeare Quarterly* 33, no. 3 (1982): 302–13, 310–11.

33 Richard A. Levin, *Love and Society in Shakespearean Comedy: A Study of Dramatic Form and Content* (Newark: University of Delaware Press, 1985).

34 Celestino Deleyto, 'Men in Leather: Kenneth Branagh's *Much Ado About Nothing* and Romantic Comedy', *Cinema Journal* 36, no. 3 (1997): 91–105.

35 Elliot Krieger, 'Social Relations and the Social Order in *Much Ado About Nothing*,' *Shakespeare Survey* 32 (1979): 49–61.

36 John Drakakis, 'Trust and Transgression: The Deceptive Practices of *Much Ado About Nothing*', in *Post-Structuralist Readings of Poetry*, ed. Richard Machin and Christopher Norris (Cambridge: Cambridge University Press, 1987), 73.

37 Jean E. Howard, *The Stage and Social Struggle in Early Modern England* (London: Routledge, 1994).

38 Nova Myhill, 'Spectatorship in/of *Much Ado About Nothing*', *Studies in English Literature, 1500–1900* 39, no. 2 (1999): 291–311.

39 Charles Prouty, *The Sources of Much Ado About Nothing* (New Haven, CT: Yale University Press, 1950).

40 John Traugott, 'Creating a Rational Rinaldo: A Study in the Mixture of the Genres of Comedy and Romance in *Much Ado About Nothing*,' *Genre* 15, nos 2/3 (1982): 157–81. Laurie E. Osborne, 'Dramatic Play in *Much Ado About Nothing*: Wedding in the Italian Novellas and English Comedy', *Philological Quarterly* 2 (1990): 167–88.

41 Martin Mueller, 'Shakespeare's Sleeping Beauties: The Sources of *Much Ado About Nothing*, and the Play of Their Repetitions', *Modern Philology* 91, no. 3 (1994): 288–311.

42 Melinda J. Gough, '"Her Filthy Feature Open Showne" in Ariosto, Spenser and *Much Ado About Nothing*', *Studies in English Literature, 1500–1900* 39, no. 1 (1999): 41–67, 44.

43 D. Cook, 'The Very Temple of Delight: The Twin Plots of *Much Ado About Nothing*', in *Poetry and Drama 1570–1700, Essays in Honour of Harold F. Brooks*, ed. Antony Coleman and Antony Hammond (Sydney: Lawbook Co. of Australasia, 1981), 32–46; Marta Straznicky, 'Shakespeare and the Government of Comedy in *Much Ado About Nothing*,' *Shakespeare Studies* 22 (1994): 141–71; Mihoko Suzuki, 'Gender, Class and the Ideology of Comic Form: *Much Ado About Nothing*', in *A Feminist Companion to Shakespeare*, ed. Dympna Callaghan (Oxford and Malden, MA: Blackwell, 2000), 121–43.

44 James Smith, '*Much Ado About Nothing*: Notes for a Book in Preparation', *Scrutiny* 13, no. 4 (1946): 242–57; A.P. Rossiter, *Angel With Horns* (New York: Theater Arts Books, 1961), 77.

45 Richard Henze, 'Deception in *Much Ado About Nothing*', *Studies in English Literature, 1500–1900* 11, no. 2 (1971): 187–201.

46 Barbara K. Lewalski, 'Love, Appearance and Reality: Much Ado About Something', *Studies in English Literature, 1500–1900* 8, no. 2 (1968): 235–51.

47 James A. McPeek, 'The Thief "Deformed" and Much Ado About "Noting"', *Boston University Studies in English* 4 (1960): 65–84, 65, 74.

48 David Lucking, 'Bringing Deformed Forth: Engendering Meaning in *Much Ado About Nothing*', *Renaissance Forum* 2, no. 1 (1997). https://web.archive.org/web/20170215210255/http://www.hull.ac.uk/renforum/v2no1/lucking.htm.

49 David Ormerod, 'Faith and Fashion in *Much Ado About Nothing*', *Shakespeare Survey* 25 (1972): 93–106; Friedman, '"For Man Is a Giddy Thing"'.

50 Robert Burton, *The Anatomy of Melancholy* (London, 1628), III, 443.

51 Leonard Digges, 'Upon Master William Shakespeare, the Deceased Author, and his Poems', in *Poems Written by Wil Shakespeare, Gent.* (London, 1640), 3.

52 Furness, *New Variorum*, 347.

53 *Bell's Edition*, 333.

54 Furness, *New Variorum*, 347.

55 *Bell's Edition*, 298, 236, 235.

56 Furness, *New Variorum*, 346.

57 G.G. Gervinus, *Shakespeare Commentaries* (1849), cited in
    Furness, *New Variorum*, 373.

58 *Boston Daily Advertiser*, 28 February 1884, cited in *Shakespeare
    in Production: Much Ado About Nothing*, ed. John F. Cox
    (Cambridge, Cambridge University Press, 1997), 41

59 Cited in Cox, *Shakespeare in Production*, 42.

60 Henry Giles, *Human Life in Shakespeare* (Boston, MA, 1868),
    cited in Furness, *New Variorum*, 352–3.

61 Mrs Anna Jameson, *Characteristics of Women, Moral, Poetical
    and Historical* (London, 1833), cited in Furness, *New Variorum*,
    280.

62 Henrietta Palmer, *The Stratford Gallery* cited in Thompson and
    Roberts, *Women Reading Shakespeare*, 112.

63 Thomas Campbell, *Dramatic Works of Shakespeare* (London,
    1838), xlvi.

64 Andrew Lang, *Harper's Magazine*, September 1891, 492.

65 Lady Martin, *On Some of Shakespeare's Female Characters*
    (Edinburgh, 1891), cited in Furness, *New Variorum*, 358.

66 Stephen B. Dobranski, 'Children of the Mind: Miscarried
    Narratives in *Much Ado About Nothing*', *Studies in
    English Literature, 1500–1900* 38, no. 2 (1998):
    233–50, 245.

67 Penny Gay, *As She Likes It: Shakespeare's Unruly Women*
    (London: Routledge, 1994), 149.

68 Maggie Steed, 'Beatrice,' in *Players of Shakespeare*, ed. Russell
    Jackson and Robert Smallwood (Cambridge: Cambridge
    University Press, 1993), 45.

69 Carol Chillington Rutter, *Clamorous Voices: Shakespeare's
    Women Today* (London: Women's Press, 1988), xvi.

70 Michael Taylor, '*Much Ado About Nothing*: The Individual in
    Society', *Essays in Criticism* 23, no. 2 (1973): 146–53.

71 Steven Rose, 'Love and Self-love in *Much Ado About Nothing*,'
    Essays in Criticism 20, no. 2 (1970): 143–50; Barbara Everett,
    '*Much Ado About Nothing*: The Unsociable Comedy', in *English*

Comedy, ed. Michael Cordner, Peter Holland and John Kerrigan (Cambridge: Cambridge University Press, 1994), 186–202.

72 William G. McCollom, 'The Role of Wit in *Much Ado About Nothing*,' *Shakespeare Quarterly* 19, no. 2 (1968): 165–74, 173.

73 Carl Dennis, 'Wit and Wisdom in *Much Ado About Nothing*', *Studies in English Literature, 1500–1900* 13, no. 2 (1973): 223–37, 229.

74 R.G. White, *Shakespeare's Scholar* (New York, 1854), cited in Furness, *New Variorum*, 6.

75 Jonas Barish, 'Pattern and Purpose in the Prose of *Much Ado About Nothing*', *Rice University Studies* 60, no. 2 (1974): 19–30; Maurice Hunt, 'The Reclamation of Language in *Much Ado About Nothing*', *Studies in Philology* 97, no. 2 (2000): 165–91.

76 Lynne Magnusson, *Shakespeare and Social Language* (Cambridge: Cambridge University Press, 1999), 160–1.

Chapter 2

1 Leonard Digges, 'Upon Master William Shakespeare, the Deceased Author, and his Poems', in *Poems Written by Wil Shakespeare, Gent.* (London, 1640), 3.

2 See Christy Desmet, 'Helen Faucit and the Shakespeare Memorial Theatre, Stratford-upon-Avon, 1879,' *Critical Survey* 24 no. 2 (2012): 4–21.

3 The radio programme *Front Row* played clips of the rediscovered footage on 9 April 2008, speculating about the reasons behind its disappearance. My investigations into the BBC archives support *Front Row*'s suggestion of possible boardroom backstabbing, though no smoking gun, and my sleuthing at the British Film Institute yielded a complete version on videotape, mislabelled but now available for viewing.

4 The BBC's first broadcast of *Much Ado*, the 1967 televised version of Franco Zeffirelli's lush Sicilian production, starring Maggie Smith and Robert Stephens, was also lost for decades until it was rediscovered at the Library of Congress in 2010.

5   David Liddiment, 'Bravo the BBC, But Keep It Up After Charter
    Renewal', *Guardian*, 14 November 2005. Available online:
    http://www.guardian.co.uk/media/2005/nov/14/
    mondaymediasection11 (accessed 1 February 2017).

6   Pamela Mason, *Text and Performance: Much Ado About
    Nothing* (London: Macmillan, 1992).

7   Michael Dobson, 'Shakespeare Performances in England, 2002',
    Shakespeare Survey 56 (2003): 256–86, 267.

8   Jami Rogers, 'Much Ado Sicilian Style,' *Birmingham Journal of
    Literature and Language* 1, no. 1 (2008): 42–51, 48.

9   Charles Spencer, 'Joyous Screwball Comedy Gives Way to the
    Glorious Glow of Love', *Telegraph*, 15 December 2006.
    Available online: http://www.telegraph.co.uk/culture/theatre/
    drama/3657145/Joyous-screwball-comedy-gives-way-to-the-
    glorious-glow-of-love.html (accessed 1 February 2017).

10 Michael Billington, 'Much Ado About Nothing', *Guardian*,
    19 May 2006. Available online: https://www.theguardian.com/
    stage/2006/may/19/theatre.rsc (accessed 1 February 2017).

11 Robert Crew, 'Tarragon's Much Ado About Nothing Not Just
    Bollywood Shakespeare', *Toronto Star*, 1 May 2015. Available
    online: https://www.thestar.com/entertainment/stage/2015/05/01/
    tarragons-much-ado-about-nothing-not-just-bollywood-
    shakespeare-review.html (accessed 1 February 2017).

12 Michael Dobson, 'The Darkness at the Heart of *Much Ado
    About Nothing*', *Guardian*, 17 June 2011. Available online:
    https://www.theguardian.com/culture/2011/jun/17/shakespeare-
    much-ado-wyndhams-globe (accessed 1 February 2017).

13 Peter Holland, *English Shakespeares* (Cambridge: Cambridge
    University Press, 1997), 35.

14 Holland, *English Shakespeares*, 36.

15 Alison Findlay, *Much Ado About Nothing: A Guide to the Text
    and the Play in Performance* (London: Palgrave Macmillan,
    2011), 113.

16 Findlay, *Much Ado*, 106.

17 On British political theatre of this era, see Michael Patterson's
    Strategies of Political Theatre (Cambridge: Cambridge University
    Press, 2003).

18 Mel Gussow, 'Stage View: Englishwomen Make an Impact as
    Directors', *New York Times*, 7 August 1988, H5. Available
    online: http://www.nytimes.com/1988/08/07/theater/stage-view-
    englishwomen-make-an-impact-as-directors.html?pagewanted=
    all (accessed 4 August 2017).

19 Di Trevis, *Being a Director* (Abingdon: Routledge, 2012).

20 Robert Smallwood, 'Shakespeare at Stratford-on-Avon, 1988',
    Shakespeare Quarterly 40, no. 1 (1989): 83–94, 85.

21 Charles Spencer, 'Much Ado About Nothing, The Old Vic,
    Review', *Telegraph*, 20 September 2013. Available at: http://
    www.telegraph.co.uk/culture/theatre/theatre-reviews/10321616/
    Much-Ado-About-Nothing-The-Old-Vic-review.html (accessed
    1 February 2017).

22 Michael Billington, '*Much Ado About Nothing* – Review,'
    Guardian, 20 September 2013. Available online: https://www.
    theguardian.com/culture/2013/sep/20/much-ado-about-nothing-
    review-rylance; Paul Taylor, 'Theatre Review: *Much Ado About
    Nothing*', *Independent*, 20 September 2013. Available online:
    http://www.independent.co.uk/arts-entertainment/theatre-dance/
    reviews/theatre-review-much-ado-about-nothing-8829937.html
    (both accessed 1 February 2017).

23 Spencer, 'Review'.

24 Smallwood, 'Shakespeare at Stratford-on-Avon, 1988', 83; the
    Financial Times and the *Guardian* both commented on her
    humourlessness in their reviews on 14 and 15 April 1988,
    respectively.

25 Dipanita Nath, 'For *Much Ado* . . . Stratford Plans a Big, Fat,
    Punjabi Wedding in India', *Indian Express*, 19 May 2012.
    Available online: http://archive.indianexpress.com/news/
    for-much-ado. . .-stratford-plans-big-fat-punjabi-wedding-in-
    india/951407 (accessed 1 February 2017).

26 Nath, 'For *Much Ado*'.

27 Harold Hobson, 'A Stage Fit for Shakespeare', *Sunday Times*,
    11 April 1976.

28 Kate Rumbold, 'Much Ado About Nothing', in *A Year of
    Shakespeare*, ed. Paul Edmondson, Paul Prescott and Erin
    Sullivan (London: Bloomsbury, 2013), 149–52, 151.

29 See Dominic Cavendish, '*Love's Labour's Lost / Love's Labour's Won*, Royal Shakespeare Theatre, Review: "Blissfully Entertaining"', *Telegraph*, 16 October 2014. Available online: http://www.telegraph.co.uk/culture/theatre/theatre-reviews/11167470/Loves-Labours-LostLoves-Labours-Won-Royal-Shakespeare-Theatre-review.html (accessed 1 February 2017).

Chapter 3

1   Marion Wynne-Davies, 'Introduction', in *Much Ado About Nothing and The Taming of the Shrew*, New Casebooks (London: Palgrave, 2001), 1–12, 1.

2   Ibid., 9.

3   Ibid., 2.

4   Leah S. Marcus, 'The Shrew as Editor/Editing *Shrews*', in *Gender and Power in Shrew-Taming Narratives, 1500–1700*, ed. David Wootton and Graham Holderness (Basingstoke: Palgrave Macmillan: 2010), 84–100, 98.

5   Ibid., 95.

6   Mihoko Suzuki, 'Gender, Class, and the Ideology of Comic Form: *Much Ado About Nothing* and *Twelfth Night*', in *A Feminist Companion to Shakespeare*, ed. Dympna Callaghan (Oxford and Malden, MA: Blackwell, 2000), 121–43, 125.

7   Ibid.

8   Ibid.

9   Ibid., 130.

10 Ibid., 131.

11 Ibid., 132.

12 Ibid., 133.

13 Ibid., 134.

14 Ibid.

15 Ibid., 141.

16 Ibid.

17 Ewan Fernie, *Shame in Shakespeare* (London: Routledge, 2002), 85.

18 Ibid., 86.

19 Ibid., 74.

20 Ibid.

21 Ibid., 87.

22 Ibid., 88.

23 Ibid.

24 Ibid.

25 Pamela Mason, 'Don Pedro, Don John and Don . . . Who?
    – Noting a Stranger in *Much Adoodle-do*', in *Shakespeare and
    His Contemporaries in Performance*, ed. Edward J. Esche
    (Aldershot: Ashgate, 2000), 241–60, 244.

26 Ibid., 246–7.

27 Ibid., 250.

28 Ibid.

29 Maurice Hunt, 'The Reclamation of Language in *Much Ado About
    Nothing*', *Studies in Philology* 97, no. 2 (2000): 165–91, 165.

30 Ibid., 186.

31 Ibid., 191.

32 Mason, 'Don Pedro, Don John', 255.

33 Ibid., 256.

34 Deborah Cartmell, *Interpreting Shakespeare on Screen* (London:
    Palgrave Macmillan, 2000), 47.

35 Ibid., 49.

36 Mason, 'Don Pedro, Don John', 242.

37 Judith Buchanan, *Shakespeare on Film* (Harlow: Longman,
    2005), 204.

38 Ibid., 206.

39 Ibid., 205.

40 Philippa Sheppard, '"Sigh No more ladies" – The Song in *Much
    Ado about Nothing*: Shakespeare and Branagh Deliver Aural
    Pleasure', *Literature/Film Quarterly* 33, no. 2 (2005): 92–100,
    95, 92.

41 Cartmell, *Interpreting Shakespeare*, 52.

42 Ibid.

43 Angela Stock, 'Recent Stage, Film and Critical Interpretations', in *Much Ado About Nothing*, ed. F.H. Mares (2nd ed., Cambridge: Cambridge University Press, 2003), 48–63, 49.

44 Ibid., 55.

45 Ibid., 56.

46 Ibid., 57.

47 Ibid., 59.

48 Claire McEachern, *Much Ado About Nothing*, Arden 3, revised edition (London: Bloomsbury, 2016), 1.

49 Ibid., 2.

50 Ibid., 354, n to line 5.4.97.

51 Hunt, 'Reclamation of Language', 178.

52 Ibid.

53 McEachern, *Much Ado*, 170

54 Ibid., 177.

55 Ibid., 178.

56 Ibid., 180.

57 Hunt, 'Reclamation of Language', 177.

58 Diana E. Henderson, 'Mind the Gaps: The Ear, the Eye, and the Senses of a Woman in *Much Ado About Nothing*', in *Knowing Shakespeare: Senses, Embodiment and Cognition*, ed. Lowell Gallagher and Shankar Raman (London: Palgrave Macmillan, 2010), 192–215, 194.

59 Ibid., 193.

60 Ibid.

61 Ibid., 194.

62 Ibid., 211.

63 Patrick Cheney, 'Halting Sonnets: Poetry and Theater in *Much Ado About Nothing*', in *A Companion to Shakespeare's Sonnets*, ed. Michael Schoenfeldt (Oxford and Malden, MA: Blackwell Publishers, 2003), 363–82, 379.

64 Ibid., 363.

65 Ibid.

66 Ibid., 369.

67 Ibid.

68 Ibid., 370.

69 Ibid., 373.

70 Ibid., 372.

71 Ibid., 371.

72 Ibid., 373.

73 Ibid., italics in the original.

74 Ibid., 375.

75 Ibid., 376.

76 Ibid., 377.

77 McEachern, *Much Ado*, 345.

78 Cheney, 'Halting Sonnets', 377.

79 Ibid., 379.

80 Alison Findlay, '*Much Ado About Nothing*', in *A Companion to Shakespeare's Works: Volume III, The Comedies*, ed. Richard Dutton and Jean E. Howard (Malden, MA: Blackwell Publishers, 2003), 393–410, 394.

81 Ibid.

82 Ibid., 398.

83 Ibid., 396.

84 Alison Findlay, 'A Day to Remember: Wedding Ceremony and Cultural Change', *Shakespeare* 8 no. 4 (2012): 411–23, 412.

85 Ibid., 415.

86 Ibid., 416.

87 Ibid., 421.

88 Ibid., 422.

89 Douglas M. Lanier, '"Good Lord, for Alliance": Joss Whedon's *Much Ado About Nothing*', *Représentations: La revue électronique du* CEMRA 1 (2014): 117–42, 136.

90 Ibid., 139.

91 Suzuki, 'Gender, Class, and the Ideology of Comic Form', 134.

92 Findlay, '*Much Ado*', 394.

93 Buchanan, *Shakespeare on Film*, 205.

Chapter 4

1   Martin Wiggins, in association with Catherine Richardson, *British Drama, 1533–1642: A Catalogue* (Oxford and New York: Oxford University Press, 2014), vol. IV, 62.

2   Claire McEachern, ed., *Much Ado About Nothing* (London and New York: Bloomsbury, rev. ed. 2015), 124, 125, 127–8, 130.

3   Jean E. Howard, 'Renaissance Antitheatricality and the Politics of Gender and Rank in *Much Ado About Nothing*', in *Shakespeare Reproduced: The Text in History and Ideology*, ed. Jean E. Howard and Marion F. O'Connor (London and New York: Methuen, 1987), 163–87. Lorna Hutson, *The Invention of Suspicion: Law and Mimesis in Shakespeare and Renaissance Drama* (Oxford and New York: Oxford University Press, 2007), 342.

4   Lena Cowen Orlin, *Locating Privacy in Tudor London* (Oxford and New York: Oxford University Press, 2007), esp. Chapter 4.

5   On Wise's publications of Shakespeare's works, see Lukas Erne, *Shakespeare and the Book Trade* (Cambridge and New York: Cambridge University Press, 2013), 161–4.

6   The name designations vary: 'Keeper.', 'Cowley.', 'Sexton.', 'Andrew.', 'Kemp.', 'Kem.', 'Kee.' And 'Cow.' in the Folio.

7   Paul Werstine, *Early Modern Playhouse Manuscripts and the Editing of Shakespeare* (Cambridge and New York: Cambridge University Press, 2013), 6–106, 138.

8   Lukas Erne, *Shakespeare as Literary Dramatist* (Cambridge and New York: Cambridge University Press, 2003), 84.

9   E.K. Chambers, *William Shakespeare: A Study of Facts and Problems* (2 vols, Oxford: Clarendon, 1930), vol. I, 384.

10 Sonia Massai, *Shakespeare and the Rise of the Editor* (Cambridge and New York: Cambridge University Press, 2007), 164. For the 'garbled' nature of *Henry V* 1600 Quarto, see my '"As Sharp as a Pen": *Henry V* and Its Texts', in *Shakespeare's Book: Essays in Reading, Writing and Reception*, ed. Richard Meek, Jane Rickard and Richard Wilson (Manchester and New York: Manchester University Press, 2008), 140–64.

11 Stanley Wells and Gary Taylor, with John Jowett and William
    Montgomery, *William Shakespeare: A Textual Companion*
    (Oxford: Clarendon Press, 1987), 371.

12 Through Line Number referencing is keyed to the play as
    published in *The Norton Facsimile: The First Folio of
    Shakespeare*, ed. Peter Blayney (2nd ed., New York and London:
    W.W. Norton, 1996), 123.

13 McEachern, *Much Ado*, 308, n.

14 Bridewell Hospital Court of Governors' Minute Books (hereafter
    BCB), 4. 370^v and 5. 102^v, The Museum of the Mind, Bethlem
    Royal Hospital, Beckenham, Kent.

15 Geoffrey Bullough, ed., *Narrative and Dramatic Sources of
    Shakespeare* (New York: Routledge, 1963), vol. II, 62–3, 82–104.

16 Ibid., 113.

17 Ibid., 114–17.

18 Ibid., 134.

19 Ben Weinreb and Christopher Hibbert, eds, *The London
    Encyclopaedia* (London and Basingstoke: Macmillan, 1983),
    962. The site of 'Whittington College' is shown in Adrian
    Prockter and Robert Taylor (eds), *The A to Z of Elizabethan
    London* (London: Guildhall and Harry Margary, Lympne Castle,
    Kent, 1979), 23.

20 BCB 1. 155^r.

21 BCB 4. 302^v.

22 London Metropolitan Archives, *Repertories of the Court of
    Aldermen*, Rep 21, 31^v (19 February 1584).

23 For the relative locations of the Poultry and Bucklersbury, see
    Prockter and Taylor, *The A to Z of Elizabethan London*, 10, 23.

24 For the Southwark 'Compter' or Counter gaol, see Sir Howard
    Roberts and Walter H. Godfrey, eds, *Survey of London,
    Bankside* (London: London County Council, 1950), 10, Plate 3.
    Also, Dorian Gerhold, *London Plotted: Plans of London
    Buildings c.1450–1720* (London: London Topographical Society,
    2016), 199–200. The Southwark Counter was closed in 1855
    and demolished.

25 BCB 2.74^r.

26 Joan Kent, *The English Village Constable, 1580–1642: A Social and Administrative Study* (Oxford: Clarendon Press, 1986), 7.

27 BCB 4.329ʳ.

28 J.O. Halliwell, *The Will of Sir Hugh Clopton, of New Place, Stratford-upon-Avon, and Citizen, Mercer and Alderman of London, 1496* (London, 1865), 6. Also William Howitt, *Visits to Remarkable Places: Old Halls, Battlefields and Scenes Illustrative . . .* (London: Longman, Orme, Brown, Green and Longmans, 1840), 132.

29 Andrew Gurr, *Playgoing in Shakespeare's London* (3rd ed., Cambridge and New York: Cambridge University Press, 2004), 84, 231.

30 LMA, St. Leonard Shoreditch, Register of burials, 1558–1654, P91/LEN/A/MS07499.

31 John Bennell, 'Spinola, Benedict (1519/20–1580)', *Oxford Dictionary of National Biography* (Oxford and New York: Oxford University Press, 2004) online edition, January 2008. Available http://www.oxforddnb.com/view/article/52156.

32 BCB 2. 235ʳ–236ʳ. The Legrande deposition is interleaved with minutes post-dating 29 February 1575/6.

33 BCB 3.141ᵛ (2 January 1576/7).

34 BCB 3.317ᵛ. For further details regarding Palavicino and Spinola, and the Copeland case, see my 'Much Ado About Italians in London', in *Shakespeare and the Italian Renaissance: Appropriation, Transformation, Opposition*, ed. Michele Marrapodi (Farnham and Burlington, VT: Ashgate, 2014), 305–16.

35 C.L. Kingsford, ed., *A Survey of London by John Stow* (2 vols, Oxford: Clarendon Press, 1908), vol. II, 262.

36 Ibid., II, 368. On the Curtain playhouse, see William Ingram, *The Business of Playing: The Beginnings of the Adult Professional Theatre in Elizabethan London* (Ithaca, NY and London: Cornell University Press, 1992), 219–38, and Tiffany Stern, 'The Curtain Is Yours', in *Locating the Queen's Men, 1583–1603: Material Practices and Conditions of Playing*, ed. Helen Ostovich, Holger Schott Syme and Andrew Griffin (Farnham and Burlington, VT: Ashgate, 2009), 77–96.

Chapter 5

1   For example, 2.3.120; 3.5.14; 5.1.50. Few characters in
    Shakespeare – Lear, Juliet and Anne Page – have their ages
    specified.

2   For Beale's much-quoted phrase see, for example, Geraldine
    Bedell, 'National Treasure', *Guardian*, 16 November 2003.
    Available online: http://www.theguardian.com/stage/2003/
    nov/16/theatre.

3   See, for example, #WomenOfACertainAge and 'Act for Change
    Launches #WomenOfACertainAge', *Equity*, 6 March 2015.
    Available online: http://www.equity.org.uk/news-and-events/
    equity-news/act-for-change-launches-womenofacertainage/.
    Recent positive developments on this front include: Deborah
    Warner casting Glenda Jackson as Lear (Old Vic, 2016) and
    Harriet Walter starring in Phyllida Lloyd's Donmar Shakespeare
    Trilogy (2016). However, while theatrical heavyweights may be
    able to challenge the prevailing casting culture, Jackson remains
    an outspoken critic of the lack of roles for older women – see,
    for example, 'Glenda Jackson: Acting Roles for Women Have
    Not Improved Because Writers Still Find Them "boring"', *The
    Telegraph*, 1 February 2017. Available online: http://www.
    telegraph.co.uk/news/2017/02/01/glenda-jackson-acting-roles-
    women-have-not-improved-writers/.

4   'Middle age' also was interpreted differently in the early modern
    period but Perdita's 'men of middle age' (4.4.108) is often a
    compliment to the more-than-middle-aged Polixenes and
    Camillo (*The Winter's Tale*, ed. John Pitcher, London:
    Bloomsbury Arden, 2010).

5   Judi Dench and Donald Sinden were 'pushing towards middle
    age' (RSC 1977) as were Elizabeth Spriggs and Derek Godfrey
    (RSC 1971) – see John F. Cox, 'Introduction', to *Much Ado
    About Nothing*, ed. John F. Cox, Shakespeare in Production
    (Cambridge: Cambridge University Press, 1997), 24. Henry
    Irving was a mature Benedick (ibid., 34) and Helena Faucit
    played Beatrice for over forty years (ibid., 35).

6   The production closed on 29 March 2008. The film recording,
    available for viewing at the National Theatre archives, is mediated
    by the use of focus, cutting and different points of view.

7   For example, Susannah Clapp, 'Much Ado, Brilliantly Done',
    Observer, 23 December 2007. Available online: https://www.
    theguardian.com/stage/2007/dec/23/theatre.shakespeare;
    Christopher Hart, 'Much Ado About Nothing', *Sunday Times*,
    23 December 2007. Available online: https://www.thetimes.co.
    uk/article/much-ado-about-nothing-l7g969gkqtz; Nicholas de
    Jongh, 'Middle-Aged Lovers Make Much the Biggest Waves',
    Evening Standard, 19 December 2007. Available online: https://
    www.standard.co.uk/goingout/theatre/middle-aged-lovers-make-
    much-the-biggest-waves-7402289.html.

8   Charles Spencer, 'Much Ado About Nothing: Happiness in the
    Last Chance Saloon', *Daily Telegraph*, 19 December 2007.
    Available online: http://www.telegraph.co.uk/culture/theatre/
    drama/3670024/Much-Ado-About-Nothing-Happiness-in-the-
    last-chance-saloon.html.

9   Jasper Rees, 'Much Ado About Nothing: We Didn't Sleep
    Together, Did We?', *Daily Telegraph*, 12 December 2007.
    Available online: http://www.telegraph.co.uk/culture/theatre/
    3669863/Much-Ado-About-Nothing-We-didnt-sleep-together-
    did-we.html.

10 Sarah Hemming, 'Theatre: Love in Sunlight and Shadows',
    Financial Times, 20 December 2007. Available online:
    https://www.ft.com/content/a4cf2f7e-af14-11dc-880f-
    0000779fd2ac.

11 Hart, 'Much Ado'.

12 Beale is a former St Paul's Cathedral choirboy so he brings a
    musician's precision to pausing. Susannah Clapp ('Much Ado,
    Brilliantly Done') notes 'inflections and daring long pauses that
    crack open the lines'.

13 For example, Michael Billington, 'Much Ado About Nothing',
    Guardian, 19 December 2007. Available online: https://www.
    theguardian.com/stage/2007/dec/19/theatre.shakespeare.

14 The following paragraph summarizes Beale's comments on
    Benedick at https://www.youtube.com/watch?v=W_MJyd1wo8c.

15 'Here, There, Gone: An Interview With Sir Nicholas Hytner
    (1974) by Will Bordell (2012)'. Available online: http://www.
    trinhall.cam.ac.uk/alumni/publications/misc/default.asp?ItemID=
    2967.

16 Laurie Maguire, 'Yours for the Talking', *Times Literary Supplement*, 11 January 2008, 17. Available online: https://www.the-tls.co.uk/articles/private/yours-for-the-talking/.

17 By contrast the programme cover has Beale gazing adoringly at Wanamaker, while Wanamaker gazes directly to camera/the audience.

18 Georgina Brown, 'Love, Loss and Much Laughter', *Mail on Sunday*, 23 December 2007. Available online: https://www.highbeam.com/doc/1G1-172734459.html.

19 Jongh, 'Middle-Aged Lovers'. There is marked contrast with Marianne Elliott's RSC production, which opened in December 2006. This was a fire and passion production, set in 1953 Cuba, and starred Tamsin Greig and Joseph Millson.

20 While Claire McEachern follows Q and F in assigning this speech to Leonato, *Much Ado* in the theatre invariably gives this line to Benedick. Oliver Ford Davies, *Shakespeare's Fathers and Daughters* (London: Bloomsbury Arden Shakespeare, 2017), 61, reports that Hytner argued that this might seem a good idea in the study but is a missed opportunity in practice. We would like to thank Davies for allowing us access to a draft of this book ahead of publication.

21 Billington, 'Much Ado'.

22 A similarly detailed and creative backstory, or subtext, was generated for Andrew Woodall's Don John who 'had once made a pass at Claudio' that had been rejected (Hytner quoted in *Much Ado About Nothing*, ed. Jonathan Bate and Eric Rasmussen, RSC edition, London: Palgrave Macmillan, 2009, 152).

23 Rehearsal Notes, Friday 30 November 2007. The period setting was vague: Rutter comments it could have been 'twentieth, nineteenth *or* sixteenth century', Carol Chillington Rutter, 'Shakespeare Performances in England (and Wales), 2008', *Shakespeare Survey* 62 (2009) 349–85, 362. Abigail Rokison-Woodall, *Shakespeare in the Theatre: Nicholas Hytner* (London: Bloomsbury Arden Shakespeare, 2017), 131, identifies the setting as 1598, the year the play was written, but this was not evident in performance.

24 Rehearsal Notes, Wednesday 14 November 2007.

25 Jane Edwardes, *Time Out, London*, January 2008. Available online: http://www.theatrerecord.org.

26 Or churchmen, as in the David Hare *Racing Demon* trilogy at the National Theatre.

27 For example, Michael Billington, 'Much Ado', observed Davies's 'towering, Lear-like rage'.

28 Davies describes this as a 'beautifully simple couplet', *Fathers and Daughters*, 60.

29 Ibid., 57.

30 Ibid., 58.

31 Ibid., 59. These are precisely the fates envisaged by Borachio (2.2.25–6).

32 Ibid., 64.

33 Ibid., 62.

34 Maguire, 'Yours for the Talking'.

35 Rehearsal Notes, Monday 29 October 2007.

36 Fielding is quoted by Davies, *Fathers and Daughters*, 64.

37 This is, of course, shorthand for a very particular, stereotypical, view of Chekhov. For possible tension between realistic production styles and *Much Ado* see Cox, *Much Ado*, 6.

38 Philip Hensher, 'The Light Infantry of the Merry War', 2007 *Much Ado* programme.

39 Hytner graduated in English from Trinity Hall, Cambridge; Beale gained a first in English from Gonville and Caius College, Cambridge. Beale embarked on a PhD (on grief). Hytner's reading of *Much Ado* was, of course, enhanced by his cutting, and rearranging, of the text.

40 Marliss C. Desens, *The Bed-Trick in English Renaissance Drama* (London: Associated University Presses, 1994), 11.

41 Rehearsal Notes, Tuesday 30 October 2007.

42 Meg was the only female character absent from the 'breakfast' rolling start. She is referred to as a 'skivvy' in the rehearsal notes.

43 Gunning graduated from Rose Bruford College of Theatre and Performance in 2007.

44 Rehearsal Notes, Wednesday 7 November 2007.

45 The BBC commissioned an eighth season of *My Family*
    while Wanamaker was playing Beatrice. *The Guardian*
    hailed it as 'one of BBC1's most popular comedies', observing
    that its seventh series, aired in 2007, peaked at 7.2 million
    viewers – see Leigh Holmwood, 'BBC Orders Two Series of
    My Family', *Guardian*, 27 March 2008. Available online:
    https://www.theguardian.com/media/2008/mar/27/bbc.
    television.

46 The programme notes encouraged such ghosting by noting that
    Wanamaker received the 'Best Mummy Award' for her
    performance as Susan.

47 For Hooch on the role most people recognize Wanamaker for,
    see Tim Lewis, 'Zoë Wanamaker: "Acting Is a Vicious Business, It
    Can Be Very Humiliating"', *Guardian*, 5 May 2013. Available
    online: http://www.theguardian.com/culture/2013/may/05/
    zoe-wanamaker-acting-vicious-business.

48 Michael L. Quinn, 'Celebrity and the Semiotics of Acting', *New
    Theatre Quarterly* 6, no. 22 (1990): 154–61, 155.

49 'Women in Theatre: How the "2:1 Problem" Breaks Down',
    Guardian, 10 December 2012. Available online: http://www.
    theguardian.com/news/datablog/2012/dec/10/women-in-theatre-
    research-full-results.

50 This data was gathered from the *Spotlight Casting Directory*
    which requires actors to categorize themselves within ten-year
    age brackets according to how old they appear, rather than their
    actual age. For a more detailed analysis of the casting situation
    see Sara Reimers, 'Casting and the Construction of Femininity in
    Contemporary Stagings of Shakespeare's Plays', PhD thesis,
    Royal Holloway, University of London, 2017.

51 'Women of a Certain Age – Act for Change', Terri Paddock
    Playlist. Available online: https://www.youtube.com/playlist?list=
    PLnNrWEwOfYXi8Csi2h8NFObG3JXP2PYor

52 The figures from the RSC and Shakespeare's Globe include new
    writing and revivals of non-Shakespearian plays, suggesting the
    problem extends beyond Shakespeare.

53 For example, Josie Rourke's 2011 production with Catherine
    Tate (42) as Beatrice; Jeremy Herrin's 2011 Globe production

starring Eve Best, who had her fortieth birthday during the run;
Iqbal Khan's 2012 'Indian' *Much Ado* for the RSC, with Meera
Syal (51).

54 For example, Michelle Terry and Claire Cox played Beatrice at
the RSC in 2014 and 2000 respectively, while Jacqueline
Defferary and Kirsty Besterman played the role at Shakespeare's
Globe in 2007 and 2008; all four of these women were under 35
when they played Beatrice and none of them had attained
celebrity status at the time.

55 Sarah Hemming, 'Much Ado About Nothing, Old Vic,
London: Review' *Financial Times*, 23 September 2013.
Available online: https://www.ft.com/content/2fc5a128-21ea-
11e3-bb64-00144feab7de; 'Much Ado About Nothing, Old
Vic – Theatre Review', *Evening Standard*, 20 September 2013.
Available online: https://www.standard.co.uk/goingout/
theatre/much-ado-about-nothing-old-vic-theatre-review-
8828894.html.

56 Simon Edge, 'Theatre review: Much Ado About Nothing, Old
Vic Theatre, London', *Express*, 19 September 2013. Available
online: http://www.express.co.uk/entertainment/theatre/430755/
Theatre-review-Much-Ado-About-Nothing-Old-Vic-Theatre-
London.

57 Ibid.

58 Billington, 'Much Ado About Nothing – Review', *Guardian*, 20
September 2013. Available online: https://www.theguardian.
com/culture/2013/sep/20/much-ado-about-nothing-review-
rylance.

59 'Casting Redgrave and Earl Jones // Old Vic Theatre, In
Conversation With Mark Rylance'. Available online: https://
www.youtube.com/watch?v=GlkJsick25M

60 Spencer, 'Happiness in the Last Chance Saloon',

61 Margaret had added lines in 2.1: 'unhand me, unhand me'.
Prompt copy.

62 This comment is made during a discussion of the character of
Iago, 'Iago on the Couch', organized by the British
Psychoanalytic Society, at the Freud Museum, Hampstead.
Available online: https://www.youtube.com/watch?v=
1tOp9cFfNpM.

Chapter 6

1   David Finkle, 'First Nighter: The Royal Shakespeare Company's
    Regal "Love's Labour's Lost" and "Love's Labour's Won"', *The
    Blog, HuffPost*, updated 1 June 2015.

2   However, as Peter J. Smith has pointed out to me, the play
    reverted to its original title once it left Stratford and *Love's
    Labour's Won* has generally been demoted to a smaller typeface.
    This suggests that Finkle may have been right about the effect of
    the renaming.

3   Quotations are taken from *Love's Labour's Lost*, ed. H.R.
    Woudhuysen (London: Arden Shakespeare, 1998) and *Much
    Ado About Nothing*, ed. Claire McEachern (London:
    Bloomsbury Arden Shakespeare, revised edition, 2015).

4   Peter J. Smith, 'Review of *Much Ado About Nothing*', *Cahiers
    Élisabéthains* 88 (2015): 184–6, 185.

5   Carol Chillington Rutter, 'Shakespeare Performances in England
    2014', *Shakespeare Survey* 65 (2015): 386–7.

6   For a synopsis of the plot, see http://illinoisshakes.com/plays/
    past/llw-2015/. For reviews of the 2015 production at Illinois
    State University, where it was performed in conjunction with
    Love's Labour's Lost, see Julie Kistler, 'Love's Labours' Lost and
    Won at the Illinois Shakespeare Festival', *A Follow Spot*, 21 July
    2017. Available at: http://www.afollowspot.com/2015/07/
    loves-labours-lost-and-won-at-illinois.html. And Patricia S.
    Stiller, 'A Winning Sequel to "Love's Labour's Lost"', *The
    Pantagraph*, 21 July 2015. Available at: http://www.pantagraph.
    com/entertainment/go/stiller-a-winning-sequel-to-love-s-labour-s-
    lost/article_f034c0d7-4a83-5890-93b0-6679f2923a1e.html.

7   Gretchen E. Minton, 'Review: Much Ado About Nothing [billed
    as *Love's Labour's Won*] (RSC) @ Royal Shakespeare Theatre,
    Stratford-upon-Avon, 2014', *Reviewing Shakespeare*, 4 October
    2014. Available at: http://bloggingshakespeare.com/reviewing-
    shakespeare/much-ado-nothing-rsc-royal-shakespeare-theatre-
    stratford-upon-avon-2014/.

8   Jami Rogers, review of *Love's Labour's Lost* and *Much Ado
    About Nothing*, *Shakespeare Bulletin* 33, no. 3 (2015): 521–7,
    521.

9   Smith, 'Review', 185; Michael Billington, 'Love's Labour's Lost/
    Love's Labour's Won – A Perceptive Painting', *The Guardian*,
    16 October 2014. Available at: https://www.theguardian.com/
    stage/2014/oct/16/loves-labours-lost-loves-labours-won-sense.

10 Peter Kirwan, 'Love's Labour's Lost (RSC/Live from Stratford)
    @ The Broadway Cinema, Nottingham', *The Bardathon*,
    14 February 2015. Available at: https://blogs.nottingham.ac.uk/
    bardathon/2015/02/14/loves-labours-lost-rsclive-from-stratford-
    the-broadway-cinema-nottingham/.

11 T.W. Baldwin, *Shakspere's Love's Labor's Won* (Carbondale, IL:
    Southern Illinois University Press, 1957).

12 *The Lost Plays Database*, ed. Roslyn L. Knutson, David McInnis
    and Matthew Steggle. See https://www.lostplays.org/lpd/Love's_
    Labour's_Won.

13 *The Lost Plays Database* prints a photograph of the bookseller's
    list.

14 In 1993–1994 the French Compagnie de Matamore, directed by
    Serge Lipszyc, performed *Love's Labour's Lost* and *Much Ado
    About Nothing* billed both under their own (translated) titles
    and as Parts One and Two of *Peines d'Amour*. There was no
    attempt to link the plays by setting or thematic cross-casting; in
    fact, the casting showcased the versatility of the actors (e.g. the
    King of Navarre reappearing as Dogberry), something on which
    one reviewer commented. See Guy Boquet, 'Review: Play: *Peines
    d'Amour! Peines d'Amour Perdues* et *Beaucoup de Bruit pour
    Rien*', *Cahiers Élisabéthains* 48 (1995): 113–14.

15 *A Midsummer Night's Dream*, in *The Norton Shakespeare*, 3rd
    edition, ed. Stephen Greenblatt et al. (New York: W.W. Norton,
    2016).

16 See David Ormerod, '*Love's Labour's Lost* and *Won:* The Case
    for *As You Like It*.' *Cahiers Élisabéthains* 44 (1993): 9–21.
    Ormerod also cites F.N. Lees, whose letter to the *Times Literary
    Supplement* (28 March 1958) he did not become aware of until
    late in his research.

17 *Love's Labour's Lost*, ed. Woudhuysen, 15–16.

18 See Peter W. Blayney, 'The Publication of Playbooks', in *A New
    History of Early English Drama*, ed. John D. Cox and David Scott
    Kastan (New York: Columbia University Press, 1997), 399.

19 Martin Wiggins and Catherine Richardson, *British Drama, 1533–1642: A Catalogue*, vol 6 (Oxford: Oxford University Press, 2015), 54.

20 Alexander Leggatt, *Shakespeare's Comedy of Love* (London: Methuen, 1974), 151.

21 Sheldon P. Zitner, ed., *Much Ado About Nothing* (Oxford: Clarendon Press, 1993), 31.

22 Zitner, *Much Ado*, 58.

23 William Shakespeare, *The Taming of the Shrew*, ed. Barbara Hodgdon (London: Arden Shakespeare, 2010).

24 Woudhuysen, *Love's Labour's Lost*, 3–5.

25 Miriam Gilbert, *Shakespeare in Performance: Love's Labour's Lost* (Manchester: Manchester University Press, 1993), 27.

26 Pamela Mason, *Text and Performance: Much Ado About Nothing* (London: Macmillan, 1992), 63.

27 *Much Ado About Nothing*, ed. John F. Cox, Shakespeare in Production (Cambridge: Cambridge University Press, 1997), 78.

28 Kenneth Branagh, *Much Ado About Nothing, by William Shakespeare. Screenplay, Introduction, and Notes on the Making of the Film* (London: Chatto & Windus, 1993), xi.

29 Music and lyrics by Leslie Arden, book by Berni Stapleton. See Douglas Lanier, 'Much Ado About Nothing in Popular Culture', in *Much Ado About Nothing: Shakespeare in Performance*, text ed. Jeffrey Kahan, Sourcebooks Shakespeare, ed. David Bevington and Peter Holland (Methuen: London, 2007), 28.

30 Ralph Berry, 'Stratford Festival, Canada,' *Shakespeare Quarterly* 31, no. 2 (1980): 167–75, 172, quoted in Gilbert, *Shakespeare in Performance*, 118.

31 Pamela Mason, 'Recent Productions of *Love's Labour's Lost*', in *Shakespeare's Early Comedies: A Casebook*, ed. Pamela Mason (Basingstoke: Macmillan, 1995), 241.

32 Rutter, 'Shakespeare Performances', 386.

33 Minton, 'Review'.

34 Gilbert, *Love's Labour's Lost*, 104.

35 The quarto attributes Rosalind's lines to Katherine. The speech prefix is corrected to Rosaline in the Folio and in most modern editions. Otherwise, one might argue that this dialogue had the effect of turning Berowne's interest toward another woman. See Woudhuysen's discussion in an appendix to his edition, 309–11.

36 Like Berowne's dialogue with Katherine/Rosaline (*LLL* 2.1.114), that of Benedick/Borachio/Balthasar with Margaret (*MA* 2.1.89) may be a false start or reflect confusion over speech prefixes. Interestingly, two speech prefixes in the quarto of *Love's Labour's Lost* refer to Maria as '*Marg*'. (See note to her name in the 'List of Roles'.) Both Rosaline and Katherine (when abbreviated to Kate) are names with strong associations elsewhere in Shakespeare.

37 Bobbyann Roesen [Anne Barton], '*Love's Labour's Lost*', *Shakespeare Quarterly* 4, no. 4 (1953): 411–26.

38 Leggatt, *Shakespeare's Comedy of Love*, 79, 81.

39 McEachern, *Much Ado*, 80–98.

40 McEachern notes that Don Pedro's telling Balthasar to 'Get us some excellent music' for the next evening (2.3.86–7) could be read two ways. Sheldon Zitner argues that Benedick's comparison of the singing to a dog howling may be accurate, since the line is addressed only to the audience (Zitner, *Much Ado*, 44).

41 Mason, *Text and Performance*, 23.

42 McEachern, *Much Ado*, 57.

43 Cox, *Much Ado*, 197, note on 4.1.313–16.

44 See Cox, *Much Ado*, notes on 5.4.35 and 83, also McEachern, *Much Ado*, 108.

Chapter 7

1 Stephen O'Neill, *Shakespeare and YouTube: New Media Forms of the Bard* (London: Bloomsbury, 2014), 26.

2 For a good account of the dynamics of YouTube searches and their many complicating factors, see O'Neill, *Shakespeare and YouTube*, Chapter 2, 25–72, *passim*.

3 I have found that searching on play titles captures some Shakespearean examples missed through other search

combinations, but brings up as well items that are not properly Shakespearean. In the case of *As You Like It*, there are videos of music composed for or based on Shakespeare's play, but other titles, such as Euge Groove's track 'As You Like It', draw on the familiar phrase without discernible reference to Shakespeare ('The Smoothjazz Loft – Euge Groove / As You Like It', YouTube, 3 April 2013. Available online: https://www.youtube.com/watch?v=QI4FaqiC9Y8, accessed 17 March 2017). On the other hand, there are, at the time of writing, a large number of short clips from productions both amateur and professional, so perhaps *As You Like It* is enjoying a surge of popularity among theatre companies and festivals.

4 'Video Summary – Much Ado About Nothing', YouTube, 19 October 2015. Available online: https://www.youtube.com/watch?v=UxuilaBWc6g (accessed 9 March 2017).

5 '"Much Ado About Nothing" | Overview: Summary & Analysis | 60second Recap#rM', YouTube, 24 April 2010. Available online: https://www.youtube.com/watch?v=wrGweMXB0jE (accessed 9 March 2017).

6 'Animated Synopsis of Love's Labour's Won (Much Ado about Nothing)', RSC Education, YouTube, 24 June 2015. Available online: https://www.youtube.com/watch?v=dMEIltCbtJ4 (accessed 9 March 2017).

7 Overly Sarcastic Productions, 'Shakespeare Summarized: Much Ado About Nothing', YouTube, 18 December 2012. Available online: https://www.youtube.com/watch?v=9-AGIUNsGgA (accessed 9 March 2017).

8 'Finger Puppet Shakespeare: Much Ado About Nothing', YouTube, 3 February 2016. Available online: https://www.youtube.com/watch?v=Pp_YxeI9vH4 (accessed 9 March 2017).

9 O'Neill, *Shakespeare and YouTube*, 55–61; The Geeky Blonde, 'Much Ado about Nothing', YouTube, 30 June 2013. Available online: https://www.youtube.com/watch?v=0H3LFpf8uFU (accessed 9 March 2017).

10 O'Neill, *Shakespeare and YouTube*, 8.

11 Henry Jenkins, *Convergence Culture: Where Old and New Media Collide* (New York: New York University Press, 2006), 3.

12 David Bell, 'On the Net: Navigating the World Wide Web', in *Digital Cultures: Understanding New Media*, ed. Glen Creeber and Royston Martin (Maidenhead: McGraw Hill, Open University Press, 2009), 35.

13 Douglas M. Lanier, '"Good Lord, for Alliance": Joss Whedon's *Much Ado About Nothing*', *Représentations: La revue électronique du CEMRA* 1 (2014): 117–42.

14 'The "Much Ado About Nothing" Cast on Meeting Joss Whedon', Backstage, YouTube, 5 June 2013. Available online: https://www.youtube.com/watch?v=RDODNaT65go; The '"Much Ado about Nothing" Cast On Shakespeare', Backstage, YouTube, 5 June 2013. Available online: https://www.youtube.com/watch?v=CPUA6wZFo8A; 'The "Much Ado About Nothing" on Shakespeare Brunches', Backstage, YouTube, 5 June 2013. Available online: https://www.youtube.com/watch?v=o_H8eBf2dAc. Whedon himself offers commentary on the film's genesis in 'My Shakespeare Story: Joss Whedon – #MySHX400', Folger Shakespeare Library, YouTube, 4 May 2016. Available online: https://www.youtube.com/watch?v=J-OL4kBJxE4 (all accessed 5 March 2017).

15 Lanier, '"Good Lord, for Alliance"', 7.

16 Rebecca Keegan, '"*Much Ado About Nothing*": A DIY Film Project at Joss Whedon's Home', *Los Angeles Times*, 31 May 2013. Available online: http://articles.latimes.com/2013/may/31/entertainment/la-et-mn-ca-much-ado-house-20130602.

17 On liquor as 'the social lubricant and principal symbol of social amity in the film', see Lanier, '"Good Lord, for Alliance"', 7.

18 For a discussion of voyeurism and scopophilia in the Whedon *Much Ado*, see Lanier, '"Good Lord, for Alliance"', 13–15.

19 For a discussion of this scene, see Lanier, '"Good Lord, for Alliance"', 11–12.

20 Lanier, '"Good Lord, for Alliance"', 6.

21 'Dr. Horrible's Sing-Along Blog Full [HD]', YouTube, 4 September 2012. Available online: https://www.youtube.com/watch?v=Of9kHpCv1ts. For the circumstances surrounding the blog's genesis and production, see 'The Making of Dr. Horrible's Sing-Along Blog', YouTube, 6 July 2013. Available online:

https://www.youtube.com/watch?v=8R3GDqqJWA0 (both accessed 3 March 2017).

22 Jenkins, *Convergence Culture*, 3.

23 The Shakespeare web series, or vlog, is a very recent phenomenon, dating from around 2013–2014. Douglas Lanier provides a good introduction to the genre and a useful list of examples in 'Vlogging the Bard: Serialization, Social Media, Shakespeare', in *Broadcast Your Shakespeare: Continuity and Change Across Media*, ed. Stephen O'Neill (London: Bloomsbury Arden Shakespeare, 2017).

24 *Nothing Much to Do* was broadcast on three channels: Benedick's, Beatrice's and the Watch's. There is also Ursula's channel, which housed musical performances and some other special episodes. The characters maintained a presence on other social media: Beatrice had a Twitter (twitter.com/beatricetheduke), Hero an Instagram account (instagram.com/herotheduke), and Ursula had a Tumblr (watchprojects.tumblr.com) ('Nothing Much to Do', Fandom: Webseries & Digital Series Wikia. Available online: http://web-series.wikia.com/wiki/Nothing_Much_to_Do, accessed 10 August 2017). While the series was running, these extra outlets provided a way for the characters to connect with their audience and keep them updated on things they might not have blogged about in the videos themselves.

25 'SHAKES', BardBox: Shakespeare and Online Video. Available online: https://bardbox.net/2016/06/04/shakes/ (accessed 10 August 2017).

26 'A Bit Much'. Available online: http://www.webserieschannel.com/bit-much/. I discovered the web series from Erica Bianca Romero, 'Shakespeare Modernized: Web Series Adaptations of William Shakespeare's Works', in *Transmedial Shakespeare: Studying Shakespeare Beyond His Texts*, 1 December 2015. Available online: https://transmedialshakespeare.wordpress.com/2015/12/01/shakespeare-modernized-web-series-adaptations-of-william-shakespeares-works/ (both accessed 10 August 2017).

27 'Much Ado About Shakespeare in Film | Bard in Multimedia', *The Shakespeare Standard*. Available online: http://

theshakespearestandard.com/shakespeare-goes-summer-camp-bard-multimedia/ (accessed 10 August 2017); and 'A Bit Much'.

28 'Much Ado About Shakespeare in Film | Bard in Multimedia'.

29 'Shakes on Snap'. Available online: https://www.facebook.com/ShakesOnSnap/ (accessed 10 August 2017).

30 I have discussed these genres in 'Paying Attention in Shakespeare Parody: From Tom Stoppard to YouTube', *Shakespeare Survey* 61 (2008): 227–38; 'YouTube Shakespeare, Appropriation, and Rhetorics of Invention', in *OuterSpeares: Shakespeare, Intermedia, and the Limits of Adaptation*, ed. Daniel Fischlin (Toronto: University of Toronto Press, 2014), 53–72; and 'The Economics of (In)Attention in YouTube Shakespeare', *Borrowers and Lenders: The Journal of Shakespeare and Appropriation* 10, no. 1 (Spring/Summer 2016). Available online: http://www.borrowers.uga.edu/783210/show (accessed 10 August 2017).

31 Patricia Lange, 'Videos of Affinity on YouTube', in *The YouTube Reader*, ed. Pelle Snickars and Patrick Vonderau (Stockholm: National Library of Sweden, 2009), 71.

32 Abigail Keating, 'Video-making, Harlem Shaking: Theorizing the Interactive Amateur', *New Cinemas: Journal of Contemporary Film* 11, no. 2/3 (2013): 99–110, 99.

33 Thomas Elsaesser, 'Tales of Epiphany and Entropy: Around the Worlds in Eighty Clicks', in *The YouTube Reader*, ed. Pelle Snickars and Patrick Vonderau (Stockholm: National Library of Sweden, 2009), 169.

Chapter 8

1 Russ McDonald, *Shakespeare and the Arts of Language* (Oxford: Oxford University Press, 2001), 122.

BIBLIOGRAPHY

Allen, John A. 'Dogberry', *Shakespeare Quarterly* 24, no. 1 (1973): 35–53.

Antinora, Sarah. 'Please Let This Be Much Ado about Nothing: "Kill Claudio" and the Laughter of Release', *Ceræ: An Australasian Journal of Medieval and Early Modern Studies* 1 (2014): 1–21.

Auden, W.H. *Lectures on Shakespeare*, edited by Arthur Kirsch. London: Faber, 2000.

Baldwin, T.W. *Shakspere's Love's Labor's Won*. Carbondale, IL: Southern Illinois University Press, 1957.

Barish, Jonas A. 'Pattern and Purpose in the Prose of *Much Ado About Nothing*'. *Rice University Studies* 60, no. 2 (1974): 19–30.

Bate, Jonathan, and Eric Rasmussen, eds. *Much Ado About Nothing*. RSC Shakespeare. London: Macmillan, 2009.

Beaumont, Matthew. *Night Walking: A Nocturnal History of London*. London: Verso, 2015.

Berger, Harry, Jr. 'Against the Sink-a-Pace: Sexual and Family Politics in *Much Ado About Nothing*'. *Shakespeare Quarterly* 33, no. 3 (1982): 302–13.

Blayney, Peter W. 'The Publication of Playbooks'. In *A New History of Early English Drama*, edited by John D. Cox and David Scott Kastan, 383–422. New York: Columbia University Press, 1997.

Boose, Lynda E., 'Scolding Brides and Bridling Scolds: Taming the Woman's Unruly Member'. *Shakespeare Quarterly* 42, no. 2 (1991): 179–213.

Branagh, Kenneth. *Much Ado About Nothing by William Shakespeare: Screenplay, Introduction, and Notes on the Making of the Film*. London: Chatto & Windus, 1993.

Brugger, William. 'Sins of Omission: Textual Deletions in Branagh's *Much Ado About Nothing*'. *Journal of the Wooden O Symposium* 3 (2003): 1–11.

Buchanan, Judith. *Shakespeare on Film*. Harlow: Longman, 2005.

Bullough, Geoffrey, ed. *Narrative and Dramatic Sources of Shakespeare*. New York: Routledge, 8 volumes, 1958 f.

Cartmell, Deborah. *Interpreting Shakespeare on Screen*. London: Palgrave Macmillan, 2000.

Cassal, Steve. 'Shakespeare's *Much Ado About Nothing*'. *Explicator* 64, no. 3 (2006): 139–41.

Cavell, Stanley. *Pursuits of Happiness: The Hollywood Comedy of Remarriage*. Cambridge, MA: Harvard Film Studies, 1984.

Cerasano, S.P. ' "Half a dozen dangerous words" '. In *Gloriana's Face: Women, Public and Private in the English Renaissance*, edited by S.P. Cerasano and Marion Wynne-Davies, 167–83. Detroit, MI: Wayne State University Press, 1992.

Chamberlain, Stephanie. 'Rotten Oranges and Other Spoiled Commodities: The Economics of Shame in *Much Ado About Nothing*'. *Journal of the Wooden O Symposium* 9 (2010): 1–10.

Chambers, E.K. *William Shakespeare: A Study of Facts and Problems*. Oxford: Clarendon Press, 2 volumes, 1930.

Cheney, Patrick. 'Halting Sonnets: Poetry and Theater in *Much Ado About Nothing*'. In *A Companion to Shakespeare's Sonnets*, edited by Michael Schoenfeldt, 363–82. Malden, MA: Blackwell Publishers, 2003.

Clegg, Cyndia Susan. 'Truth, Lies, and the Law of Slander in *Much Ado About Nothing*'. In *The Law in Shakespeare*, edited by Constance Jordan and Karen Cunningham, 167–88. Basingstoke and New York: Palgrave Macmillan, 2007.

Collington, Philip D. 'A "Pennyworth" of Marital Advice: Bachelors and Ballad Culture in *Much Ado About Nothing*'. In *Shakespeare's Comedies of Love*, edited by Karen Bamford and Richard Knowles, 30–54. Toronto: University of Toronto Press, 2008.

Collington, Philip D. ' "Stuffed With All Honourable Virtues": *Much Ado About Nothing* and *The Book of the Courtier*'. *Studies in Philology* 103, no. 3 (2006): 281–312.

Cook, Carol. ' "The Sign and Semblance of Her Honor": Reading Gender Difference in *Much Ado About Nothing*'. *Publications of the Modern Language Association of America* 101, no. 2 (1986): 186–202.

Cook, D. ' "The Very Temple of Delight": The Twin Plots of *Much Ado About Nothing*'. In *Poetry and Drama 1570–1700: Essays in Honour of Harold F. Brooks*, edited by Antony Coleman and Antony Hammond, 32–46. Sydney: Lawbook Co. of Australasia, 1981.

Cox, John F., ed. *Much Ado About Nothing*, Shakespeare in Production. Cambridge: Cambridge University Press, 1997.

Cox, John F. 'The Stage Representation of the "Kill Claudio" Sequence in *Much Ado About Nothing*'. *Shakespeare Survey* 32 (1979): 27–36.

Cummings, Peter. 'Verbal Energy in Shakespeare's *Much Ado About Nothing*'. *Shakespeare Yearbook* 8 (1997): 448–58.

Davis, Lloyd. 'Rethinking Misogyny: Shakespeare, Gender, and the Critical Tradition'. *Shakespearean International Yearbook* 6 (2006): 185–211.

Deleyto, Celestino. 'Men in Leather: Kenneth Branagh's *Much Ado About Nothing* and Romantic Comedy'. *Cinema Journal* 36, no. 3 (1997): 91–105.

Dennis, Carl. 'Wit and Wisdom in *Much Ado About Nothing*'. *Studies in English Literature, 1500–1900* 13, no. 2 (1973): 223–37.

Desens, Marliss C. *The Bed-Trick in English Renaissance Drama*. London: Associated University Presses, 1994.

Desmet, Christy. 'Helen Faucit and the Shakespeare Memorial Theatre, Stratford-upon-Avon, 1879'. *Critical Survey* 24, no. 2 (2012): 4–21.

Dobranski, Stephen B. 'Children of the Mind: Miscarried Narratives in *Much Ado About Nothing*'. *Studies in English Literature, 1500–1900* 38, no. 2 (1998): 233–50.

Dobson, Michael. 'Shakespeare Performances in England, 2002'. *Shakespeare Survey* 56 (2003): 256–86.

Drakakis, John. 'Trust and Transgression: The Deceptive Practices of *Much Ado About Nothing*'. In *Post-Structuralist Readings of Poetry*, edited by Richard Machin and Christopher Norris, 59–84. Cambridge: Cambridge University Press, 1987.

Erne, Lukas. *Shakespeare and the Book Trade*. Cambridge and New York: Cambridge University Press, 2013.

Erne, Lukas. *Shakespeare as Literary Dramatist*. Cambridge and New York: Cambridge University Press, 2003.

Everett, Barbara. '*Much Ado About Nothing*: The Unsociable Comedy'. In *English Comedy*, edited by Michael Cordner, Peter Holland and John Kerrigan, 68–84. Cambridge: Cambridge University Press, 2007.

Fabiszak, Jacek. 'Kenneth Branagh's Multicultural and Multi-Ethnic Filmed Shakespeare(s)'. *Multicultural Shakespeare: Translation, Appropriation, and Performance* 12, no. 27 (2015): 75–86.

Fernie, Ewan. *Shame in Shakespeare*. London: Routledge, 2002.

Fernie, Ewan. *Shakespeare for Freedom: Why the Plays Matter*. Cambridge: Cambridge University Press, 2017.

Findlay, Alison. 'A Day to Remember: Wedding Ceremony and Cultural Change'. *Shakespeare* 8, no. 4 (2012): 413–23.

Findlay, Alison. *Illegitimate Power: Bastards in Renaissance Drama*. Manchester: Manchester University Press, 1994.

Findlay, Alison. '*Much Ado About Nothing*'. In *A Companion to Shakespeare's Works: Volume III, The Comedies*, edited by Richard Dutton and Jean E. Howard, 393–410. Malden, MA: Blackwell Publishers, 2003.

Findlay, Alison. *Much Ado About Nothing: A Guide to the Text and the Play in Performance*. London: Palgrave Macmillan, 2011.

Fleck, Andrew. 'The Ambivalent Blush: Figural and Structural Metonymy, Modesty, and *Much Ado About Nothing*'. *ANQ: A Quarterly Journal of Short Articles, Notes and Reviews* 19, no. 1 (2006): 16–23.

Friedman, Michael D. '"For Man Is a Giddy Thing and This Is My Conclusion": Faith and Fashion in *Much Ado about Nothing*'. *Text and Performance Quarterly* 13, no. 3 (1993): 267–82.

Friedman, Michael D. '"Hush'd on Purpose to Grace Harmony": Wives and Silence in *Much Ado About Nothing*'. *Theatre Journal* 42, no. 3 (1990): 350–63.

Friedman, Michael D. 'The Editorial Recuperation of Claudio'. *Comparative Drama* 25, no. 4 (1991): 369–86.

Gay, Penny. *As She Likes It: Shakespeare's Unruly Women*. London: Routledge, 1994.

Gay, Penny. *Cambridge Introduction to Shakespeare's Comedies*. Cambridge: Cambridge University Press, 2008.

Gilbert, Miriam. *Shakespeare in Performance: Love's Labour's Lost*. Manchester: Manchester University Press, 1993.

Gough, Melinda J. '"Her Filthy Feature Open Showne" in Ariosto, Spenser, and *Much Ado About Nothing*'. *Studies in English Literature, 1500–1900* 39, no. 1 (1999): 41–67.

Greer, Germaine. 'Shakespeare and the Marriage Contract'. In *Shakespeare and the Law*, edited by Paul Raffield and Gary Watt, 51–63. Oxford: Hart, 2008.

Gurr, Andrew. *Playgoing in Shakespeare's London*. 3rd ed. Cambridge and New York: Cambridge University Press, 2004.

Harlan, Susan. ' "Returned From the Wars": Comedy and Masculine Post-War Character in Shakespeare's *Much Ado About Nothing*'. *Upstart: A Journal of English Renaissance Studies*, 24 June 2013. https://upstart.sites.clemson.edu/Essays/returned-from-the-wars/returned-from-the-wars.xhtml.

Hazlitt, William. *Characters of Shakespeare's Plays*. London: Rowland Hunter, 1817.

Henderson, Diana E. 'Mind the Gaps: The Ear, the Eye, and the Senses of a Woman in *Much Ado About Nothing*'. In *Knowing Shakespeare: Senses, Embodiment and Cognition*, edited by Lowell Gallagher and Shankar Raman, 192–215. London: Palgrave Macmillan, 2010.

Hodgdon, Barbara, ed. *The Taming of the Shrew*. London: Arden Shakespeare, 2010.

Holland, Peter. *English Shakespeares*. Cambridge: Cambridge University Press, 1997.

Howard, Jean E. 'Renaissance Antitheatricality and the Politics of Gender and Rank in *Much Ado About Nothing*'. In *Shakespeare Reproduced: The Text in History and Ideology*, edited by Jean E. Howard and Marion F. O'Connor, 163–87. New York: Methuen, 1987.

Howard, Jean E. *The Stage and Social Struggle in Early Modern England*. London: Routledge, 1994.

Hunt, Maurice. 'The Reclamation of Language in *Much Ado About Nothing*'. *Studies in Philology* 97, no. 2 (2000): 165–91.

Hutson, Lorna. *The Invention of Suspicion: Law and Mimesis in Shakespeare and Renaissance Drama*. Oxford and New York: Oxford University Press, 2007.

Ingram, William. *The Business of Playing: The Beginnings of the Adult Professional Theatre in Elizabethan London*. Ithaca, NY and London: Cornell University Press, 1992.

Johnson, Samuel. *Selections from Johnson on Shakespeare*, edited by Bertrand H. Bronson with Jean M. O'Meara. New Haven, CT and London: Yale University Press, 1986.

Kathman, David. 'Actors' Names as Textual Evidence'. *Theatre Notebook* 63, no. 2 (2009): 70–9.

Kazimierczak, Karolina. 'Adapting Shakespeare for *Star Trek* and *Star Trek* for Shakespeare: The Klingon *Hamlet* and the Spaces of Translation'. *Studies in Popular Culture* 32, no. 2 (2010): 35–47.

Kent, Joan. *The English Village Constable, 1580–1642: A Social and Administrative Study*. Oxford: Clarendon Press, 1986.

King, Ros. 'Plays, Playing, and Make-Believe: Thinking and Feeling in Shakespearean Drama'. In *Embodied Cognition and Shakespeare's Theatre: The Early Modern Body-Mind*, edited by Laurie Johnson, John Sutton and Evelyn Tribble, 27–45. New York and Abingdon: Routledge, 2014.

Knutson, Roslyn L., David McInnis and Matthew Steggle, eds. *The Lost Plays Database*. https://www.lostplays.org/lpd/Love's_Labour's_Won.

Kreps, Barbara. 'Two-Sided Legal Narratives: Slander, Evidence, Proof, and Turnarounds in *Much Ado About Nothing*'. In *Taking Exception to the Law: Materializing Injustice in Early Modern English Literature*, edited by Donald Beecher, Travis DeCook, Andrew Wallace and Grant Williams, 162–78. Toronto: University of Toronto Press, 2015.

Krieger, Elliot. 'Social Relations and the Social Order in *Much Ado About Nothing*'. *Shakespeare Survey* 32 (1979): 49–61.

Lane, Robert. '"Foremost in Report": Social Identity and Masculinity in *Much Ado About Nothing*'. *The Upstart Crow* 16 (1996): 31–47.

Lanier, Douglas M. '*Much Ado About Nothing* in Popular Culture'. In *Much Ado About Nothing: Shakespeare in Performance*, edited by David Bevington and Peter Holland, 25–35. London: Methuen, 2007.

Lanier, Douglas M. '"Good Lord, for Alliance": Joss Whedon's *Much Ado About Nothing*'. *Représentations: La revue électronique du CEMRA* 1 (2014): 117–42.

Leggatt, Alexander. *Shakespeare's Comedy of Love*. London: Methuen, 1974.

Lenz, Carolyn Ruth Swift, Gayle Greene and Carol Thomas Neely, eds. *The Woman's Part: Feminist Criticism of Shakespeare*. Urbana: University of Illinois Press, 1980.

Levin, Richard A. *Love and Society in Shakespearean Comedy: A Study of Dramatic Form and Content*. Newark: University of Delaware Press, 1985.

Lewalski, Barbara K. 'Love, Appearance and Reality: Much Ado About Something'. *Studies in English Literature, 1500–1900* 8, no. 2 (1968): 235–51.

Lucking, David. 'Bringing Deformed Forth: Engendering Meaning in *Much Ado About Nothing*'. *Renaissance Forum* 2, no. 1 (1997). https://web.archive.org/web/20170215210255/http://www.hull.ac.uk/renforum/v2no1/lucking.htm.

Madelaine, R.E.R. 'Oranges and Lemans: *Much Ado About Nothing*, IV.i.31', *Shakespeare Quarterly* 33, no. 4 (1982): 491–2.

Magnusson, Lynne. *Shakespeare and Social Language*. Cambridge: Cambridge University Press, 1999.

Marcus, Leah S. 'The Shrew as Editor/Editing *Shrews*'. In *Gender and Power in Shrew-Taming Narratives, 1500–1700*, edited by David Wootton and Graham Holderness, 84–100. Basingstoke: Palgrave Macmillan, 2010.

Mares, F.H., ed. *Much Ado About Nothing*. Cambridge: Cambridge University Press, 2003.

Mason, Pamela. 'Don Pedro, Don John and Don . . . Who? – Noting a Stranger in *Much Adoodle-do*'. In *Shakespeare and His Contemporaries in Performance*, edited by Edward J. Esche, 241–60. Aldershot: Ashgate, 2000.

Mason, Pamela. *Text and Performance: Much Ado About Nothing*. London: Macmillan, 1992.

Massai, Sonia. *Shakespeare and the Rise of the Editor*. Cambridge and New York: Cambridge University Press, 2007.

Maurer, Margaret. 'Leonato and Beatrice in Act 5, Scene 5, Line 97 of *Much Ado About Nothing*'. In *Reading What's There: Essays on Shakespeare in Honor of Stephen Booth*, edited by Michael J. Collins, 89–98. Newark: University of Delaware Press, 2014.

McCollom, William G. 'The Role of Wit in *Much Ado About Nothing*'. *Shakespeare Quarterly* 19, no.2 (1968): 165–74.

McEachern, Claire. 'Fathering Herself: A Source Study of Shakespeare's Feminism'. *Shakespeare Quarterly* 39, no. 3 (1988): 269–90.

McEachern, Claire, ed. *Much Ado About Nothing*. London: Arden Shakespeare, 2015.

McKeown, Roderick Hugh. '"I Will Stop Your Mouth": The Regulation of Jesting in *Much Ado About Nothing*'. *Shakespeare* 12, no. 1 (2016): 33–54.

McPeek, James A. 'The Thief "Deformed" and Much Ado About "Noting"'. *Boston University Studies in English* 4 (1960): 65–84.

Moisan, Thomas. 'Deforming Sources: Literary Antecedents and Their Traces in *Much Ado About Nothing*'. *Shakespeare Studies* 31 (2003): 165–83.

Morgan, William W. 'Verse and Prose in *Much Ado About Nothing*: An Analytic Note'. *English* 20, no. 108 (1971): 89–92.

Moseley, Charles. '"Men Were Deceivers Ever"'. In *Critical Essays on Much Ado About Nothing*, edited by Linda Cookson and Bryan Loughrey, 45–53. Harlow: Longman, 1989.

Moulton, Ian Frederick. 'Courtship, Sex, and Marriage'. In *The Ashgate Research Companion to Popular Culture in Early Modern England*, edited by Andrew Hadfield, Matthew Dimmock and Abigail Shinn, 133–48. Farnham: Ashgate, 2014.

Mowat, Barbara A., and Paul Werstine, eds. *Much Ado About Nothing*. New York: Folger Shakespeare Library, 1995.

Mueller, Martin. 'Shakespeare's Sleeping Beauties: The Sources of *Much Ado About Nothing* and the Play of Their Repetitions'. *Modern Philology* 91, no. 3 (1994): 288–311.

Munro, Ian. 'Shakespeare's Jestbook: Wit, Print, Performance'. *English Literary History* 71, no.1 (2004): 89–113.

Myhill, Nova. 'Spectatorship in/of *Much Ado About Nothing*'. *Studies in English Literature, 1500–1900* 39, no. 2 (1999): 291–311.

Nelson, Brent. 'Faith and Sheep's Guts in *Much Ado About Nothing*'. *Shakespeare* 12, no. 2 (2016): 161–74.

Oppenheimer, Jean. 'An Indie Twist on Shakespeare', *American Cinematographer* 94, no. 7 (2013): 56–63.

Orlin, Lena Cowen. *Locating Privacy in Tudor London*. Oxford and New York: Oxford University Press, 2007.

Ormerod, David. 'Faith and Fashion in *Much Ado About Nothing*'. *Shakespeare Survey* 25 (1972): 93–106.

Ormerod, David. '*Love's Labour's Lost* and *Won*: The Case for *As You Like It*'. *Cahiers Élisabéthains* 44 (1993): 9–21.

Osborne, Laurie E. 'Dramatic Play in *Much Ado About Nothing*: Wedding in the Italian Novellas and English Comedy'. *Philological Quarterly* 69, no. 2 (1990): 167–88.

Patterson, Michael. *Strategies of Political Theatre*. Cambridge: Cambridge University Press, 2003.

Pellegrini, Ann. 'Closing Ranks, Keeping Company: Marriage Plots and the Will to be Single in *Much Ado About Nothing*'. In *Shakesqueer: A Queer Companion to the Complete Works of Shakespeare*, edited by Madhavi Menon, 245–53. Durham, NC: Duke University Press, 2011.

Peterson, Kaara L. 'Shakespearean Revivifications: Early Modern Undead' *Shakespeare Studies* 32 (2004): 240–66.

Potter, Nicholas. 'Romance and Realism in *Much Ado About Nothing*'. In *Critical Essays on Much Ado About Nothing*, edited by Linda Cookson and Bryan Loughrey, 54–62. Harlow: Longman, 1989.

Prouty, Charles. *The Sources of Much Ado About Nothing*. New Haven, CT: Yale University Press, 1950.

Quinn, Michael L. 'Celebrity and the Semiotics of Acting'. *New Theatre Quarterly* 6, no. 22 (1990): 154–61.

Roesen, Bobbyann [Anne Barton]. '*Love's Labour's Lost*'. *Shakespeare Quarterly* 4, no. 4 (1953): 411–26.

Rogers, Jami. 'Much Ado Sicilian Style'. *Birmingham Journal of Literature and Language* 1, no. 1 (2008): 42–51.

Rose, Steven. 'Love and Self-Love in *Much Ado About Nothing*'. *Essays in Criticism* 20, no. 2 (1970): 143–50.

Rossiter, A.P. *Angel With Horns*. New York: Theater Arts Books, 1961.

Rutter, Carol Chillington. *Clamorous Voices: Shakespeare's Women Today*. London: Women's Press, 1988.

Rutter, Carol Chillington. 'Shakespeare Performances in England (and Wales), 2008'. *Shakespeare Survey* 62 (2009): 349–85.

Rutter, Carol Chillington. 'Shakespeare Performances in England 2014'. *Shakespeare Survey* 65 (2015): 368–407.

Ryan, Kiernan. *Shakespeare's Comedies*. Basingstoke: Palgrave Macmillan, 2009.

Salingar, Leo. 'Borachio's Indiscretion: Some Noting about *Much Ado*'. In *The Italian World of English Renaissance Drama*, edited by Michele Marrapodi, 225–38. London: Associated University Presses, 1998.

Salkeld, Duncan. 'Much Ado About Italians in London'. In *Shakespeare and the Italian Renaissance: Appropriation, Transformation, Opposition*, edited by Michele Marrapodi, 305–16. Farnham and Burlington, VT: Ashgate, 2014.

Schafer, Elizabeth. *Ms-Directing Shakespeare: Women Direct Shakespeare*. Basingstoke: Palgrave Macmillan, 2000.

Sheppard, Philippa. '"Sigh No More Ladies" – The Song in *Much Ado about Nothing*: Shakespeare and Branagh Deliver Aural Pleasure'. *Literature/Film Quarterly* 33, no. 2 (2005): 92–100.

Slights, Camille Wells. *Shakespeare's Comic Commonwealths*. Toronto: University of Toronto Press, 1993.

Smallwood, Robert. 'Shakespeare at Stratford-on-Avon, 1988'. *Shakespeare Quarterly* 40, no. 1 (1989): 83–94.

Smith, James. '*Much Ado About Nothing*: Notes for a Book in Preparation'. *Scrutiny* 13, no. 4 (1946): 242–57.

Smith, Peter J. *Social Shakespeare: Aspects of Renaissance Dramaturgy and Contemporary Society*. Basingstoke: Macmillan, 1995.

Smith, Philip. '"I Look'd Upon Her With a Soldier's Eye": The Normalization of Surveillance Culture in Whedon's *Much Ado*'. *Slayage: The Journal of Whedon Studies* 14, no. 1 [43] (2016). http://www.whedonstudies.tv/uploads/2/6/2/8/26288593/smith_slayage_14.1.pdf.

Steed, Maggie. 'Beatrice'. In *Players of Shakespeare 3*, edited by Russell Jackson and Robert Smallwood, 42–51. Cambridge: Cambridge University Press, 1993.

Stern, Tiffany. 'The Curtain is Yours'. In *Locating the Queen's Men, 1583–1603: Material Practices and Conditions of Playing*, edited by Helen Ostovich, Holger Schott Syme and Andrew Griffin, 77–96. Farnham and Burlington, VT: Ashgate, 2009.

Stock, Angela. 'Recent Stage, Film and Critical Interpretations'. In *Much Ado About Nothing*, edited by F.H. Mares, 48–63. 2nd ed. Cambridge: Cambridge University Press, 2003.

Straznicky, Marta. 'Shakespeare and the Government of Comedy: *Much Ado About Nothing*'. *Shakespeare Studies* 22 (1994): 141–71.

Suzuki, Mihoko. 'Gender, Class and the Ideology of Comic Form: *Much Ado About Nothing* and *Twelfth Night*'. In *A Feminist Companion to Shakespeare*, edited by Dympna Callaghan, 121–43. Oxford and Malden, MA: Blackwell, 2000.

Taylor, Michael. '*Much Ado About Nothing*: The Individual in Society'. *Essays in Criticism* 23, no. 2 (1973): 146–53.

Thompson, Ann, and Sasha Roberts, eds. *Women Reading Shakespeare 1660–1900: An Anthology of Criticism*. Manchester: Manchester University Press, 1997.

Trevis, Di. *Being a Director*. Abingdon: Routledge, 2012.

Turner, John. 'Claudio and the Code of Honour'. In *Critical Essays on Much Ado About Nothing*, edited by Linda Cookson and Bryan Loughrey, 21–30. Harlow: Longman, 1989.

Weinreb, Ben, and Christopher Hibbert, eds. *The London Encyclopaedia*. London and Basingstoke: Macmillan, 1983.

Weller, Philip. '"Kill Claudio": A Laugh Almost Killed by the Critics'. *Journal of Dramatic Theory and Criticism* 11, no. 1 (1996): 101–10.

Wells, Stanley, and Gary Taylor, with John Jowett and William Montgomery. *William Shakespeare: A Textual Companion*. Oxford: Clarendon Press, 1987.

Werstine, Paul. *Early Modern Playhouse Manuscripts and the Editing of Shakespeare*. Cambridge and New York: Cambridge University Press, 2013.

Wiggins, Martin, in association with Catherine Richardson. *British Drama, 1533–1642: A Catalogue*. Oxford and New York: Oxford University Press, 2014.

Wilcox, Rhonda V. 'Joss Whedon's Translation of Shakespeare's *Much Ado About Nothing*: Historical Double Consciousness, Reflections, and Frames'. *Slayage: The Journal of Whedon Studies* 11:2–12:1 (2014). http://www.whedonstudies.tv/uploads/2/6/2/8/26288593/wilcox_slayage_11.2–12.1.pdf.

Wiles, David. *Shakespeare's Clown: Actor and Text in the Elizabethan Playhouse*. Cambridge: Cambridge University Press, 2005.

Womack, Mark. 'Balthasar's Song in *Much Ado About Nothing*'. In *Shakespeare Up Close: Reading Early Modern Texts*, edited by Russ McDonald, Nicholas D. Nace and Travis D. Williams, 57–63. London: Arden Shakespeare, 2012.

Woudhuysen, H.R., ed. *Love's Labour's Lost*. London: Arden Shakespeare, 1998.

Wright, Nancy E. 'Legal Interpretation of Defamation in Shakespeare's *Much Ado About Nothing*'. *Ben Jonson Journal* 13, no. 1 (2006): 93–108.

Wynne-Davies, Marion, ed. *Much Ado About Nothing and The Taming of the Shrew*. New Casebooks. Basingstoke: Palgrave, 2001.

Zitner, Sheldon P., ed. *Much Ado About Nothing*, Oxford Shakespeare. Oxford: Clarendon Press, 1993.

INDEX